Embedded Sensor Technology

By

Dr. NEELAPALA ANIL KUMAR

Mr. MADHUSUDAN DONGA

Department of ECE

Alliance University.

Preface

Embedded sensor technology has revolutionized the way we interact with and understand the world around us. With the capability to seamlessly integrate sensors into various devices and systems, this technology has unlocked a multitude of applications across industries, ranging from healthcare and automotive to environmental monitoring and industrial automation.

At its core, embedded sensor technology involves the incorporation of small, intelligent, and often specialized sensors into everyday objects or larger systems. These sensors can detect and measure a wide array of parameters, such as temperature, pressure, humidity, light, motion, and more. What sets this technology apart is its ability to collect and process data in real-time, enabling informed decision-making, automation, and enhanced functionalities.

The development of embedded sensor technology has been driven by continuous advancements in microelectronics, wireless communication, and data processing. Miniaturization of components has made it possible to create sensors that are not only highly accurate but also compact enough to be seamlessly integrated into various devices, even those with limited space. Furthermore, wireless connectivity has untethered sensors from traditional wired setups, enabling remote monitoring, control, and data transmission.

However, with the remarkable potential come certain challenges. Power efficiency remains a concern, as sensors need to operate for extended periods without frequent battery replacements. Additionally, ensuring data security and privacy is crucial, especially as sensors gather sensitive information. Calibrating and maintaining sensor accuracy over time, despite harsh environmental conditions, is another hurdle that researchers and engineers continue to address.

In conclusion, embedded sensor technology's seamless integration of intelligent sensors into devices and systems has significantly transformed various industries. Its ability to collect, process, and transmit data in real- time has enabled unprecedented levels of automation, efficiency, and insight. As technology continues to evolve, the potential applications of embedded sensors are bound to expand, shaping a smarter and more interconnected world.

The author Express his Gratitude and sincere thanks to management, All the Professors and Students of Alliance college of Engineering and Design who have expressed their desire of this book. The Author hopes this book will serve the purpose.

Dr. Neelapala Anil Kumar

Mr. Madhusudan Donga

Authors Biography

Dr. Neelapala Anil Kumar boasts a strong academic background with B. Tech, M. E, Ph. D degrees from JNTU Hyderabad, Andhra University, Visvesvaraya Technological University respectively. Currently working as Associate Professor in Alliance University, Bangalore, Karnataka. He has seasoned teaching experience across diverse institutions, enriching his skills in different states. A prolific researcher, he has presented and published extensively on medical image processing in international forums. Moreover, he has authored international and national textbooks, actively contributing to academia. Recognized for his dedication and excellence, Professor Kumar has received several awards, including the Pratibha Award, Sastra Award, Best Engineering Teacher Award, and Teaching Excellency Award.

Madhusudan Donga is an Embedded Engineer and Educator with expertise in Robotics and embedded systems. Currently working as R&D director at Electropro India involves in developing electronic products. He holds M.Tech in Electronics and Communicational Engineering from JTNUK and has over 15 years of experience in teaching and research with industrial exposure. His publications include Image processing, Antennas and communications with optimizing Techniques. Professor is passionate about making complex concepts accessible to learners of all levels. Recognized for his dedication and excellence, he has recognised with several awards with Pratibha award for best teaching, with Sastra Award for his continuous research contribution and with Visistaseva Award for long service in an organization.

Dedicated to our

Parents

Smt & Shri Nirmala Venkateswara Rao,

Smt & Shri Thirumala Rao

And

Faculty, Students Alliance College

of Engineering and Design

Alliance University.

Bangalore

Karnataka.

INDEX

Unit-1 An Introduction to Embedded Sensors

Unit Structure

1.0 Objectives

1.1 Introduction to Embedded Sensors

1.2 Embedded Sensor Characteristics

1.3 Basic blocks of Embedded Sensors

1.4 Types of Embedded Sensors

1.5 Performance of Embedded Sensors

1.6 Error analysis characteristics of Embedded Sensors

1.0 Objective

- Aims to provide readers with fresh insights and perspectives on embedded sensor technology.

- The introduction provides a clear and concise explanations of embedded sensors are, highlighting their significance in modern technology.

- Relevance of embedded sensors across various industries and applications.

- Addressing the challenges associated with embedded sensor technology, such as power efficiency, data security, and sensor calibration.

- Establishing a foundation of knowledge that readers can build upon as they delve deeper into the topic of embedded sensors.

1.1 Introduction to Embedded Sensors

The landscape of modern technology is being dramatically reshaped by the integration of embedded sensors, a transformative innovation that is altering the way we perceive and interact with the world around us. These unassuming yet powerful devices have ushered in a new era of possibilities, driving advancements across diverse industries, and enabling unprecedented levels of automation, intelligence, and convenience.

At its core, embedded sensor technology involves seamlessly incorporating tiny, specialized sensors into various objects and systems. These sensors possess the remarkable capability to detect and quantify a wide spectrum of physical parameters, including temperature, pressure, motion, and light. What truly set them apart is their real-time data processing and transmission, endowing devices, and systems with the ability to respond instantaneously to changing conditions, thereby amplifying their overall functionality and operational efficiency.

The rapid evolution of embedded sensors can be attributed to significant progress in microelectronics, wireless communication, and data processing. These technological leaps have not only facilitated the creation of highly accurate sensors but also made them energy-efficient and versatile enough to be seamlessly integrated into an array of applications. From smart home devices that intuitively adjust settings based on user preferences to industrial machinery that optimizes performance through real-time sensor insights, the influence of embedded sensors is far-reaching.

The impact of this technology resonates across a wide spectrum of industries. In the realm of healthcare, wearable devices equipped with embedded sensors are capable of continuously monitoring vital signs, physical activity, and even identifying potential health anomalies, thereby offering personalized and actionable information to users and healthcare providers alike. In the automotive sector, embedded sensors are the cornerstone of advanced driver-assistance systems, contributing to safer and more autonomous driving experiences. Additionally, domains such as environmental monitoring, agriculture, and manufacturing have all embraced embedded sensors to facilitate precise data collection and informed decision-making processes.

Nevertheless, as with any innovative frontier, embedded sensor technology is not without its challenges. Ensuring the durability of sensor accuracy in the face of harsh environmental conditions and extended operational periods remains a critical consideration. The pursuit of optimal power efficiency is another ongoing endeavour, as these sensors often operate with limited power resources, necessitating innovative solutions. Moreover, striking the delicate balance between data collection and the preservation of privacy is of utmost importance in a digital landscape where data security is paramount.

As we embark on a comprehensive exploration of embedded sensors, it becomes evident that they constitute a cornerstone of modern technological progress. By understanding the foundational principles, diverse applications, and potential advancements of embedded sensors, we gain insight into how these unassuming components are quietly shaping our world and reshaping our relationship with technology. This chapter introduces the reader to the world of embedded Sensors. Exploration, Classification, Application, Performance, Error characteristics and analysis were discussed primarily in this Chapter.

1.2   Embedded Sensor Characteristics

Embedded sensors are characterized by several distinctive features that collectively define their significance and impact on modern technology. These characteristics underscore their ability to gather and process data seamlessly, enabling a wide range of applications across industries. Distinctive characteristics of embedded sensors encompass their compact size, real-time processing, versatility, integration, wireless connectivity, energy efficiency, cost-effectiveness, enhanced functionality, data-driven insights, and role in interconnectivity. These characteristics collectively underscore their role as foundational elements in shaping the way we interact with technology and the world around us.

Miniaturization: One of the most defining features of embedded sensors is their compact size. Through advancements in microelectronics, these sensors have become incredibly small, allowing them to be integrated into devices and systems without occupying significant space. This miniaturization has facilitated their incorporation into objects and environments where traditional sensors wouldn't fit.

Real-Time Data Processing: Embedded sensors are designed to process data in real time. This characteristic enables them to swiftly capture information from their surroundings and provide immediate feedback. This real-time processing capability is vital for applications that require quick decision-making and rapid response, such as in industrial automation, healthcare monitoring, and autonomous vehicles.

Versatility: Embedded sensors exhibit versatility in their ability to measure and detect various physical parameters. They can be tailored to monitor factors like temperature, pressure, humidity, light intensity, motion, and more. This adaptability allows them to serve a diverse range of applications, from climate control systems to wearable fitness trackers.

Energy Efficiency: Many embedded sensors are designed to operate efficiently on limited power sources. This energy-conscious design ensures that they can function for extended periods without frequent battery replacements. This feature is particularly important for devices that require continuous, long-term monitoring.

Cost-Effectiveness: The miniaturization and advancements in manufacturing processes have contributed to making embedded sensors more cost-effective to produce. This affordability has led to their widespread adoption in various consumer and industrial products, democratizing access to advanced sensing capabilities.

Enhanced Functionality: By integrating sensors directly into objects and systems, these sensors enhance the overall functionality of devices. For instance, embedded sensors in smart phones enable features like automatic screen rotation and ambient light adjustment. In industrial settings, embedded sensors provide critical data for optimizing processes and maintenance.

Data-Driven Insights: Embedded sensors generate a wealth of data that can be leveraged for insights and decision-making. When aggregated and analysed, this data offers valuable information for improving efficiency, predicting maintenance needs, optimizing resource utilization, and more.

Interconnectivity: Embedded sensors contribute to the interconnected nature of the Internet of Things (IoT). They enable devices and systems to communicate with each other, enabling seamless automation and data exchange across a wide spectrum of applications.

1.3   Basic blocks of Embedded Sensors

Embedded sensors are constructed based on a sophisticated amalgamation of components and principles that enable them to detect and process various physical phenomena. Understanding their construction and working principles sheds light on how these devices seamlessly gather and interpret data.

Embedded sensors are typically composed of several key components:

Sensing Element: This is the core component responsible for detecting the specific physical parameter of interest, such as temperature, pressure, light, or motion. Sensing elements can be based on a variety of materials, including semiconductors, piezoelectric materials, and optical fibers.

Transducer: The transducer converts the physical change detected by the sensing element into an electrical signal. It translates the sensed parameter into a form that can be processed and interpreted by electronic circuits.

Signal Conditioning Circuitry: The raw signal from the transducer might need amplification, filtering, or modification to ensure accuracy and compatibility with further processing. Signal conditioning circuitry prepares the signal for precise interpretation.

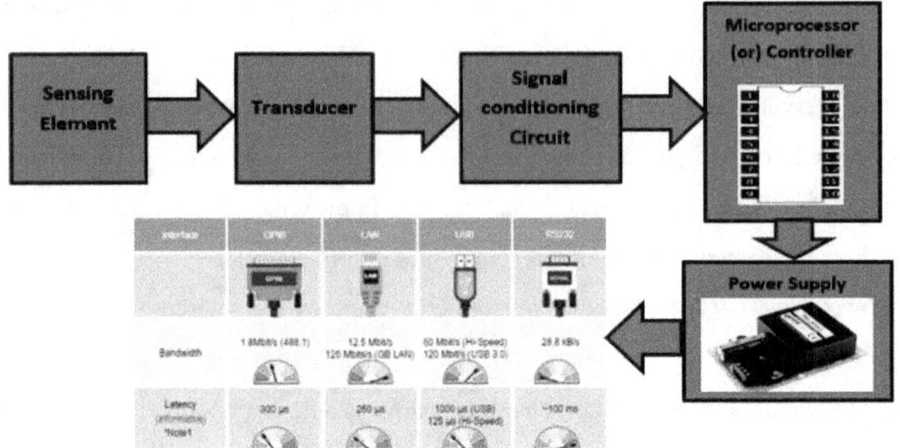

Communication Interfaces

Fig 1.1 Components and flow of data in an embedded sensor system

Microcontroller/Processor: Embedded sensors are equipped with microcontrollers or processors that handle data processing, analysis, and communication. These components make the sensor "smart," enabling it to make decisions based on collected data and transmit information if required.

Power Supply: Sensors require a power source to function. Depending on the application, this could range from batteries to energy harvesting mechanisms, ensuring sustained operation.

Communication Interface: In modern applications, embedded sensors often incorporate wireless communication capabilities. This interface allows the sensor to transmit data to other devices or systems, enabling real-time monitoring and control.

1.4   Types of Embedded Sensors

Embedded sensor construction involves key components like sensing elements, transducers, signal conditioning circuitry, microcontrollers/processors, power supplies, and communication interfaces. Their working principles depend on the specific parameter being measured, and they rely on the interaction between the sensing element and the physical phenomenon. These principles, coupled with innovative design and miniaturization, allow embedded sensors to seamlessly capture and process data across a wide range of applications. Embedded sensors vary based on the type of parameter they're designed to measure. The well knows sensors for the embedded applications are as follows:

Temperature Sensors: These sensors utilize temperature-dependent electrical properties of materials. Common types include thermocouples, resistance temperature detectors (RTDs), and thermistors.

Pressure Sensors: Pressure sensors measure mechanical pressure and convert it into an electrical signal. This is achieved through the deformation of sensing elements like diaphragms or piezoelectric crystals.

Light Sensors: Light sensors, such as photodiodes or phototransistors, detect changes in light intensity or wavelength. These changes lead to variations in electrical current, enabling the sensor to measure light levels.

Motion Sensors: Motion sensors use various technologies like accelerometers, gyroscopes, or passive infrared (PIR) sensors to detect movement or changes in position. Accelerometers, for instance, measure acceleration forces.

Gas Sensors: Gas sensors detect the presence of specific gases by reacting with the target gas and producing an electrical response. This can involve changes in conductivity or potential difference.

Proximity Sensors: Proximity sensors detect the presence or absence of an object within a certain range. Capacitive, inductive, and ultrasonic sensors are commonly used for this purpose.

Humidity Sensors: Humidity sensors measure the moisture content in the air using materials that change their electrical properties with humidity variations, such as capacitive or resistive humidity sensors.

1.5   Performance of Embedded Sensors

The performance of embedded sensors plays a pivotal role in determining the effectiveness and reliability of various applications in which they are deployed. Several key aspects collectively define the performance of these sensors, influencing their accuracy, responsiveness, and overall functionality.

Accuracy and Precision: The accuracy of an embedded sensor refers to its ability to provide measurements that closely match the true value of the parameter being sensed. Precision, on the other hand, relates to the consistency and repeatability of measurements. High accuracy and precision are crucial, especially in applications like medical devices or industrial control systems, where small deviations can lead to significant consequences.

Sensitivity: Sensitivity refers to the ability of a sensor to detect even minor changes in the parameter it is measuring. Sensors with high sensitivity can detect subtle variations, making them suitable for applications where precise monitoring is essential, such as environmental monitoring or scientific research.

Resolution: Resolution refers to the smallest detectable change in the parameter that a sensor can measure. A higher resolution allows the sensor to capture finer details, providing more nuanced data for analysis. For example, in temperature sensors, higher resolution can differentiate between slight temperature fluctuations.

Response Time: The response time of a sensor indicates how quickly it can detect and react to changes in the measured parameter. In applications that require real-time monitoring or rapid adjustments, such as in automated manufacturing or safety systems, a fast response time is critical to maintaining optimal performance.

Drift and Stability: Drift refers to the gradual change in a sensor's output over time, even in constant conditions. Stable sensors exhibit minimal drift, ensuring consistent and reliable measurements over extended periods. Stability is essential in applications where long-term accuracy is required, like calibration instruments.

Linearity: A linear sensor produces a response that is directly proportional to the input signal. Non-linearity can introduce inaccuracies, particularly when measuring a wide range of values. High linearity is essential in applications like data acquisition systems and feedback control loops.

Calibration and Compensation: Embedded sensors often undergo calibration processes to align their output with known reference values. Some sensors also incorporate compensation techniques to mitigate factors like temperature changes that can influence readings. Well-calibrated and compensated sensors offer improved accuracy and reliability.

Environmental Robustness: The ability of a sensor to perform consistently in various environmental conditions, including temperature extremes, humidity, and electromagnetic interference, is crucial. Sensors intended for outdoor use or industrial environments must be designed to withstand harsh conditions.

Power Efficiency: Embedded sensors should operate efficiently to prolong battery life or reduce power consumption in energy-harvesting scenarios. Minimizing energy usage is particularly important for remote or inaccessible locations.

Dynamic Range: The dynamic range of a sensor indicates the span between the lowest and highest values it can accurately measure. A wide dynamic range ensures the sensor remains accurate across a broad range of input values, accommodating diverse applications.

In summary, the performance of embedded sensors encompasses accuracy, sensitivity, resolution, response time, stability, linearity, calibration, environmental robustness, power efficiency, and dynamic range. Achieving optimal performance in these aspects is crucial for enabling reliable data collection, real-time decision-making, and successful integration into a wide spectrum of applications.

1.6   Error analysis characteristics of Embedded Sensors

Error analysis is a fundamental aspect when assessing the performance and reliability of embedded sensors. These characteristics shed light on the accuracy, limitations, and overall quality of sensor measurements. By understanding these traits, engineers and designers can enhance the precision and credibility of data collected by embedded sensors in various applications.

Embedded sensors, while powerful in their ability to capture real-world data, are not immune to errors. This introduction explores the distinct error analysis characteristics that can affect the measurements generated by these sensors. These characteristics encompass both systematic and random errors, offering insights into their sources and methods of mitigation. Understanding the intricacies of error analysis in embedded sensors is essential for refining their performance and ensuring their effectiveness across diverse applications.

Certainly, here are the error analysis characteristics of embedded sensors:

Systematic Errors (Bias): Embedded sensors can exhibit systematic errors that consistently deviate measurements from the true values. These errors can arise due to imperfect calibration, sensor drift over time, or inaccuracies in signal conditioning. Identifying and addressing systematic errors is crucial for accurate measurements.

Random Errors (Noise): Random errors introduce fluctuations in measurements that are unpredictable and inconsistent. They often result from external interference, electronic noise, or variations in the environment. Employing statistical techniques like averaging or filtering can mitigate the impact of random errors.

Resolution Limitation: Embedded sensors have finite resolution, leading to quantization errors when converting analog measurements into digital values.

Higher-resolution sensors provide finer increments and reduce quantization errors.

Interference and Crosstalk: External factors, such as electromagnetic fields or nearby sensors, can introduce interference or crosstalk in measurements. Proper shielding, grounding, and isolation techniques help minimize the influence of external signals.

Non-Linearity: Non-linear behaviour occurs when a sensor's response is not directly proportional to the input. Non-linearity can introduce inaccuracies, especially when operating across a wide range of values. Calibration and compensation methods can mitigate non-linearity.

Temperature Effects: Temperature variations can impact sensor accuracy. Changes in temperature affect sensor characteristics and signal conditioning circuits, leading to errors. Temperature compensation techniques, such as using temperature sensors or mathematical corrections, can counteract these effects.

Drift and Aging: Drift refers to gradual changes in sensor performance over time, affecting measurements. Aging is similar and involves changes due to prolonged usage. Regular recalibration or compensation can minimize drift and aging effects.

Environmental Influences: Embedded sensors can be sensitive to environmental factors like humidity, pressure, and ambient light. Understanding how these variations affect sensor readings is essential for accurate measurements.

Sampling Rate Limitation: Sampling rate determines how often a sensor's value is recorded. Inadequate sampling rates might miss rapid changes, leading to inaccurate representation of the signal. Ensuring an appropriate sampling rate is essential for capturing dynamic changes accurately.

Processing Algorithm Errors: Errors can emerge during data processing and interpretation. Incorrect algorithms or flawed data analysis techniques can propagate errors from sensor readings to final outcomes. Validating and refining processing algorithms is vital for minimizing these errors.

By recognizing and addressing these error analysis characteristics, developers and engineers can optimize the performance of embedded sensors, leading to more accurate and reliable measurements in various applications.

References & Further Reading

1. **"Principles of Embedded Computing System Design"** by Wayne Wolf, edition-1 2000.

2. **"Embedded Systems: A Contemporary Design Tool"** by James K. Peckol edition-2 2018.

UNIT-II Embedded Temperature Sensors

Unit Structure

2.0 Objectives.

2.1 Introduction.

2.2 Resistive temperature transducers

    2.2.1 Metallic resistive temperature sensor

    2.2.2 Thermistors

    2.2.3 Resistance temperature sensor bridge circuits

2.3 Thermocouples.

    2.3.1 Thermocouple Compensation

    2.3.2 Multiple thermocouple arrangements

2.4 Bimetallic temperature sensors

2.5 PN junction sensors

2.6 Liquid crystal temperature sensor

2.7 Pyrometry

References & Further Reading

2.0 Objectives

- Aims to provide readers with fresh insights and perspectives on embedded temperature sensor.

- The introduction provides a clear and concise explanation for basic embedded temperature sensors, highlighting their significance in modern technology.

- To provide concise explanation for different types of embedded temperature sensors, highlighting their significance in modern technology.

- Establishing a foundation of knowledge that readers can build upon as they delve deeper into the topic of embedded temperature sensors.

2.1 Introduction

Embedded temperature sensors are fundamental components of modern technology, seamlessly integrating into various systems to measure and monitor temperature variations. These sensors, often compact and unobtrusive, play a crucial role in a wide spectrum of applications, from industrial processes to consumer devices. This introduction provides an overview of the basic principles and significance of embedded temperature sensors.

Embedded temperature sensors are designed to accurately detect and quantify temperature changes within their environment. Their integration within systems allows for real-time temperature monitoring, facilitating informed decision-making and automation. By converting temperature changes into electrical signals, these sensors enable precise data collection and analysis, contributing to enhanced efficiency, safety, and control. The versatility of embedded temperature sensors lies in their ability to cater to diverse requirements. They offer valuable insights into industrial processes by optimizing manufacturing conditions, ensuring product quality, and maintaining equipment integrity. In homes and commercial buildings, these sensors drive energy-efficient climate control, enhancing comfort and sustainability.

Moreover, embedded temperature sensors have a pivotal role in safety-critical domains. They can identify early warnings of overheating in machinery, preventing malfunctions and potential hazards. In healthcare, these sensors facilitate accurate patient temperature monitoring, essential for diagnoses and treatments. They even extend their utility to scientific research, environmental monitoring, and space exploration, adapting to various contexts and challenges. The subsequent exploration will delve deeper into the principles, types, and applications of embedded temperature sensors, shedding light on their technical intricacies and diverse implementations. By grasping the fundamental concepts surrounding these sensors, we uncover their transformative potential in shaping our interconnected world. This chapter provides concise explanation for different types of embedded temperature sensors, highlighting their construction and operational performance and significance in modern technology.

2.2 Resistive temperature transducers

A temperature transducer is employed to measure the temperature of a physical object. Ordinarily, a transducer is nothing but transforming a physical quantity into electrical energy. Thus, a temperature transducer is an instrument used to convert the thermal energy of the substances into electrical form. In other words, it is a piece of electrical equipment applied for automated measuring of temperature. The latest purpose of the temperature transducer is to measure the heat of the material in a readable format.

Principle Features of Temperature Transducers

Although there are various types and applications for temperature transducers, the basic principle, and features of them are quite similar, which can be summarized as the following:

- The input to a temperature transducer is invariably the thermal quantities.
- They regularly transform the thermal amount into an electrical one.
- They are typically utilized for the determination of the temperature and heat flow.

Resistive temperature sensors are probably the most common type in use .They may be based on metals or semiconductors. The semiconductor versions are the most common and probably cheapest. They are sometimes known as (RTD) Resistance Temperature Detectors. This are another sort of temperature transducer, relatively high accuracy temperature sensors fabricated from high purity conducting metals, such as copper, platinum, or nickel, bound into a coil.

Their electrical resistance varies similarly to that of the thermistor corresponding to the temperature change.

A RTD is an electronic device used to determine the temperature by measuring the resistance of an electrical wire. This wire is referred to as a temperature sensor. If we want to measure temperature with high accuracy, an RTD is the ideal solution, as it has good linear characteristics over a wide range of temperatures.RTD or resistance temperature detector is an electrical sensor used to measure the temperature of the environment by measuring the change in electrical resistance of a metallic wire.

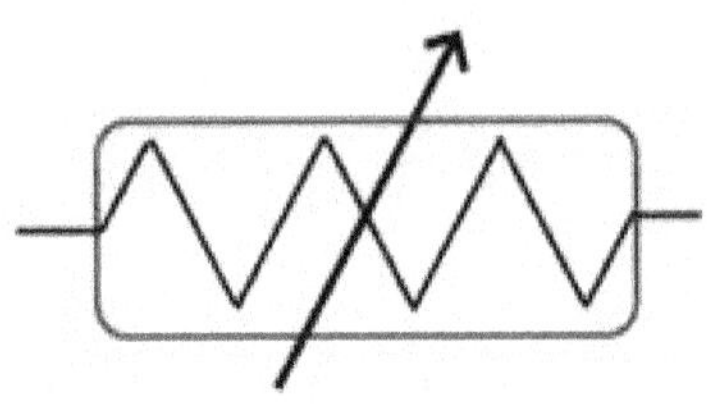

Fig 2.1 RTD- Resistance Temperature Detector

The metallic wire is referred to as the temperature sensor whose resistance varies with the temperature. The resistance is measured using any other device to translate into temperature. It has high accuracy and linear characteristics as compared to other temperature sensors.

Construction of RTD

An RTD or resistance temperature detector is made by wounding the resistive material around a mica base. The material used is drawn into a fine wire to form the elements of the RTD. The wire is wounded in helical shape &it's both terminals are brought out at the same side. The element is protected by a stainless-steel case or sheath. There is an insulator between the element and the outer sheath.

The element is designed in a helical shape to reduce the effects due to tension on it. As we know that the resistance of a wire depends on the temperature as well as the length of the wire. Due to thermal expansion, the wire length increase with temperature which also affects the resistance of the elements. It causes an error in the reading because we want the only temperature to change the resistance & not the physical strain on the wire. Therefore, the element is designed in a helical shape.

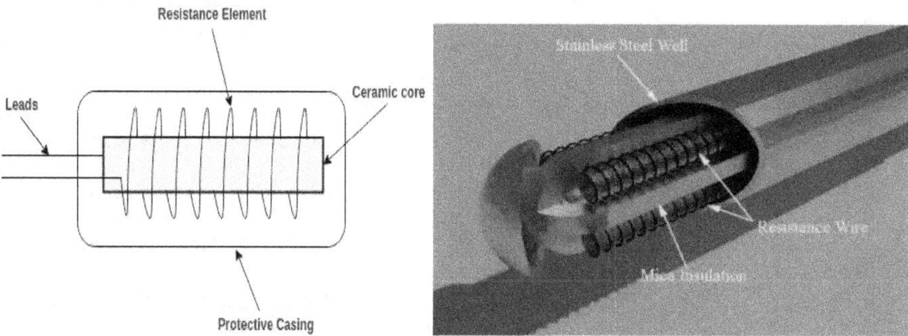

Fig 2.2 (a) Construction of RTD- Resistance Temperature Detector (b) Structural view of an Industrial Resistance Temperature Detector.

The outer protective sheath is made of Inconel, an alloy made of nickel, iron & chromium. It has excellent corrosion resistive properties to protect the inner element from harsh environments. It is an excellent heat conductor that quickly reaches the surrounding temperature and passes it to the element.

Types of Material used in RTD Construction

The RTD element consists of a pure metal whose electrical resistance is directly proportional to the change in temperature i.e., their resistance increases with an increase in temperature and vice versa. The resistance is converted into a voltage signal that represents the proportional temperature value. Almost every conductor shows a change in resistance as its temperature changes. However, they are not that significant due to their low temperature coefficient. But there are certain metals that show properties that offer best performance and linear characteristics. They must possess the following characteristics to be used as an RTD element.

- It must have high temperature coefficient to provide high resistance change per degree of temperature.

- It must have a linear relationship between temperature and resistance.

- It must provide repeatability i.e., its resistance must not change for the same temperature over a span of time.

- It must be durable.

- It must be able to withstand the temperature that is being measured.

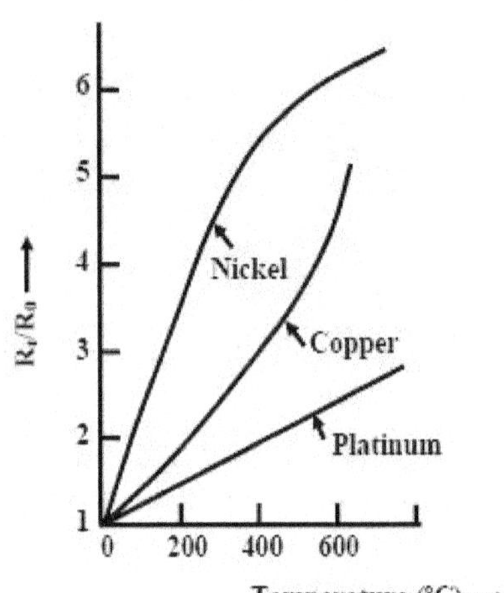

Fig 2.3   Temperature-resistance curve of RTD

The element of RTD is usually made of metals having positive temperature coefficients such as platinum, nickel, copper, or nickel alloy. These materials show stability as well as high temperature coefficient.

Copper

The copper shows linear characteristics with a relatively high temperature coefficient i.e. high resistance change per degree of temperature. However, their operating temperature range is low with low accuracy. It is cheaper than other elements, therefore, it is used in applications where high accuracy & high temperature range is not required such as in motor windings, etc.

Nickel

Nickel shows the highest temperature coefficient of all RTD elements. However, the relation between temperature and resistance is less linear. It results in lower accuracy. Its temperature range is wider than copper but lower than platinum. Since it has lower accuracy, it is used due to its cheaper price as compared to platinum.

Platinum

Platinum shows the most linear characteristics of all three. It provides operation over a wide range of temperatures with high accuracy and repeatability. It has a high temperature coefficient but is expensive as compared to other RTD elements. The platinum RTD elements are used more commonly in industrial applications.

Working Principle of Resistance Temperature Detector

The RTD device works on the principle that the resistance of a conductor changes due to a change in temperature. As we know the resistance of a given conductor having length "l" & area "a" is given by;

$$R = \rho\, l\, /\, a$$

Where
- R = Resistance of the wire
- ρ = Resistivity of the material
- l = length of wire
- a = cross-sectional area of the wire

ρ is the resistivity of the material which is measured in ohm-cm. It depends on the type of material as well as its temperature. Since the length & the area of the wire remains constant throughout RTD operation, the resistance becomes the function of only temperature. Therefore, the resistance of a metal at a given temperature 't' is given by.

$$R_t = R_0\,(1 + \alpha t)$$

- R_t = Resistance at temperature t
- R_0 = Resistance at a reference temperature
- α = coefficient of temperature

The resistance value depends on α, the coefficient of temperature. It is different for different metals. Therefore, such metals are best suited for the RTD element that has the highest α value.

Advantages & Disadvantages of RTD

Advantages

Here are some advantages of RTD.

- It can operate at a wide range of temperatures.
- Its readings are consistent and highly repeatable at high temperature.
- They are resistant to corrosion & best for extreme environments.
- It has more linear characteristics.
- It has excellent accuracy over a wide range of temperatures.
- It is stable & has a longer life span at high temperature measurement.
- The RTD is constructed, installed, and replaced easily.
- It can measure differential temperature.
- They are suitable for monitoring remote areas.

Disadvantages

Here are some disadvantages of RTD.

- It requires a current source.
- Its accuracy depends on the battery's health.
- Heat is generated due to I2R losses in the element also known as self-heating which inflicts error in the measurement thus affecting the accuracy.
- It has a large size, therefore, unable to sense temperature at small points.
- It is affected by physical shock and vibration.
- It has a limited temperature operating range as compared to thermocouple.
- It has a higher initial cost as compared to thermocouple.
- It has complex operating circuitry or signal conditioning unit.

- It requires an external circuit to operate such as a bridge circuit with a power supply.
- It has low sensitivity & slower response time.

Applications of RTD's

RTD is generally used for continuous monitoring of temperature in various applications. Some of these applications are given below.

- It is used in applications where temperature control is important.
- It is used in remote areas where it is difficult to get access.
- It is used to measure the temperature of the engine & the air intake in automotive.
- In different industrial processes such as food handling and manufacturing, it is used to monitor the temperature.
- In different power electronics, medical & military electronics use RTD.
- It is also used in multiple communication and instrumentation for temperature measurement.

2.2.1 Metallic resistive temperature sensor

Principle of Operation:

A metallic resistive temperature sensor operates based on the principle of the temperature-dependent change in electrical resistance of a metallic material. According to the fundamental concept of electrical resistance, the resistance of a conductor increases with an increase in temperature. This phenomenon is utilized in metallic resistive temperature sensors to measure temperature accurately.

Construction:

It is the most frequently used sensor element in industrial thermometers and changes its ohmic resistance depending on the temperature. Connected to an evaluation unit, the sensor temperature can be determined from the measured resistance. Usually used as a platinum chip temperature sensor and consists of a ceramic carrier to which a thin platinum layer is applied by a sputtering process. Due to the very thin layer thickness, the term thin film sensors are also commonly used. The platinum coating is then structured in a meandering pattern using a photolithographic process. The connecting wires are welded onto pads and these contact surfaces are strain-relieved with a glass layer. A further - melted - glass layer acts as a cover layer to protect the platinum meanders from external influences and serves as insulation.

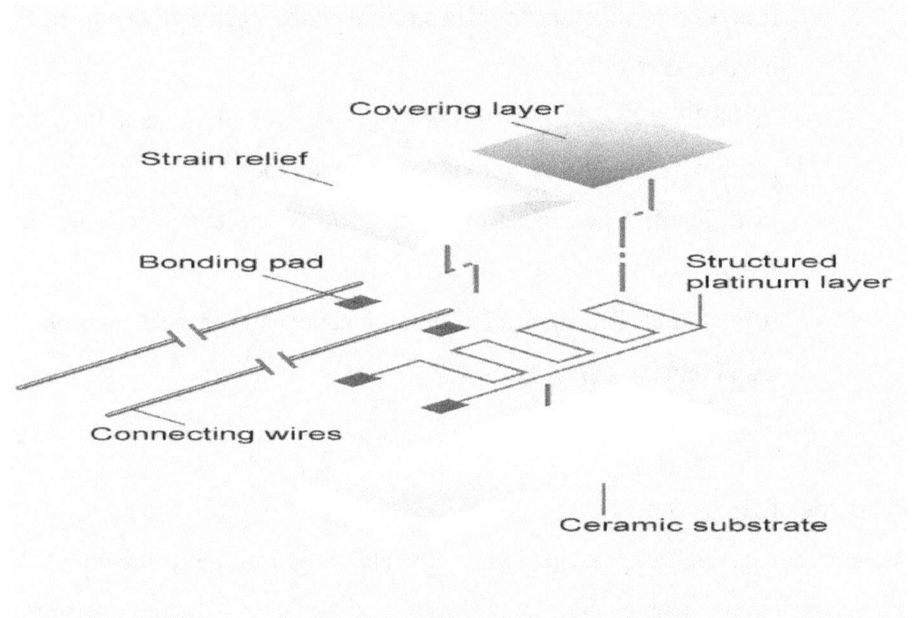

Fig 2.4 Miniature Platinum Resistance Transducer

Furthermore, the thin film sensors are available in Surface Mounted Device design, SMD design for short. These do not have any wire connections but are soldered directly onto the circuit board via solderable connection caps. "Pt" is the designation for platinum and the number 100 designates the basic resistance of 100 ohms at 0 °C. At 0 °C, a Pt100 has a basic resistance of 100 Ohm. With increasing temperature, the sensor changes its resistance by about 0.38 ohm/kelvin (i.e. per °C temperature change). The characteristic curve is standardized (DIN EN 60751) and thus evaluation units can determine the sensor temperature from the measured resistance.

For metallic temperature sensors a polynomial can be used to calculate which sensor resistance results for different sensor temperatures. The basic formula for the second order polynomial is:

$$R(T) = R0 \times (1 + A \times \vartheta + B \times \vartheta 2)$$

R0: Basic resistance at 0 °C :   **ϑ:** Temperature in °C: **A, B:** Individual coefficients of the sensor.

For a P_t=100, the base resistance is 100 Ω **and the coefficients** are 3.9083×10-3 ° C-1 (A) and -5.775×10-7 °C-2(B). Substituted into the polynomial, the Pt 100 formula is:

R(T) = 100 Ω x (1 + 3.9083 ×10-3 °C-1 x ϑ - 5.775 ×10-7 °C-2x ϑ2)

The formula is valid for positive temperatures. Platinum sensors also exist with basic resistances such as 1000 ohms (at 0 °C). Other nominal resistances are also producible, but rare. The thin film technology allows measurements in a range from -70 to +600 °C.

Working and Operational Principle:

The sensor consists of a metallic material, typically platinum (P_t), nickel (N_i), or copper (Cu), that exhibits a predictable change in resistance with temperature. Platinum is commonly used due to its stable and linear temperature-resistance relationship over a wide range of temperatures. The sensor is often constructed in the form of a wire or thin film.

When the metallic sensor is subjected to a temperature change, the resistance of the material changes proportionally. This change in resistance is measured using a Wheatstone bridge circuit or a simple voltage divider configuration. The sensor is usually connected in a circuit with a known excitation voltage, and the resulting voltage across the sensor is measured. By analysing the change in voltage or current, the temperature can be accurately determined based on the resistance-temperature characteristics of the specific metallic material.

Merits:

- **High Accuracy:** Metallic resistive temperature sensors provide high accuracy and precision in temperature measurement, making them suitable for various critical applications such as industrial processes, scientific research, and medical equipment.

- **Wide Temperature Range:** Depending on the choice of metallic material, these sensors can operate over a wide temperature range, from cryogenic temperatures to high temperatures.

- **Stability:** Platinum-based sensors, in particular, offer excellent long-term stability and repeatability of temperature measurements due to their consistent resistance-temperature relationship.

- **Linearity:** Metallic resistive temperature sensors often exhibit a linear relationship between resistance and temperature, simplifying the calibration process.

Demerits:

Limited Sensitivity: While these sensors offer good accuracy, their sensitivity might be limited compared to other types of temperature sensors like thermocouples or thermistors.

Self-Heating: When current flows through the metallic sensor to measure its resistance, it can lead to self-heating, causing inaccuracies in temperature measurements, especially at low temperatures.

Slower Response Time: The response time of metallic resistive temperature sensors might be slower compared to some other sensor types, which could be a limitation in applications requiring rapid temperature changes to be detected.

Cost: Platinum-based sensors, which are widely considered the most accurate, can be expensive due to the cost of the platinum material itself.

2.2.2 Thermistors

The word thermistor is a summarized form of "Thermal Resistor". As the name implies, it is a device in which resistance varies with the temperature change. They are extensively employed for the measurements of the temperature due to their high sensitivity. They are regularly called the ideal temperature transducer. Thermistors are commonly comprised of a mixture of metallic oxides.

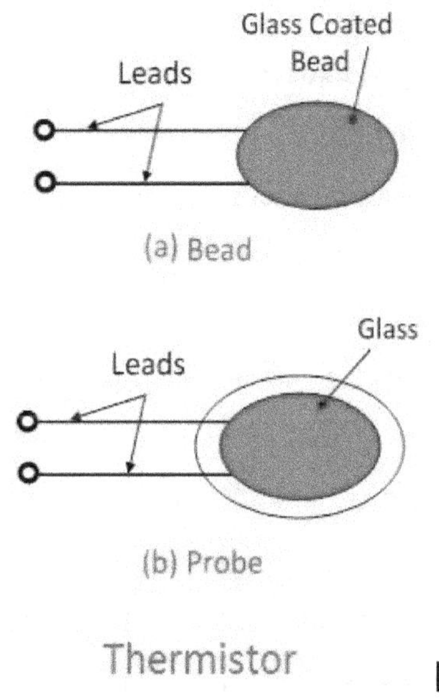

Fig 2.5 Schematic view of thermistors (Reference: **electrical4u.com**)

Bead Thermistors:

Bead thermistors, also known as bead-type thermistors, are a type of thermistors where the sensing element is encapsulated within a small bead-like package. This bead is usually made of ceramic material that is highly sensitive to changes in temperature. The ceramic material's resistance changes significantly with temperature variations, and this change in resistance is used to calculate the temperature. Bead thermistors are often small and rugged, making them suitable for various applications, such as temperature monitoring in industrial settings, HVAC systems, and automotive applications.

Probe Thermistor:

A probe thermistor is a thermistor sensor that is encapsulated within a probe-like housing. This housing can be made of materials like stainless steel or plastic, and it typically has a pointed or cylindrical shape, which makes it easy to insert into liquids, gases, or other substances to measure their temperature. Probe thermistors are commonly used for applications where direct contact with the substance being measured is required, such as in food processing, laboratory experiments, and medical equipment.

Characteristics of Thermistors

Thermistors have various types and applications; however, they have some common characteristics as follows:

- They have a "Negative Thermal Coefficient", i.e., the thermistor resistance diminishes with an increment in temperature.
- They are produced from semiconductor materials.
- They are generally more sensitive than "Thermocouples" and "Resistance Thermometers".
- Their resistance extends within 0.5 Ω to 0.75 MΩ.
- They are generally employed in applications with a temperature range between -60degree C to 15-degreeC.

Thermistor is a solid-state temperature sensing device which acts a bit like an electrical resistor but is temperature sensitive. Thermistors can be used to produce an analogue output voltage with variations in ambient temperature and as such can be referred to as a transducer. This is because it creates a change in its electrical properties due to an external and physical change in heat.

The thermistor is basically a two-terminal solid state thermally sensitive transducer constructed using sensitive semiconductor-based metal oxides with metallised or sintered connecting leads formed into a ceramic disc or bead.

This allows the thermistor to change its resistive value in proportion to small changes in ambient temperature. In other words, as its temperature changes, so too does its resistance and as such its name, "Thermistor" is a combination of the words THERM-ally sensitive res-ISTOR.

While the change in resistance due to heat is generally undesirable in standard resistors, this effect can be put to good use in many temperature detection circuits. Thus, being non-linear variable-resistive devices, thermistors are commonly used as temperature sensors having many applications to measure the temperature of both liquids and ambient air.

Also, being a solid-state device made from highly sensitive metal oxides, they operate at the molecular level with the outermost (valence) electrons becoming more active producing a negative temperature coefficient, or less active producing a positive temperature coefficient as the temperature of the thermistor is increased.

This means they have very good resistance verses temperature characteristics allowing them to operate at temperatures up to200-degree C.

Typical Thermistor

While the principal use of thermistors is as resistive temperature sensors, they can also be connected in series with another component or device to control an electrical current flowing through them. In other words, they can be used as thermally sensitive current-limiting devices.

Thermistors are available in a whole range of types, materials and sizes characterised by their response time and operating temperature. Also, hermetically sealed thermistors eliminate errors in resistance readings due to moisture penetration while still offering high operating temperatures and a compact size. The three most common types are: Bead thermistors, Disk thermistors, and Glass encapsulated thermistors.

These heat-dependent resistors can operate in one of two ways, either by increasing or decreasing their resistive value with changes in temperature. Then there are two types of thermistors available: negative temperature coefficient (NTC) of resistance and positive temperature coefficient (PTC) of resistance.

Negative Temperature Coefficient Thermistors

Negative temperature coefficient of resistance thermistors, or *NTC thermistors* for short, reduce or decrease their resistive value as the operating temperature around them increases. Generally, NTC thermistors are the most used type of temperature sensors as they can be used in virtually any type of equipment where temperature plays a role.

NTC temperature thermistors have a negative electrical resistance versus temperature (R/T) relationship. The relatively large negative response of an NTC thermistor means that even small changes in temperature can cause significant changes in their electrical resistance. This makes them ideal for accurate temperature measurement and control.

We said previously that a thermistor is an electronic component whose resistance is highly dependent on temperature so if we send a constant current through the thermistor and then measure the voltage drop across it, we can thus determine its resistance at a particular temperature.

An NTC thermistors reduces its resistance with an increase in temperature and are available in a variety of base resistances and temperature curves. NTC thermistors are usually characterised by their base resistance at room temperature that is 25-degree C, (77oF) as this provides a convenient reference point. So for example, 2k2Ω at 25-degree C, 10kΩ at 25oC or 47kΩ at 25-degree C, etc.

Another important characteristic of a thermistor is its "B" value. The B value is a material constant which is determined by the ceramic material from which it is made. it describes the gradient of the resistive (R/T) curve over a particular temperature range between two temperature points. Each thermistor material will have a different material constant and therefore a different resistance versus temperature curve.

Thus, the B value will define the thermistors resistive value at a first temperature or base point, (which is usually 25-degree C), called T1, and the thermistors resistive value at a second temperature point, for example 100oC, called T2.

Therefore, the B value will define the thermistors material constant between the range of T1 and T2. That is BT1/T2 or B25/100 with typical NTC thermistor B values given anywhere between about 3000 and about 5000.

Note however, that both the temperature points of T1 and T2 are calculated in the temperature units of Kelvin where 00C = 273.15 Kelvin. Thus, a value of 25-degree C is equal to 25-degree C + 273.15 = 298.15K, and 100oC is equal to 100o + 273.15 = 373.15K, etc.

So, by knowing the B value of a particular thermistor (obtained from manufacturers datasheet), it is possible to produce a table of temperature versus resistance to construct a suitable graph using the following normalised equation:

Thermistor Equation

$$B_{\left(T_1/T_2\right)} = \frac{T_2 X T_1}{T_2 - T_1} X \, ln(\frac{R_1}{R_2}$$

Where:
- T1 is the first temperature point in Kelvin.
- T2 is the second temperature point in Kelvin.
- R1 is the thermistors resistance at temperature T1 in Ohms
- R2 is the thermistors resistance at temperature T2 in Ohms

Thermistors Example No.1

A 10kΩ NTC thermistor has a "B" value of 3455 between the temperature range of 25 degree-C and 100 degree-C. Calculate its resistive value at 25 degree-C and again at 100 degree-C.

Data given:

B = 3455, R1 = 10kΩ at 25degree-C. To convert the temperature scale from degrees Celsius, degree-C to degrees Kelvin add the mathematical constant 273.15.

The value of R1 is already given as 10kΩ base resistance, thus the value of R2 at 100degree-C is calculated as:

$$B_{(25/100)} = \frac{(100 + 273.15)X(25 + 273.15)}{(100 + 273.15) - (25 + 273.15)} X \ln\left(\frac{10000}{R_x}\right)$$

$$3455 = \frac{111254.6725}{75} X \ln\left(\frac{10000}{R_x}\right)$$

$$3455 = 1483.4 \, X \, \ln\left(\frac{10000}{R_x}\right)$$

$$e^{\left[\frac{3455}{1483.4}\right]} = \ln\left(\frac{10000}{R_x}\right)$$

$$R_x = \frac{10000}{e^{2.33}} = 973 \, ohms$$

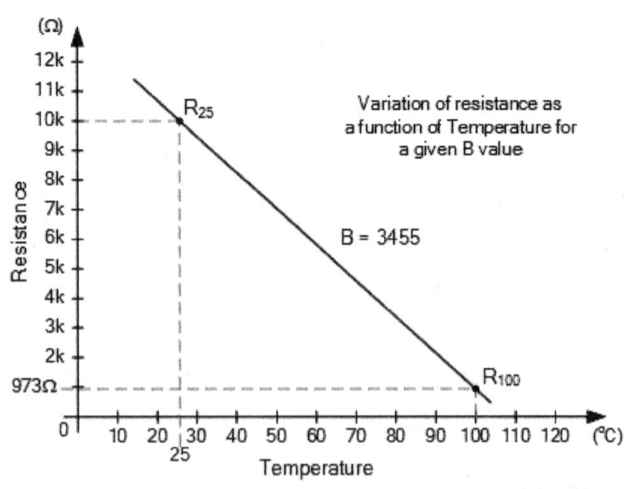

Fig 2.6 Two-point characteristics graph a Thermistor.

Note that in this simple example, only two points were found, but generally thermistors change their resistance exponentially with changes in temperature so their characteristic curve is nonlinear, therefore the more temperature points are calculated the more accurate will be the curve. These points can be plotted as shown to give a more accurate characteristics curve for the 10kΩ NTC Thermistor which has a B-value of 3455.

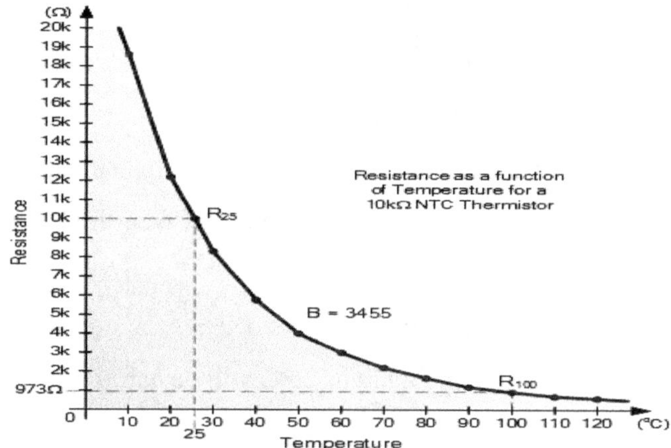

Fig 2.7 NTC Thermistor Characteristics Curve

Notice that it has a negative temperature coefficient (NTC) that is its resistance decreases with increasing temperatures.

Thermistors to Measure Temperature.

So how can we use a thermistor to measure temperature. Hopefully by now we realise that a thermistor is a resistive device and therefore according to Ohms law, if we pass a current through it, a voltage drop will be produced across it. As a thermistor is a passive type of a sensor, that is, it requires an excitation signal for its operation, any changes in its resistance because of changes in temperature can be converted into a voltage change.

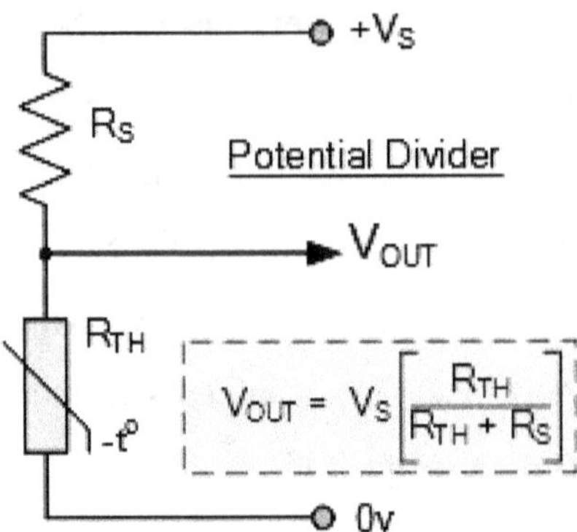

Fig 2.8 Thermistor as part of a potential divider circuit

The simplest way of doing this is to use the thermistor as part of a potential divider circuit as shown. A constant supply voltage is applied across the resistor and thermistor series circuit with the output voltage measured from across the thermistor.

If for example we use a 10kΩ thermistor with a series resistor of 10kΩ, then the output voltage at the base temperature of 25°C will be half the supply voltage as 10Ω/(10Ω+10Ω) = 0.5.

When the resistance of the thermistor changes due to changes in temperature, the fraction of the supply voltage across the thermistor will also change producing an output voltage which is proportional to the fraction of the total series resistance between the output terminals.

Thus, the potential divider circuit is an example of a simple resistance to voltage converter where the resistance of the thermistor is controlled by temperature with the output voltage produced being proportional to the temperature. So the hotter the thermistor gets, the lower the output voltage. If we reversed the positions of the series resistor, RS and the thermistor, RTH, then the output voltage would change in the opposite direction, that is the hotter the thermistor gets, the higher the output voltage.

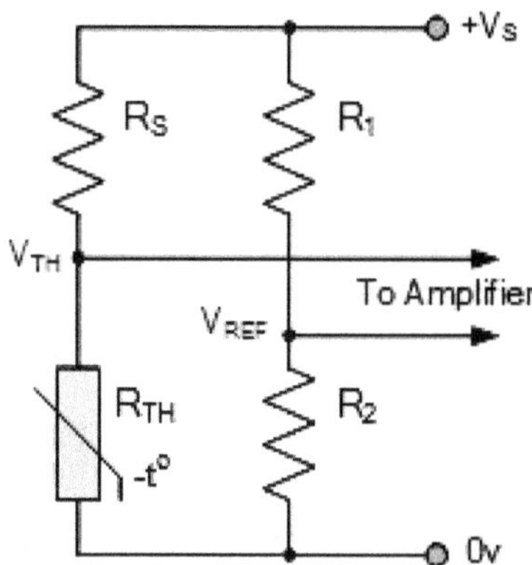

Fig 2.9 Potential divider circuit with series resistors

We can use NTC thermistors as part of a basic temperature sensing configuration using a bridge circuit as shown. The relationship between resistors R1 and R2 sets the reference voltage, V$_{REF}$ to the value required. For example, if both R1 and R2 are of the same resistive value, the reference voltage will be equal to half of the supply voltage as before. That is Vs/2.

As the temperature and therefore the resistive value of the thermistor changes, the voltage at VTH will also change, either higher or lower than that at VREF producing a positive or negative output signal to the connected amplifier. The amplifier circuit used for this basic temperature sensing bridge circuit could act as a differential amplifier for high sensitivity and amplification, or a simple Schmitt-trigger circuit for ON-OFF switching.

The problem with passing a current through a thermistor in this way, is that thermistors experience what is called a self-heating effect, that is the I2*R power loss could be high enough to create more heat than can be dissipated by the thermistor affecting its resistive value producing false results.

Thus, it is possible that if the current through the thermistor is too high it would result in increased power dissipation and as the temperature increases, its resistance decreases causing more current to flow, which increases the temperature further resulting in what is known as *Thermal Runaway*. In other words, we want the thermistor to be hot due to the external temperature being measured and not by itself heating up. The value for the series resistor, RS above should be chosen to provide a reasonably wide response over the expected range of temperatures for which the thermistor is likely to be used while at the same time limiting the current to a safe value at the highest temperature.

One way of improving on this and having a more accurate conversion of resistance against temperature (R/T) is by driving the thermistor with a constant current source. The change in resistance can be measured by using a small and measured direct current, or DC, passed through the thermistor to measure the output voltage drop produced.

Applications

Some most important applications of thermistors are as the following:

- They can be utilized as current-limiting devices for circuit security as replacements for fuses.
- They can be employed as timers in the degaussing coil circuit of most Cathode-ray tube (CRT) displays.
- They can be employed as a heater in the automotive industry to produce additional heat inside the cabin with a diesel engine.
- They can also be utilized in the protection circuits of lithium batteries.
- They can be used as a resistance thermometer for very low-temperature measurements in the order of 10 K.
- They are also employed as sensors in automotive applications to monitor fluid temperatures like the cabin air, engine coolant, engine oil temperature, or external air, and supply the relative readings to regulate units like the ECU.

- Thermistors are also regularly used in modern digital thermostats and monitor battery packs' temperature during charging.

- During the purchaser appliance industry for estimating temperature. Toasters, freezers, refrigerators, hairdryers, etc., depending on thermistors for precise temperature control.

- They are used to determine the temperature profile inside the sealed hole of a convective (thermal) inertial sensor.

2.2.3 Resistance temperature sensor bridge circuits

The Wheatstone bridge configuration is a classic circuit used for accurate resistance measurement, including RTDs. It consists of four resistive arms in a diamond shape, with the RTD forming one of the arms. The other three arms consist of precision resistors, usually known as 'balancing resistors.' When the bridge is balanced, meaning the voltage across its output terminals is zero, the ratio of resistances in the arms can be used to calculate the resistance of the RTD, which is directly related to the temperature.

A typical electrical circuit designed to measure temperature with RTDs measures a change in *resistance* of the RTD, which is then used to calculate a change in temperature. The resistance of an RTD increases with increasing temperature, just as the resistance of a strain gage increases with increasing strain. Figure below shows a basic bridge circuit which consists of three known resistances, R1, R2, and R3 (variable), an unknown variable resistor RX (RTD), a source of voltage, and a sensitive ammeter.

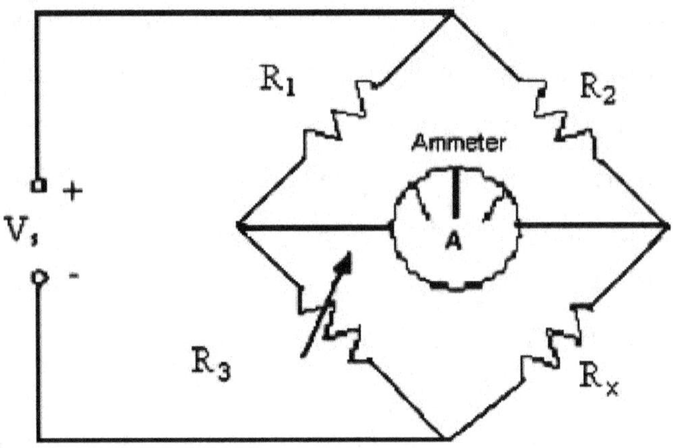

Fig 2.10 Basic bridge circuit

Resistors R1 and R2 are the ratio arms of the bridge. They ratio the two variable resistances for current flow through the ammeter. R3 is a variable resistor known as the standard arm that is adjusted to match the unknown resistor. The sensing ammeter visually displays the current that is flowing through the bridge circuit. Analysis of the circuit shows that when R3 is adjusted so that the ammeter reads zero current, the resistance of both arms of the bridge circuit is the same. The relationship of the resistance between the two arms of the bridge can be expressed as $\dfrac{R_1}{R_3} - \dfrac{R_2}{R_X}$

Since the values of R1, R2, and R3 are known values, the only unknown is Rx. The value of Rx can be calculated for the bridge during an ammeter zero current condition. Knowing this resistance value provides a baseline point for calibration of the instrument attached to the bridge circuit. The unknown resistance, Rx, is given by $R_X = \dfrac{R_2 R_3}{R_1}$

Advantages of Wheatstone Bridge for RTDs:

- High precision and accuracy in temperature measurement.
- Minimized effects of lead wire resistance and supply voltage variations.
- Suitable for both 2-wire and 4-wire RTD configurations.

Disadvantages:

- Requires precision resistors, making it relatively more complex and potentially expensive.
- Changes in resistors' values over time or due to temperature can affect accuracy.

2.3   Thermocouples.

Thermocouples are temperature sensors that operate on the principle of the Seebeck effect, where a voltage is generated at the junction of two dissimilar metals in response to a temperature difference. To achieve accurate temperature measurements using thermocouples, compensation techniques are employed to account for errors and ensure reliable results. Thermocouples are very common temperature sensors in process plants. Thermocouples have few benefits that makes them widely used. They can be used to measure very high temperatures, much higher than with RTDs (Resistance temperature detector). The thermocouple is also a very robust sensor, so it does not break easily.

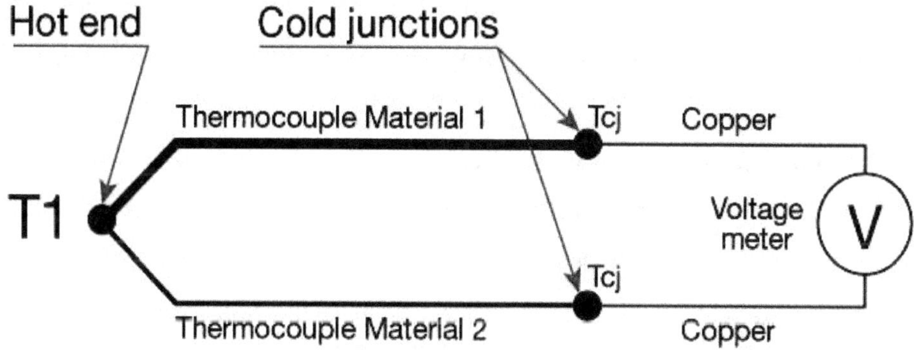

Fig 2.11 Simplified thermocouple

Although thermocouples are not as accurate as RTD sensors, they are accurate enough in many applications. Thermocouples are also relatively cheap sensors, and the thermocouple measurement circuit does not require excitation current like an RTD circuit does, so the circuit is in that sense, simpler to make. As discovered back in 1821 by Thomas Johann See beck, when the connection point of these wires is taken into different temperatures, there will be a thermo-electric current generated, causing a small voltage between the wires in the open end. The voltage depends on temperature and on the materials of the conductive wires being used. This effect was named as **Seebeck effect.**

In the above figure the "Thermocouple material 1 and 2" represent the two different materials the thermocouple is made of. "T1" is the hot end of the thermocouple, i.e. the point that is used to measure temperature. The two "Tcj" are the temperatures of the cold junctions.

A thermocouple is a device for measuring temperature. It comprises two dissimilar metallic wires joined together to form a junction. When the junction is heated or cooled, a small voltage is generated in the electrical circuit of the thermocouple which can be measured, and this corresponds to temperature.

In theory, any two metals can be used to make a thermocouple but in practice, there are a fixed number of types that are commonly used. They have been developed to give improved linearity and accuracy and comprise specially developed alloys.

Thermocouples can be made to suit almost any application. They can be made to be robust, fast responding and to measure a very wide temperature range. The thermocouple can be defined as a kind of temperature sensor that is used to measure the temperature at one specific point in the form of the EMF or an electric current. This sensor comprises two dissimilar metal wires that are connected at one junction. The temperature can be measured at this junction, and the change in temperature of the metal wire stimulates the voltages. The amount of EMF generated in the device is very minute (millivolts), so very sensitive devices must be utilized for calculating the e.m.f produced in the circuit. The common devices used to calculate the e.m.f are voltage balancing potentiometer and the ordinary galvanometer. From these two, a balancing potentiometer is utilized physically or mechanically.

The thermocouple diagram is shown in the below picture. This circuit can be built with two different metals, and they are coupled together by generating two junctions. The two metals are surrounded by the connection through welding. In the below diagram, the junctions are denoted by P & Q, and the temperatures are denoted by T1, & T2. When the temperature of the junction is dissimilar from each other, then the electromagnetic force generates in the circuit.

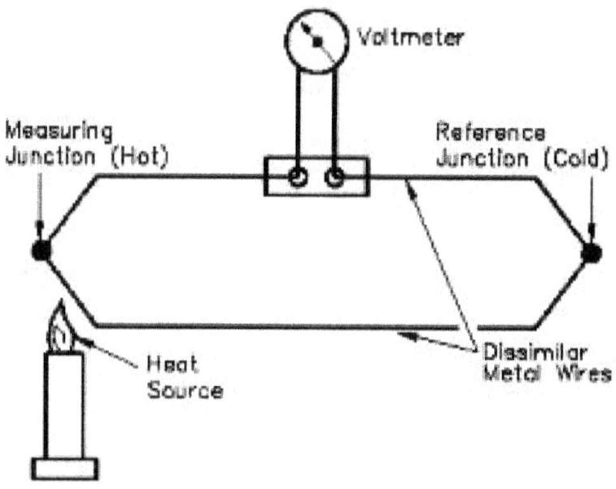

Fig 2.12 Operational diagram of thermocouple

If the temperate at the junction end turn into equivalent, then the equivalent, as well as reverse electromagnetic force, produces in the circuit, and there is no flow of current through it. Similarly, the temperature at the junction end becomes imbalanced, and then the potential variation induces in this circuit.

The magnitude of the electromagnetic force induces in the circuit relies on the sorts of material utilized for thermocouple making. The entire flow of current throughout the circuit is calculated by the measuring tools.

The electromagnetic force induced in the circuit is calculated by the following equation.

$$E = a\,(\Delta\Theta) + b\,(\Delta\Theta)2$$

Where $\Delta\Theta$ is the temperature difference among the hot thermocouple junction end as well as the reference thermocouple junction end, a & b are constants.

Advantages & Disadvantages

The advantages of thermocouples include the following.

- Accuracy is high.
- It is Robust and can be used in environments like harsh as well as high vibration.
- The thermal reaction is fast.
- The operating range of the temperature is wide.
- Wide operating temperature range
- Cost is low and extremely consistent.

The disadvantages of thermocouples include the following.

- Nonlinearity
- Least stability
- Low voltage
- Reference is required.
- least sensitivity
- The thermocouple recalibration is hard.

Applications

- Some of the **applications of thermocouples** include the following.
- These are used as the temperature sensors in thermostats in offices, homes, offices & businesses.
- These are used in industries for monitoring temperatures of metals in iron, aluminium, and metal.
- These are used in the food industry for cryogenic and Low-temperature applications. Thermocouples are used as heat pumps for performing thermoelectric cooling.

- These are used to test temperature in chemical plants, petroleum plants.
- These are used in gas machines for detecting the pilot flame.

2.3.1 Thermocouple Compensation

Thermocouples are widely used temperature sensors based on the Setback effect, which generates a voltage proportional to the temperature difference between two junctions of dissimilar metals. However, accurate temperature measurement with thermocouples requires compensation techniques to account for various sources of error that can affect the measurement accuracy.

Cold Junction Compensation (CJC): The fundamental principle of thermocouple compensation is Cold Junction Compensation (CJC). The measurement junction where the thermocouple wires connect to the measurement instrument is referred to as the "cold" junction. To accurately determine the temperature at the "hot" junction (the point being measured), the temperature at the cold junction must be known.

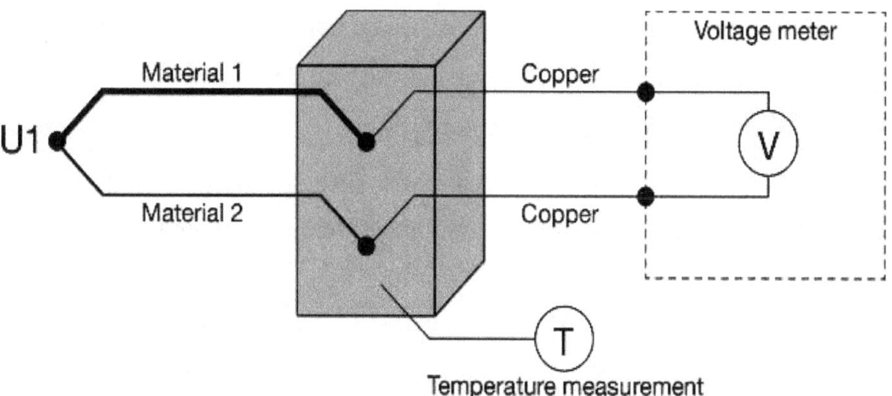

Fig 2.13 Operational diagram of Cold Junction Compensation (CJC) thermocouple

CJC involves measuring the temperature at the cold junction using a separate temperature sensor, typically a thermistor or an RTD (Resistance Temperature Detector). This cold junction temperature is used to adjust the thermocouple's output voltage. By referencing the temperature at the cold junction, compensation can be applied to eliminate errors introduced by temperature variations at this point.

Mathematical Compensation: Once the cold junction temperature is known, the voltage generated by the thermocouple can be compensated mathematically. This compensation involves applying a correction to the thermocouple's output based on the known cold junction temperature and the specific characteristics of the thermocouple material. Calibration tables, polynomial equations, or digital signal processing algorithms can be used to perform this compensation and convert the voltage reading into an accurate temperature measurement.

Extension or "Lead Wire" Compensation: Another source of error in thermocouple measurements is the temperature gradient along the thermocouple wires (lead wires) between the measurement point and the cold junction. These temperature gradients can introduce inaccuracies. Extension or "lead wire" compensation involves using thermocouple wires of the same material as the thermocouple, thus ensuring that any temperature-induced voltage drop along the leads is uniform and can be compensated for.

Advantages of Thermocouple Compensation:

Enhanced Accuracy: Compensation techniques significantly improve the accuracy of thermocouple temperature measurements by mitigating errors introduced by the cold junction and lead wire effects.

Wide Temperature Range: Compensation allows accurate measurements over a wide temperature range, making thermocouples suitable for various applications.

Simplicity: Compensation can be implemented through simple mathematical calculations or lookup tables, making it accessible for practical use.

Limitations:

Complexity: Compensation techniques may introduce additional complexity to the measurement setup, requiring proper calibration and adjustment.

Cost: Additional sensors, such as thermistors or RTDs, might be needed for CJC, leading to increased costs.

Calibration Requirements: Compensation accuracy relies on proper calibration and understanding of the thermocouple characteristics.

2.3.2 Multiple thermocouple arrangements

In temperature measurement applications, different arrangements of multiple thermocouples can be utilized to enhance accuracy, extend temperature ranges, provide redundancy, and address specific measurement challenges. These arrangements take advantage of the characteristics of various thermocouple types and their unique properties.

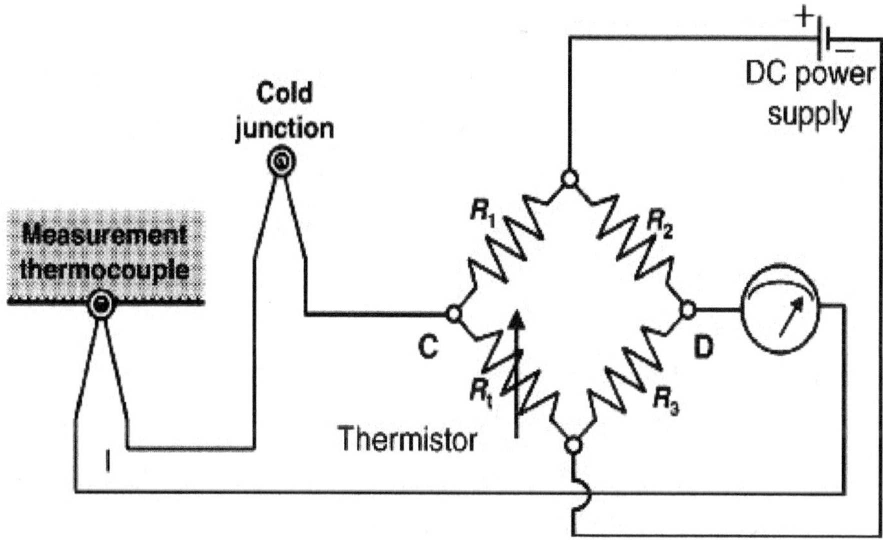

Fig 2.14 Cold junction compensation of a thermocouple.

Differential Arrangement:

A differential thermocouple configuration employs two different thermocouple types to measure the temperature difference between two points. One thermocouple measures the actual temperature at the measurement point, while the other measures the temperature at a reference point. The difference in the outputs of the two thermocouples provides an accurate measurement of the temperature difference. This arrangement is particularly useful in applications where temperature gradients need to be measured.

Parallel (Homogeneous) Arrangement:

In a parallel arrangement, multiple thermocouples of the same type are connected in parallel. This configuration helps increase accuracy and redundancy by averaging the outputs of the individual thermocouples. It is particularly useful in critical applications where precision and reliability are essential. The parallel arrangement helps mitigate potential errors caused by a single thermocouple's drift or failure.

Series (Heterogeneous) Arrangement:

A series arrangement involves connecting two or more thermocouples of different types in series. This arrangement allows measurements over a wider temperature range, as different thermocouples have distinct temperature ranges where they exhibit accurate and linear behaviour. By combining the outputs of multiple thermocouples, accurate measurements can be obtained across a broader span of temperatures.

Thermopile Configuration:

A thermopile consists of multiple thermocouples connected in series. This arrangement generates a higher output voltage, which is beneficial in applications where the thermocouple's voltage output needs to be amplified for further signal processing. Thermopiles are often used in situations where the temperature difference between the measurement point and the reference junction is relatively small.

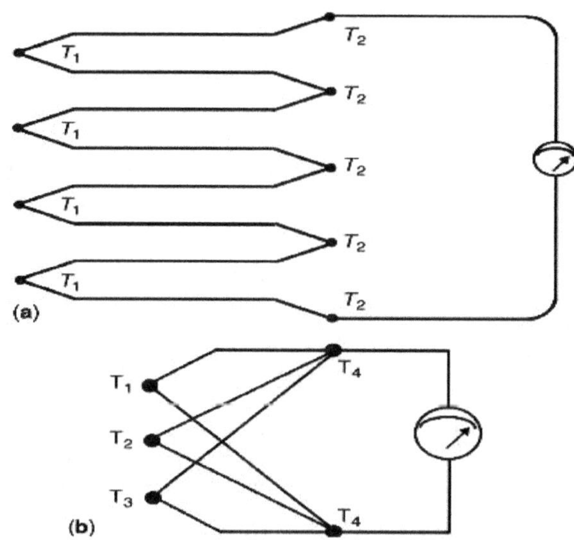

Fig 2.15(a) A serial thermopile and (b) Averaging with parallel connected thermocouples.

Advantages of Multiple Thermocouple Arrangements:

Enhanced Accuracy: Multiple thermocouple arrangements can improve measurement accuracy by compensating for individual thermocouple drift and nonlinearity.

Wider Temperature Range: Series and differential arrangements extend the usable temperature range by combining the strengths of different thermocouple types.

Redundancy and Reliability: Parallel arrangements provide redundancy, ensuring reliable measurements even if one thermocouple fails.

Customized Solutions: Different arrangements can be chosen to suit specific temperature measurement requirements.

Limitations:

Complexity: Some arrangements, such as series and differential configurations, require careful calibration and consideration of the characteristics of each thermocouple type.

Increased Wiring: Multiple thermocouples may require more complex wiring and signal conditioning.

Cost: The use of multiple thermocouples and specialized arrangements may lead to higher costs.

2.4 Bimetallic temperature sensors

Definition: The bimetallic thermometer uses the bimetallic strip which converts the temperature into mechanical displacement. The working of the bimetallic strip depends on the thermal expansion property of the metal.

Thermal expansion is the tendency of metal in which the volume of metal changes with the variation in temperature. Every metal has a different temperature coefficient. The temperature coefficient shows the relation between the change in the physical dimension of metal and the temperature that causes it. The expansion or contraction of metal depends on the temperature coefficient, i.e., at the same temperature the metals have different changes in the physical dimension.

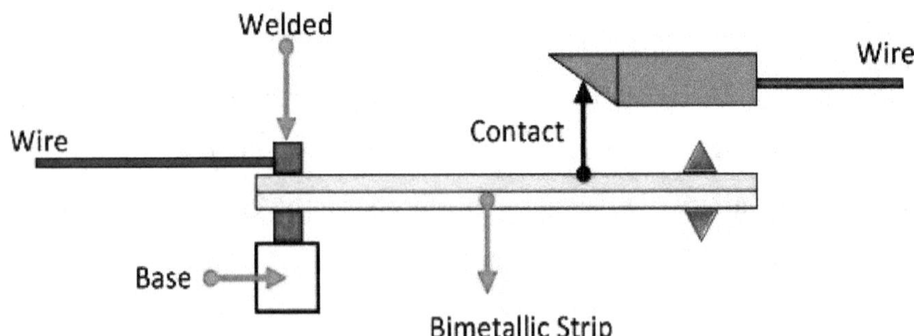

Fig 2.16A Bimetallic Thermometer

Working Principle of Bimetallic Thermometer

The working principle of bimetallic thermometer depends on the two fundamental properties of the metal.

1. The metal has the property of thermal expansion, i.e., the metal expands and contract concerning the temperature.

2. The temperature coefficient of all the metal is not the same. The expansion or contraction of metals is different at the same temperature.

Constructions of Bimetallic Thermometer

The bimetallic strip is constructed by bonding together the two thin strips of different metals. The metals are joined together at one end with the help of the welding. The bonding is kept in such a way that there is no relative motion between the two metals. The physical dimension of the metals varies with the variation in temperature.

Since the bimetallic strip of the thermometer is constructed with different metals. Thereby, the length of metals changes at different rates. When the temperature increases, the strip bends towards the metal which has a low-temperature coefficient. And when the temperature decreases, the strip bends towards the metal which has a high-temperature coefficient. The figure below shows the bimetallic strip in the form of the straight cantilever beam. The strip is fixed at one end and deflects at the other end.

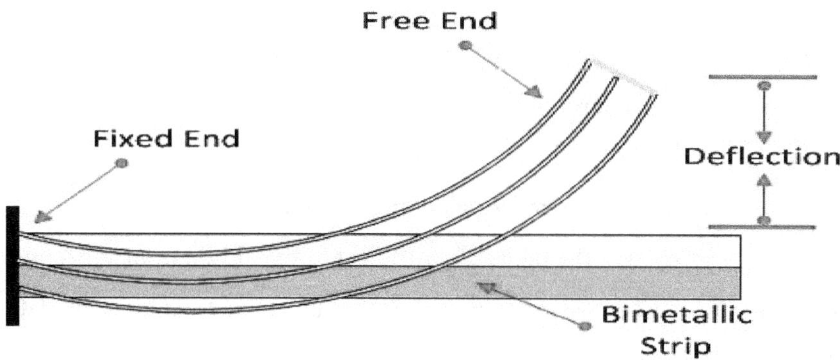

Fig 2.17A bimetallic strip fixed at one end.

The range of deflection of bimetallic strip depends on the type of metals used for construction. The deflection of the metal is directly proportional to the length of the strip and the variation of temperature and is inversely proportional to the thickness of the strips.

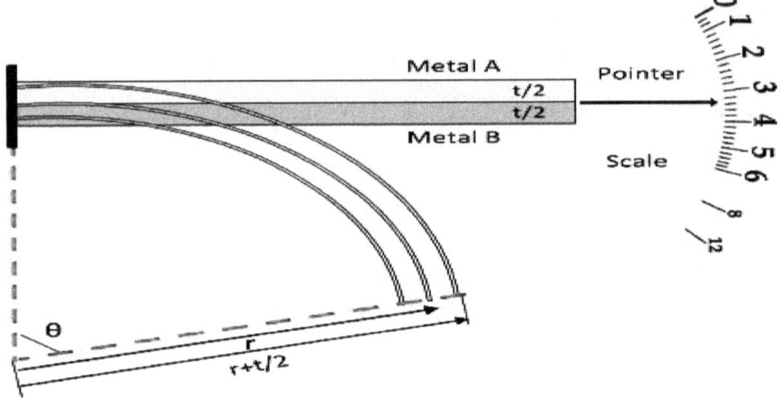

Fig 2.18 Deflection of Bimetallic Strain.

Let understand this with the help of the mathematical formula. Consider the bimetallic strip is made of two different metals, i.e., metal A and metal B. Both the metals have a different temperature coefficient. The T2 – T1 shows the variation of temperature, which causes the expansion of the string.

$$r = \frac{t[3(1+m)^2 + (1+mn)(m^2 + 1/mn)]}{6(\alpha_A - \alpha_B)(T_2 - T_1)(1+m)^2}$$

Where,   t – the total thickness of the strip

n – the ratio of moduli of elasticity = EB/EA

m – the ratio of the thickness

$T_2 - T_1$ – change in temperature

t_A, t_B – the thickness of metal A and metal B.

α_A, α_B– the thermal coefficient of expansion of metal A and B.

The expansion causes the strip to move in the uniform circular arc. The radius of the arm is given by the formula shown below.

$$r = \frac{2t}{6(\alpha_A - \alpha_B)(T_2 - T_1)}$$

The above equation shows that the strip bends towards the metals which have a low-temperature coefficient (when the temperature increases) and the inverse will happen when the temperature decreases. For practical applications, the strip is made of metals whose moduli of elasticity and thickness are same. The moduli of elasticity show the ability of the material to regain its original position or shape after the removal of force or load. Consider the strip is fixed at one end and free to move at the other end. When the temperature surrounding the strip varies, the strip bends towards the circular arc. Consider the strip is made of metal having thickness t/2.

$$\frac{r + t/2}{r} = \frac{expanded\ length\ of\ strip\ A}{expanded\ length\ of\ strip\ B}$$

$$= \frac{L[1 + \alpha_A(T_2 - T_1)]}{L[1 + \alpha_B(T_2 - T_1)]}$$

$$r = \frac{t}{2}\left|\frac{[1 + \alpha_B(T_2 - T_1)]}{[(\alpha_A - \alpha_B)(T_2 - T_1)]}\right|$$

$$r = \frac{t}{2\alpha_A(T_2 - T_1)}$$

If one of the metals has a very small temperature coefficient, then the above equation shows that if one end of the metal is fixed, the deflection of the free end of metals shows the variation of temperature. This thermometer is not used for industrial application because of low sensitivity and small deflection. The sensitivity of the thermometer increases with the increase of the length of the strip.

Types of Bimetallic Strip

The linear strip shows a small deflection. If the length of strip increases, the size of the thermometer also increases. For keeping the size of the thermometer in the manageable limit, the helix or spiral strip is used for making the thermometer.

Spiral Strip bimetallic thermometer – In bimetallic strip thermometer, the spiral-shaped strip is used. This type of thermometer is used for measuring ambient temperature. Because of the thermal expansion property of metal deformation occurs in the spring with the variation of temperature. The pointer and dials attached to the spring, which indicates the variation of temperature.

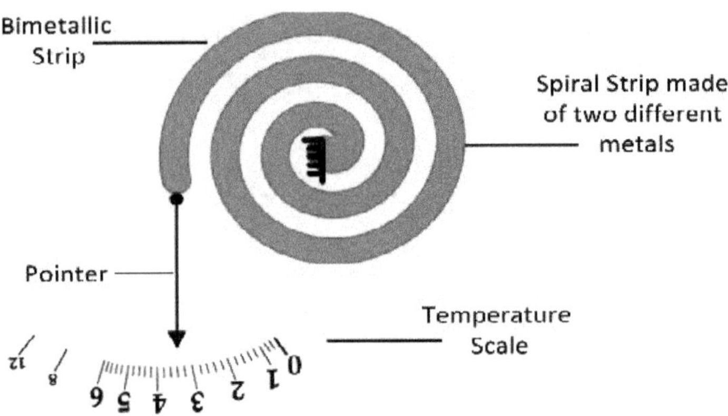

Fig 2.19 Spiral strip Bimetallic Strain.

Helical Types Bimetallic Strip – The helix type bimetallic strip is mostly used for industrial applications. In this thermometer, the helix shape strip is used for measuring the temperature. The free end of the strip is connected to the pointer. The deflection of the strip shows the variation of temperature.

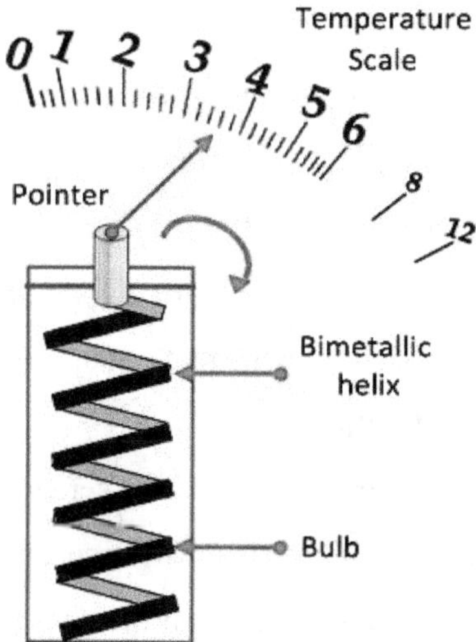

Fig 2.20 Industrial type Bimetallic Thermometer.

Advantages

- The thermometer is simple in construction, robust and less expensive.

Disadvantages

- The thermometer gives the less accurate result while measuring the low temperature.

- Applications of Bimetallic Thermometer

- The bimetallic thermometer is used in household devices like oven, air conditioner, and in industrial apparatus like refineries, hot wires, heater, tempering tanks etc. for measuring the temperature.

2.5   PN junction sensors

P-N Junction Temperature Transducing Circuit Construction and Operation:

A P-N junction temperature transducing circuit utilizes the temperature-dependent characteristics of a semiconductor's P-N junction to measure changes in temperature. The P-N junction acts as a diode, and its forward voltage drop varies with temperature. This principle is harnessed to create a temperature sensor circuit that converts temperature changes into voltage variations.

Construction:

The circuit consists of a semiconductor diode with a P-N junction, typically a silicon diode, and supporting components for signal conditioning and measurement. Here's a basic construction:

Semiconductor Diode (P-N Junction): A silicon diode is used due to its well-defined temperature-dependent voltage behaviour. The diode is often connected in a forward-biased configuration.

Resistor Network: A resistor is connected in series with the diode to limit the current flowing through it. This resistor is often chosen based on the diode's characteristics and the desired sensitivity of the circuit.

Voltage Measurement Circuit: The voltage drop across the diode is measured using a voltage measurement circuit. This circuit can include an operational amplifier configured as a differential amplifier to amplify and condition the voltage signal.

Operation:

The P-N junction temperature Transducing circuit operates based on the temperature-dependent voltage drop across the diode:

Temperature Sensing: As temperature changes, the voltage drops across the P-N junction (diode) changes due to the temperature coefficient of the semiconductor material. This change in voltage is used to infer the temperature at the diode.

Forward Voltage Measurement: The voltage drop across the diode is typically a forward voltage (around 0.6 - 0.7 volts for silicon diodes). This voltage is sensitive to temperature variations and can be correlated to the ambient temperature.

Signal Conditioning: The voltage drop across the diode may be small, so an operational amplifier configured as a differential amplifier can be used to amplify and condition the signal. This allows for better accuracy and compatibility with measurement systems.

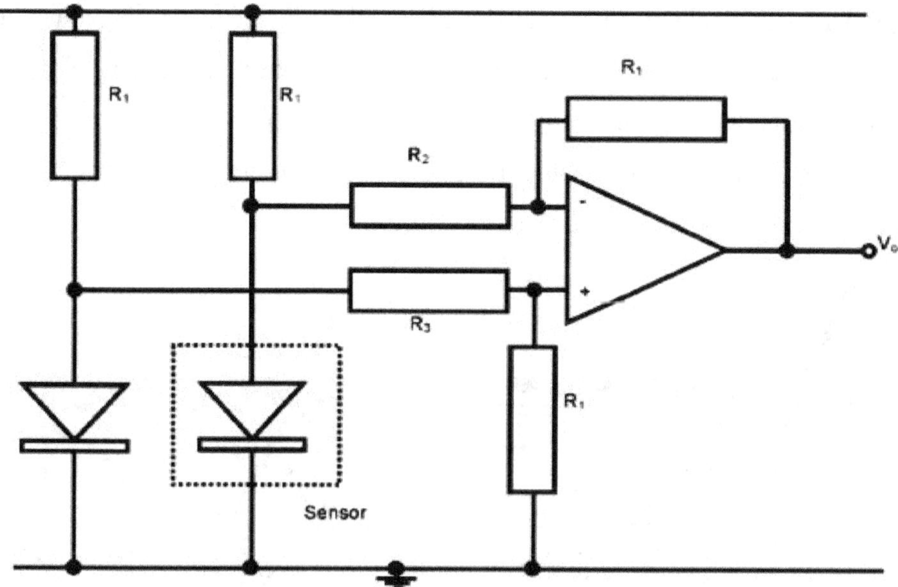

Fig 2.21 PN Junction temperature transducing circuit

Output: The amplified and conditioned voltage signal is then processed and measured using analog-to-digital converters (ADCs) for further data analysis.

Advantages:

Simplicity: The circuit is relatively simple, with few components required for basic operation. Wide Temperature Range: Depending on the choice of semiconductor material, the circuit can cover a wide temperature range.

Accuracy: With proper calibration and compensation, the circuit can provide accurate temperature measurements.

Limitations:

Nonlinearity: The relationship between temperature and diode voltage drop is nonlinear, requiring calibration or correction techniques.

Sensitivity to Diode Variability: The sensitivity of the circuit may vary due to manufacturing tolerances of the diode.

2.6   Liquid crystal temperature sensor

A liquid crystal temperature sensor operates by utilizing the unique optical properties of liquid crystals to reflect changes in temperature. Its construction involves sandwiching liquid crystals between substrates with alignment layers and electrodes. The liquid crystals' orientation and subsequent color shift in response to temperature changes enable the sensor to accurately measure temperature within a specific range.

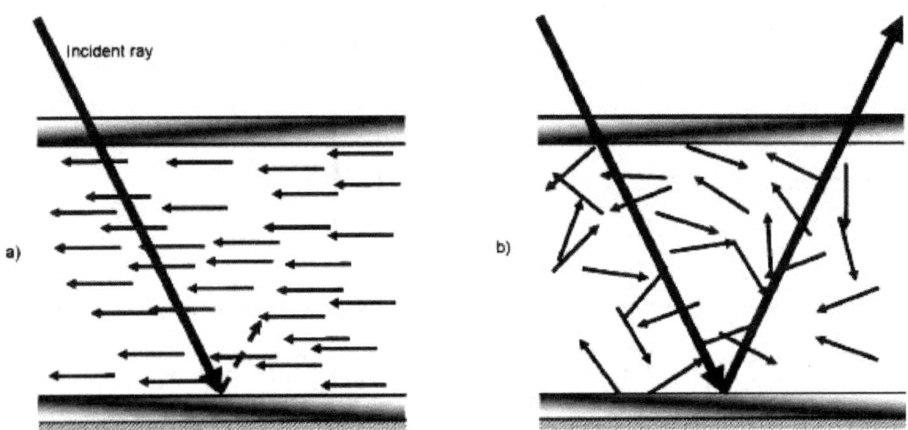

Fig 2.22 Liquid Crystal temperature sensing (a) Destructive interface (b) No interface

A liquid crystal temperature sensor is a device that utilizes the unique optical properties of liquid crystals to measure changes in temperature. Here's a description of its construction and operation without plagiarism:

Construction:

A liquid crystal temperature sensor consists of the following key components:

Liquid Crystal Material: The sensor employs a specific type of liquid crystal material that exhibits changes in color or optical properties in response to temperature fluctuations. Cholesteric liquid crystals are commonly used due to their ability to reflect different wavelengths of light based on temperature.

Substrate: The liquid crystal material is sandwiched between two transparent substrates, typically made of glass or plastic. These substrates provide a stable platform for the liquid crystal and protect it from external factors.

Alignment Layers: Thin alignment layers are coated onto the inner surfaces of the substrates. These layers help orient the liquid crystal molecules in a specific direction, allowing them to respond consistently to temperature changes.

Electrodes: Transparent conductive electrodes are patterned onto the substrate surfaces. These electrodes apply an electric field to the liquid crystal material, influencing its optical properties.

Operation:

The operation of a liquid crystal temperature sensor involves the following steps:

Initial Alignment: The liquid crystal molecules are aligned parallel to the substrates due to the influence of the alignment layers. In this state, the liquid crystal material reflects specific wavelengths of light, resulting in a characteristic color or optical appearance.

Temperature Change: When the temperature changes, the liquid crystal molecules also experience a change in their orientation. This alters the reflective properties of the liquid crystal, leading to a shift in color or optical appearance. The relationship between temperature and optical response is calibrated during the sensor's manufacturing process.

Electrostatic Influence: The conductive electrodes on the substrate can apply an electric field to the liquid crystal material. By adjusting the voltage applied across the electrodes, the sensor can be fine-tuned to enhance or modulate its response to temperature changes.

Observation and Measurement: The change in color or optical appearance of the liquid crystal material is observed and analysed. This can be done visually or through specialized optical equipment. The extent of the color shift corresponds to the temperature change, allowing accurate temperature measurement within a certain range.

Calibration: To ensure accurate temperature readings, the sensor is calibrated using known temperature references. This calibration process establishes a reliable relationship between the sensor's optical response and actual temperature values.

2.7   Pyrometry

Temperature measurement by pyrometry is a non-contact method that involves the measurement of the thermal radiation emitted by an object to determine its temperature.

Principle of Pyrometry:

Pyrometry is based on the fundamental principle that all objects with a temperature above absolute zero emit thermal radiation. This radiation is a form of electromagnetic radiation that includes infrared (IR) wavelengths. The intensity and spectrum of the emitted radiation depend on the object's temperature, emissivity (a material property describing how efficiently it emits radiation), and surface characteristics.

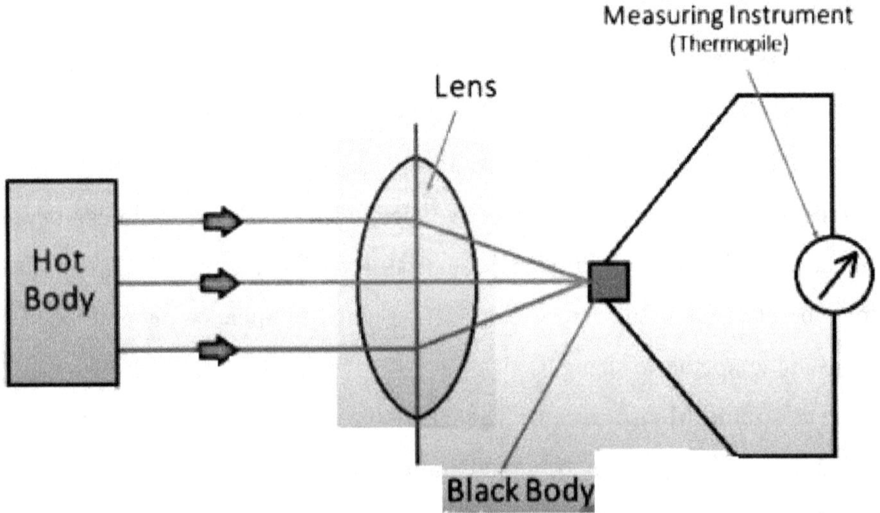

Fig 2.23 Radiation Pyrometry

Operation:

Emission of Thermal Radiation: When an object is heated, it emits thermal radiation according to its temperature. The hotter the object, the more intense the radiation. This radiation includes a range of wavelengths, with a significant portion falling within the infrared region.

Optical Collection: A pyrometer collects the emitted radiation using optical components like lenses or mirrors. These components focus the emitted radiation onto a detector or sensor element.

Detector Response: The detector or sensor element is designed to respond to the specific wavelength range of the emitted thermal radiation, usually in the infrared spectrum. The intensity of the radiation that reaches the detector is proportional to the object's temperature.

Signal Processing: The detector generates an electrical signal based on the intensity of the collected radiation. This signal is then processed by electronic circuitry within the pyrometer.

Temperature Calculation: The processed signal is used to calculate the temperature of the object using the principles of blackbody radiation and the Stefan-Boltzmann law. These laws relate the intensity of emitted radiation to temperature and emissivity.

Emissivity Compensation: Emissivity is a crucial factor in accurate pyrometric temperature measurement. Since real surfaces don't behave as ideal blackbodies, the pyrometer may include features to adjust for the object's emissivity. Some pyrometers allow users to input or measure the emissivity of the object being measured, or they might have algorithms to estimate emissivity based on the material.

Display and Output: The calculated temperature is typically displayed on the pyrometer's screen. Additionally, the pyrometer might offer options for data output, such as analog signals, digital interfaces, or data logging.

Advantages of Pyrometry:

Non-Contact: Pyrometry allows temperature measurement without physical contact, making it suitable for measuring extremely high or hazardous temperatures.

Wide Temperature Range: Pyrometers can measure a wide range of temperatures, from relatively low temperatures (a few hundred degrees Celsius) to extremely high temperatures (several thousand degrees Celsius).

Fast Response: Pyrometers provide rapid temperature readings, making them useful for dynamic processes.

Versatility: Pyrometry can be applied in various industrial, scientific, and research settings, including metalworking, glass manufacturing, furnace control, and material analysis.

References & Further Reading

1. "Temperature Measurement and Control "byA. C. Fischer-Cripps, CRC Press, 1st Edition (2001)

2. Instrumentation for Engineers and scientists by John Turner, Oxford University Press 2014.

UNIT-III Embedded Displacement Sensors

Unit Structure

3.0 Objectives.

3.1 Introduction.

3.2 Potentiometers.

3.3. Inductive type Displacement sensor

3.4. Capacitive type Displacement sensor

3.5 Optic motion Sensor

3.6 Ultrasonic displacement Sensor.

3.7 References & Further Reading

3.0 Objectives

- The primary objective of displacement sensors is to accurately measure the position or movement of an object. This information can be crucial for various applications such as robotics, manufacturing, and automation.

- Objectives might involve using displacement measurements to adjust parameters and maintain desired positions or movements in real-time.

- Objectives may involve selecting displacement sensors with the appropriate resolution and minimizing measurement errors, optimizing production efficiency, reducing downtime, and improving overall process control.

- Objectives could include leveraging this data to gain insights into operational efficiency, trends, and performance optimization and may involve selecting the most suitable sensor type for the application's unique requirements.

3.1 Introduction

Displacement sensors are vital components in modern industries and technologies, playing a crucial role in measuring the movement, position, or distance between objects. These sensors enable precise and accurate monitoring of shifts, deviations, or changes in position, making them indispensable in a wide range of applications, from manufacturing and robotics to automotive systems and scientific research. By converting physical movement into measurable data, displacement sensors empower engineers, researchers, and technicians to optimize processes, enhance safety, and improve overall performance.

As technology evolves, displacement sensors continue to improve in terms of accuracy, sensitivity, and integration capabilities. Miniaturization allows for their integration into compact devices, while wireless connectivity and IoT integration enable real-time data monitoring and analysis. Advancements in nanotechnology and photonics hold promise for even more precise and versatile displacement sensing technologies, further expanding their applications across industries.

In conclusion, displacement sensors represent a pivotal intersection of physics, engineering, and innovation. Their ability to convert physical movement into quantifiable data empowers industries to achieve higher levels of precision, safety, and efficiency, propelling us into a future of enhanced technological capabilities and transformative advancements.

3.2 Potentiometers.

Potentiometric-based displacement sensors are widely used devices in various industries and applications to measure and monitor changes in position or movement. These sensors operate on the principle of changing electrical resistance as the position of a sliding contact (wiper) moves along a resistive element. This resistance change is directly proportional to the displacement being measured.

Potentiometer displacement sensor is a primary sensor which converts the linear motion or the angular motion of shat into changes in resistance. It is a type of resistive displacement sensor. Linear potentiometers are sensors that produce a resistance output proportional to the linear displacement or position. Linear potentiometers are essentially variable resistors whose resistance is varied by the movement of a slide over a resistance element.

Rotary potentiometers are sensors that produce resistance output proportional to the angular displacement or position. They can be either wire wound or conductive plastic, and either rectangular or cylindrical.

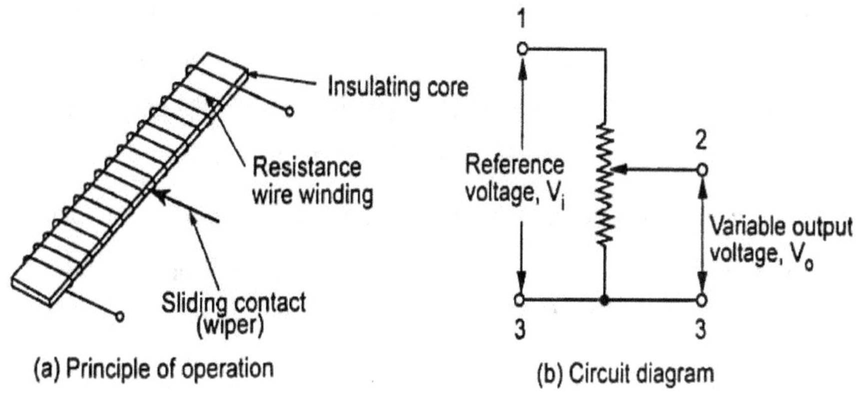

Fig 3.1 The linear potentiometer

Illustrates the basic principle of a linear potentiometer. The linear potentiometer employs an electrically conductive linear slide member (also called wiper) connected to a variable wire wound resistor (winding) that changes resistance to be equated to the linear position of the device that is monitored. As the sliding contact moves along the winding, the resistance changes in linear relationship with the distance from one end of the potentiometer. To measure displacement, a potentiometer is typically wired as a 'voltage divider' so that the output voltage is proportional to the distance travelled by the wiper. A known voltage is applied to the resistor ends.

The contact is attached to the moving object of interest. The output voltage at the contact is proportional to the displacement. The resolution is defined by the number of turns per unit distance, and loading effects of the voltage divider circuit should be considered. A rotary potentiometer employs a rotary slide member connected to a variable wire wound resistor that changes resistance to be equated to the angular position of the device that is monitored. Other principles of operations are same as that of linear potentiometer.

The potentiometer can be used as a voltage divider to obtain a manually adjustable output voltage at the slider (wiper) from a fixed input voltage applied across the two ends of the resistance wire winding. A potentiometer circuit with a resistive load and circuit with equivalent fixed resistors respectively. The voltage across RL can be calculated by: Potentiometer Displacement Sensors

$$V_L = (R_2 R_L) R_1 R_L + R_2 R_L + R_3 R_L) \times V_S$$

If R_L is large compared to the other resistances (like the input to an operational amplifier), the output voltage can be approximated by the simpler equation.

$$V_L = R_2 R_1 + R_2 \times V_S$$

As an example, assume.

$V_s = 12V$, $R_1 = 1k\Omega$, $R_2 = 3k\Omega$, and $R_L = 200k\Omega$.

Since the load resistance is large compared to the other resistance, the output voltage V_L will be approximately,

$V_L = 3 1 + 3 \times 12 = 9V$

Due to the load resistance, however, it will be slightly lower: $\approx 8.966V$.

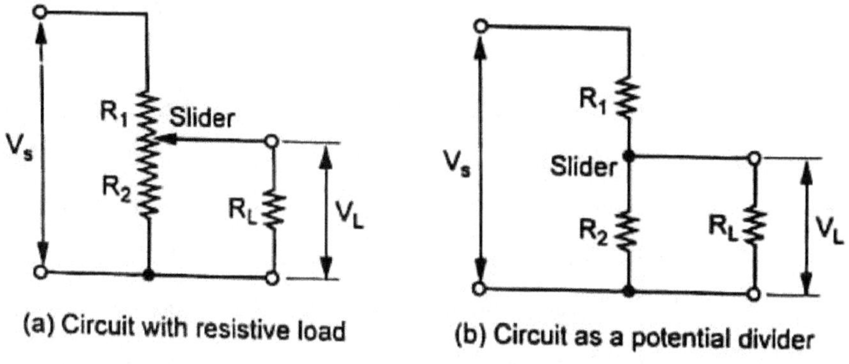

(a) Circuit with resistive load   (b) Circuit as a potential divider

Fig 3.2 The linear potentiometer with resistive load and potential divider.
One of the most common uses for modern low power potentiometer sensor is as audio control devices. Both sliding pots (also known as faders) and rotary potentiometers (commonly called knobs) are regularly used to adjust loudness, frequency attenuation and other characteristics of audio signals.

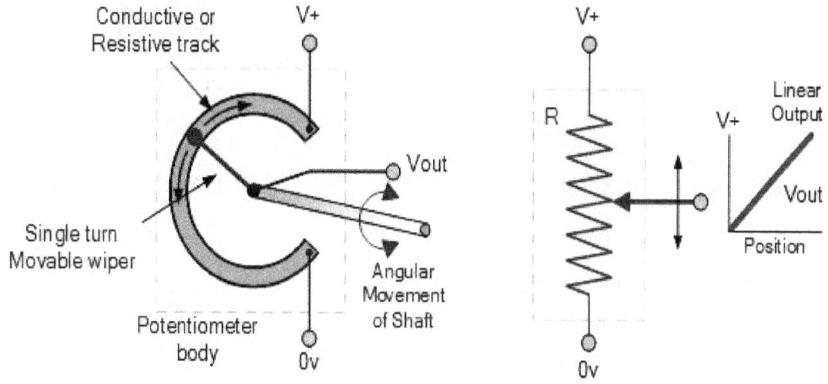

Fig 3.3 Principle of operation and circuit diagram for Circular potentiometer

The output signal (V_{out}) from the potentiometer is taken from the centre wiper connection as it moves along the resistive track and is proportional to the angular position of the shaft. While resistive potentiometer position sensors have many advantages: low cost, low tech, easy to use etc, as a position sensor they also have many disadvantages: wear due to moving parts, low accuracy, low repeatability, and limited frequency response.

But there is one main disadvantage of using the potentiometer as a positional sensor. The range of movement of its wiper or slider (and hence the output signal obtained) is limited to the physical size of the potentiometer being used.

For example, a single turn rotational potentiometer generally only has a fixed mechanical rotation of between 0o and about 240 to 330o maximum. However, multi-turn pots of up to 3600o (10 x 360o) of mechanical rotation are also available.

Most types of potentiometers use carbon film for their resistive track, but these types are electrically noisy (the crackle on a radio volume control), and also have a short mechanical life.

Wire-wound pots also known as rheostats, in the form of either a straight wire or wound coil resistive wire can also be used, but wire wound pots suffer from resolution problems as their wiper jumps from one wire segment to the next producing a logarithmic (LOG) output resulting in errors in the output signal. These to suffer from electrical noise.

For high precision low noise applications conductive plastic resistance element type polymer film or cermet type potentiometers are now available. These pots have a smooth low friction electrically linear (LIN) resistive track giving them a low noise, long life and excellent resolution and are available as both multi-turn and single turn devices. Typical applications for this type of high accuracy position sensor are in computer game joysticks, steering wheels, industrial and robot applications.

The following factors to be considered while selecting the potentiometers:

- Operating temperature
- Shock and vibration
- Humidity

- Contamination and seals
- Life cycle

Advantages and Disadvantages of Potentiometers

Advantages:

- Easy to use.
- Low cost.
- High-amplitude output signal.
- Proven technology.
- Rugged construction.
- Very high electrical efficiency.
- Availability in different forms, ranges and sizes.

Disadvantages

- Limited bandwidth
- Frictional loading
- Inertial loading
- Limited life due to wear

3.3. Inductive type Displacement sensor

The most widely used variable-inductance displacement transducer in industry is LVDT (Linear Variable Differential Transformer). It is a passive type of sensor. It is an electro-mechanical device designed to produce an AC voltage output proportional to the relative inductive displacement sensor of the transformer and the ferromagnetic core.

The physical construction of a typical LVDT consists of a movable core of magnetic material and three coils comprising the static transformer as shown in image. One of the three coils is the primary coil or excitation coil and the other two are secondary coils or pick-up coils. An AC current (typically 1 kHz) is passed through the primary coil, and an AC voltage is induced in the secondary coils. The magnetic core inside the coil winding assembly provides the magnetic flux path linking the Primary and secondary Coils.

When the magnetic core is at the centre position or null position the output voltages are equal and opposite in polarity and, therefore, the output voltage is zero. The Null Position of an LVDT is extremely stable and repeatable. When the magnetic core is displaced from the Null Position, a certain number of coil windings are affected by the proximity of the sliding core and thus an electromagnetic imbalance occurs. This imbalance generates a differential AC output voltage across the secondary coil which is linearly proportional to the direction and magnitude of the displacement. The output voltage to displacement plot is a straight line within a specified range. Beyond the nominal range, the output deviates from a straight line in a gentle curve as shown in image.

The Rotational Variable Differential Transformer (RVDT) is used to measure rotational angles and operates under the same principles as the LVDT sensor. Whereas the LVDT uses a cylindrical iron core, the RVDT uses a rotary ferromagnetic core.

Calculation of output voltage

Motion of a magnetic core changes the mutual inductance of two secondary coils relative to a primary coil

Primary coil voltage: $V_{in} = \sin(\omega t)$

Secondary coils induced emf: $V_1 = k_1 \sin(\omega t)$ and $V_2 = k_2 \sin(\omega t)$

The value of k_1 and k_2 depend on the amount of coupling between the primary and the secondary coils, which is proportional to the position of the coil.

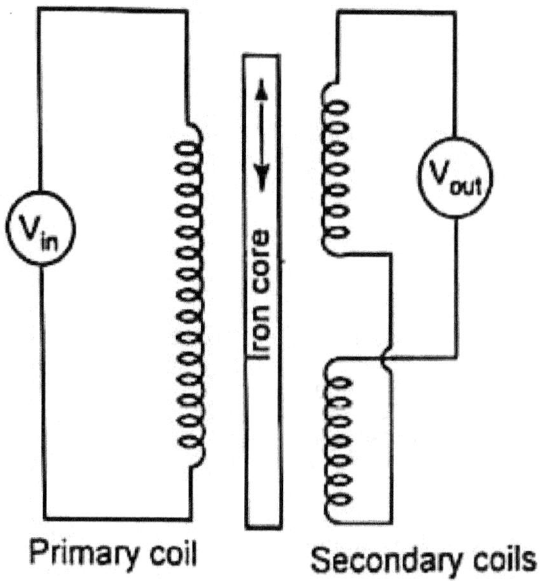

Fig 3.4 Principle of operation of LVDT

When the coil is in the central position, $k_1=k_2$; $V_{out} = V_1 - V_2 = 0$

When the coil is displaced x units, $k_1 \neq k_2$; $V_{out} = (k_1 - k_2)\sin(\omega t)$

Positive or negative displacements are determined from the phases of V_{out}.

Applications

LVDT can be used to measure the displacement, deflection, position, and profile of a work piece.

Advantages:

- Relatively low cost due to its popularity.

- Solid and robust, capable of working in a wide variety of environments.

- No friction resistance, sin2ce the iron core does not contact the transformer coils, resulting in an infinite (very long) service life.

- High signal to noise ratio and low output impedance.

- Negligible hysteresis.

- Short response time, only limited by the inertia of the iron core and the rise time of the amplifiers.

- No permanent damage to the LVDT if measurements exceed the designed range.

- It can operate over a temperature range of -2650C to 600 0c

- High sensitivity up to 40 V/mm.

- Less power consumption (less than 1W)

Disadvantages:

The performance of these sensors is likely affected by vibration etc.

- Relatively large displacements are required for appreciable output.

- Not suitable for fast dynamic measurements because of the mass of the core.

- Inherently low power output.

- Sensitive to stray magnetic fields but shieling is not possible.

3.4. Capacitive type Displacement sensor

Capacitive-type displacement sensors are versatile devices that use changes in capacitance to measure the distance between an object and a sensor element. These sensors are widely used in various applications for their ability to provide accurate and non-contact measurements of position, thickness, and displacement.

A simple **capacitive sensor** has been available commercially for many years for the detection of non-metallic objects, although they are restricted to short ranges, normally below 1 cm. Generally, a capacitor sensor is one type of proximity sensor used to detect nearby objects through their electrical field effect formed through the sensor. These types of sensors have some similarities with radar in their capacity to sense conductive materials while observing through insulating materials like plastic or wood. The differences are significant as compared to radar. Capacitive sensors are smaller, simpler, less expensive & use less power. So, this article briefly explains a **capacitive sensor** and its works with applications.

Capacitive Sensor

An electronic device that is used to detect the targets like liquids or solids

without any physical contact is known as a capacitive sensor. For detecting these targets, the capacitive sensor will produce an electrical field from the sensor's detecting end. Any target that can interrupt this electrical field can be detected through this sensor.

Fig 3.5 Capacitive Sensor

The solid materials which can be detected by a capacitor sensor are paper, plastic, glass, cloth, and wood. The liquids which can be detected by a capacitor sensor are oil, paint, water, etc.

Working Principle of Capacitive Sensor

A capacitive sensor works like a normal capacitor. In this sensor, a metal plate within the sensing face is electrically connected to an oscillator circuit and the target which is detected can act as the next plate of the capacitor. Not like an inductive sensor that generates an electromagnetic field, a capacitive sensor generates an electrostatic field.

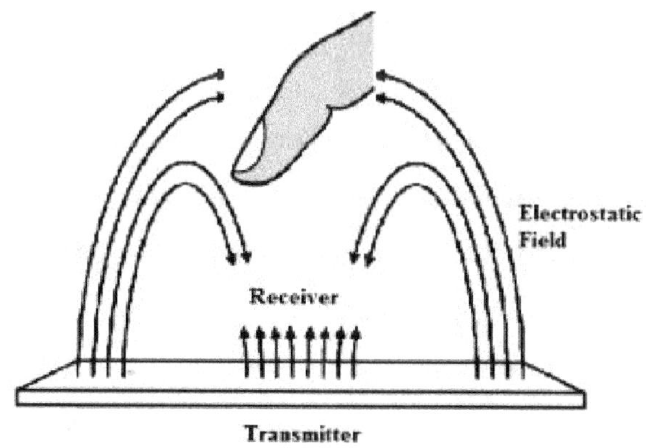

Fig 3.6 Electrostatic Field Generation of a capacitive sensor

The block diagram of the capacitive sensor is shown below. The internal capacitive diagram is shown above. This sensor includes a high-frequency oscillator with a sensing surface that is formed through two metal electrodes. Once an object approach close to the sensing surface, then it moves into the electrostatic field of the electrodes & changes the oscillator's capacitance.

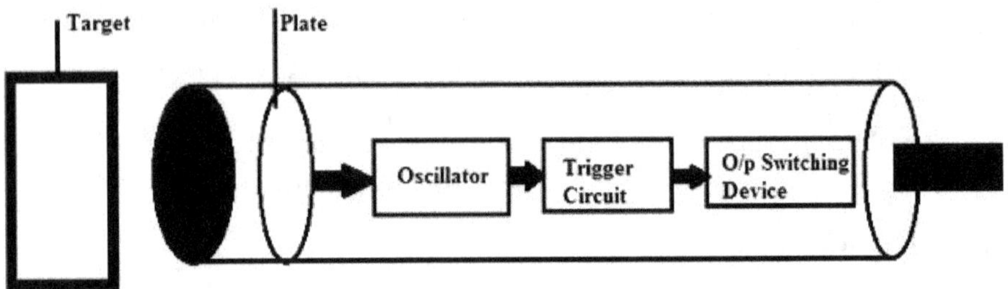

Fig 3.7 Block diagram of capacitive transducer

Capacitive Sensor Working

Consequently, the oscillator circuit will begin to oscillate & change the sensor's output condition once it arrives at a certain amplitude. Once the target goes away from the capacitive sensor, the amplitude of the oscillator will reduce, switching the capacitive sensor back to its original position.

This sensor's typical detecting range is about 1 inch or 25 mm whereas some sensors' range is extended up to 2 inches.

These sensors detect the superior dielectric constant of an object simply. So, this makes achievable the detection of the material within non-metallic containers because the dielectric constant of liquid is much higher as compared to the container. So, this provides the sensor ability to observe throughout the container & detect the liquid. For better operation, they must utilize in a situation with a quite constant temperature & humidity.

Capacitive Sensor Formula

The capacitive sensor is one kind of device used for capacitive sensing. It is mainly based on the capacitive coupling principle. This sensor can simply detect & measure different things like motion, chemical composition, displacement, electric field & indirectly detect many other variables which can be changed into dielectric constant or motion like acceleration, pressure, fluid composition & fluid level.

A capacitance sensor includes two metal plates which are separated by a distance'd' and area 'A'. So the capacitance 'C' between two terminals can be given through the following expression.

$C = \varepsilon0*\varepsilon r*A/h$

Where,

'C' is capacitance within Faradays.

'εr' is Insulator's relative dielectric constant.

'εo' is dielectric constant for free space.

'A' is the overlapping area of two plates.

'h' is the width of the gap between two plates.

Advantages of Capacitive Displacement Sensors:

Non-Contact Measurement: Capacitive sensors do not require physical contact with the object being measured, preventing wear and minimizing potential damage.

High Accuracy: Capacitive sensors offer high resolution and accuracy, making them suitable for precise measurements.

Wide Range of Materials: They can measure the displacement of various materials, including conductive, insulating, and non-metallic substances.

Environmentally Friendly: Capacitive sensors can be used in clean or vacuum environments without introducing contaminants.

Applications:

- **Semiconductor Manufacturing:** Used for wafer thickness measurement and alignment in semiconductor production.

- **Automotive Industry:** Measuring piston position, valve position, and brake pad wear in vehicles.
- **Micromachining:** Monitoring of microelectromechanical systems (MEMS) during fabrication.
- **Quality Control:** Measuring thickness and flatness of materials in manufacturing processes.
- **Robotics:** Providing feedback for precise positioning of robot arms and grippers.
- **Non-Destructive Testing:** Detecting defects or variations in materials without damaging them.
- **Medical Devices**: Measuring fluid levels, detecting object presence, and controlling positions in medical equipment.

Challenges and Considerations:

- **Environmental Factors:** Capacitance can be affected by changes in humidity, temperature, and nearby conductive materials.
- **Sensitivity to Dielectric Changes:** Changes in the material between the plates can impact the capacitance and measurement accuracy.
- **Calibration:** Calibration may be required to account for variations caused by different materials and environmental conditions.

Conclusion:

Capacitive-type displacement sensors are powerful tools that provide accurate and non-contact measurements of position and displacement. Their ability to work with various materials and in diverse applications, coupled with their high accuracy, makes them essential components in industries ranging from manufacturing to robotics and beyond. While challenges like environmental influences should be considered, ongoing advancements continue to enhance the capabilities of capacitive displacement sensors, making them an integral part of modern technology and innovation.

3.5 Optic motion Sensor

An optical motion sensor, also known as an optical motion detector or optical motion sensor module, is a device that detects movement or motion in its surroundings using optical technology. These sensors rely on changes in light levels, patterns, or reflections to determine the presence or movement of objects within their field of view. Optical motion sensors are commonly used in a variety of applications for detecting motion, triggering actions, and enhancing automation. Here's an overview of optical motion sensors:

Working Principle:

Optical motion sensors use light-based principles to detect movement. They typically consist of a light source (often an infrared LED) and a photodetector (such as a phototransistor or photodiode). The sensor emits light and measures the reflected or interrupted light to determine changes in the environment.

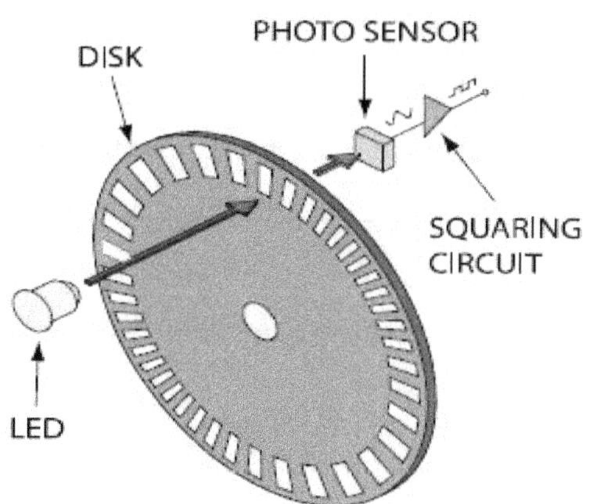

Fig 3.8RotaryEncoder

Rotary Encoders are another type of position sensor which resemble potentiometers mentioned earlier but are non-contact optical devices used for converting the angular position of a rotating shaft into an analogue or digital data code. In other words, they convert mechanical movement into an electrical signal (preferably digital).

All optical encoders work on the same basic principle. Light from an LED or infra-red-light source is passed through a rotating high-resolution encoded disk that contains the required code patterns, either binary, grey code or BCD. Photo detectors scan the disk as it rotates, and an electronic circuit processes the information into a digital form as a stream of binary output pulses that are fed to counters or controllers which determine the actual angular position of the shaft.

There are two basic types of rotary optical encoders, **Incremental Encoders** and **Absolute Position**

Incremental Encoder

Incremental Encoders, also known as quadrature encoders or relative rotary encoders, are the simplest of the two position sensors. Their output is a series of square wave pulses generated by a photocell arrangement as the coded disk, with evenly spaced transparent and dark lines called segments on its surface, moves, or rotates past the light source. The encoder produces a stream of square wave pulses which, when counted, indicates the angular position of the rotating shaft.

Incremental encoders have two separate outputs called "quadrature outputs". These two outputs are displaced at 90o out of phase from each other with the direction of rotation of the shaft being determined from the output sequence.

The number of transparent and dark segments or slots on the disk determines the resolution of the device and increasing the number of lines in the pattern increases the resolution per degree of rotation. Typical encoded discs have a resolution of up to 256 pulses or 8-bits per rotation.

The simplest incremental encoder is called a tachometer. It has one single square wave output and is often used in unidirectional applications where basic position or speed information only is required. The "Quadrature" or "Sine wave" encoder is the more common and has two output square waves commonly called *channel A* and *channel B*. This device uses two photo detectors, slightly offset from each other by 90o thereby producing two separate sine and cosine output signals.

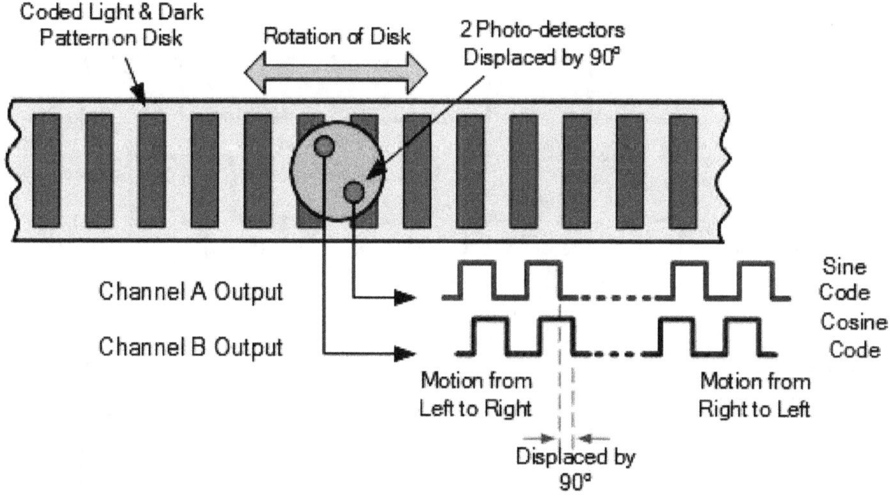

Fig 3.9Simple Incremental Encoder

By using the *Arc Tangent* mathematical function, the angle of the shaft in radians can be calculated. Generally, the optical disk used in rotary position encoders is circular, then the resolution of the output will be given as: $\theta = 360/n$, where n equals the number of segments on coded disk.

Then for example, the number of segments required to give an incremental encoder a resolution of 1o will be: 1o − 360/n, therefore, n = 360 windows, etc. Also, the direction of rotation is determined by noting which channel produces an output first, either channel A or channel B giving two directions of rotation, A leads B or B leads A. This arrangement is shown below.

Incremental Encoder Output

One main disadvantage of incremental encoders when used as a position sensor, is that they require external counters to determine the absolute angle of the shaft within a given rotation. If the power is momentarily shut off, or if the encoder misses a pulse due to noise or a dirty disc, the resulting angular information will produce an error. One way of overcoming this disadvantage is to use absolute position encoders.

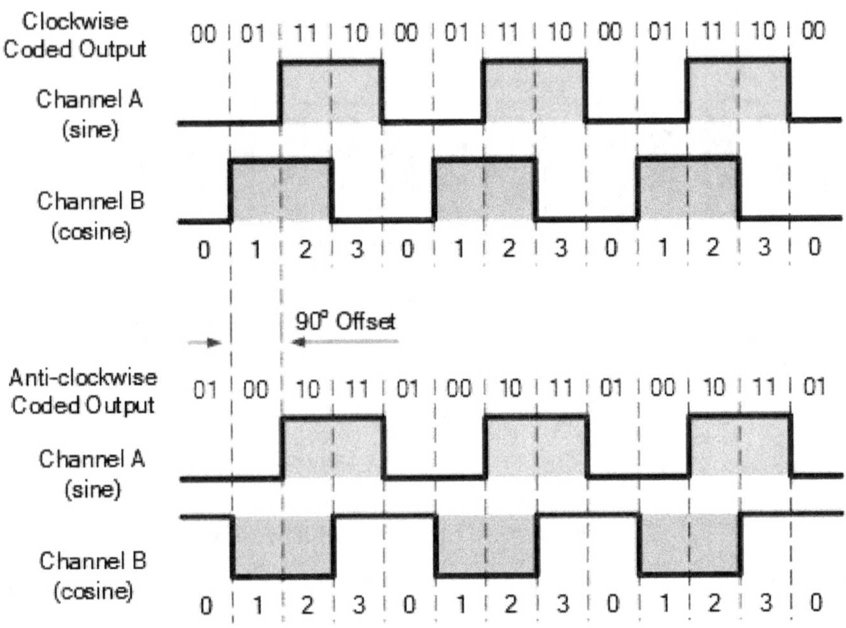

Fig 3.10Simple Incremental Encoder output

Absolute Position Encoder

Absolute Position Encoders are more complex than quadrature encoders. They provide a unique output code for every single position of rotation indicating both position and direction. Their coded disk consists of multiple concentric "tracks" of light and dark segments. Each track is independent with its own photo detector to simultaneously read a unique coded position value for each angle of movement. The number of tracks on the disk corresponds to the binary "bit"-resolution of the encoder so a 12-bit absolute encoder would have 12 tracks and the same coded value only appears once per revolution.

4-bit Binary Coded Disc

One main advantage of an absolute encoder is its non-volatile memory which retains the exact position of the encoder without the need to return to a "home" position if the power fails. Most rotary encoders are defined as "single turn" devices, but absolute multi-turn devices are available, which obtain feedback over several revolutions by adding extra code disks.

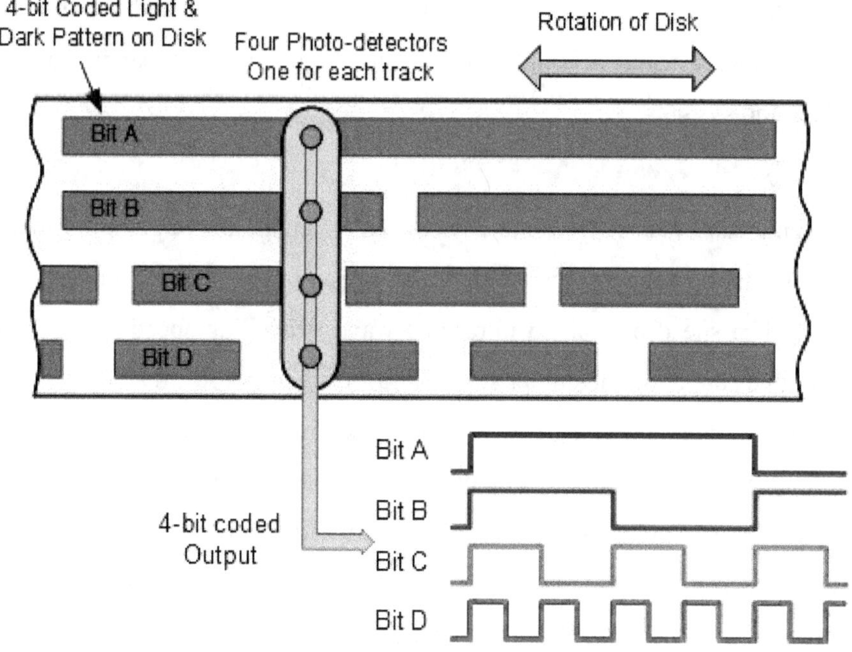

Fig 3.114-bit Binary Coded Disc

Typical application of absolute position encoders is in computer hard drives and CD/DVD drives were the absolute position of the drives read/write heads are monitored or in printers/plotters to accurately position the printing heads over the paper. In this tutorial about **Position Sensors**, we have looked at several examples of sensors that can be used to measure the position or presence of objects. In the next tutorial we will look at sensors that are used to measure temperature such as thermistors, thermostats, and thermocouples, and as such are known commonly as Temperature Sensors.

Conclusion:

Optical motion sensors are essential components in various industries and applications, enabling the detection of motion and movement through light-based principles. Their versatility, energy efficiency, and ability to provide touch less interaction make them invaluable for enhancing automation, security, and user experiences. Despite potential challenges, ongoing advancements in optical technology continue to improve the performance and reliability of optical motion sensors, driving their integration into an ever-expanding array of devices and systems.

3.6 Ultrasonic displacement Sensor

Ultrasonic sensors are electronic devices that calculate the target's distance by emission of ultrasonic sound waves and convert those waves into electrical signals. The speed of emitted ultrasonic waves travelling speed is faster than the audible sound. A transmitter sends ultrasonic waves toward an object, and a receiver receives the reflected waves back from it. This type of sensor determines the distance by calculating the relationship between the time required for the ultrasonic waves to be sent and received, and the speed of sound. There are mainly two essential elements which are the transmitter and receiver. Using the piezoelectric crystals, the transmitter generates sound, and from there it travels to the target and gets back to the receiver component.

To know the distance between the target and the sensor, the sensor calculates the amount of time required for sound emission to travel from transmitter to receiver. The calculation is done as follows:

$$\mathbf{D = 1/2\ T * C}$$

Where 'T' corresponds to time measured in seconds.
'C' corresponds to sound speed = 343 measured in mts/sec

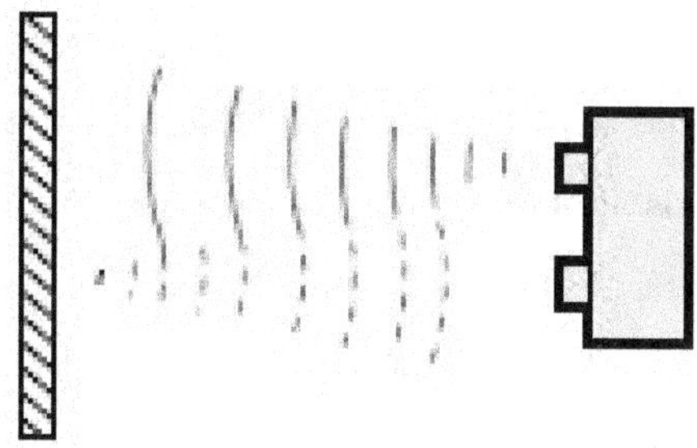

Fig 3.12Ultrasonic displacement Sensor

Ultrasonic sensor working principle.

This is either like sonar or radar which evaluates the target/object attributes by understanding the received echoes from sound/radio waves correspondingly. These sensors produce high-frequency sound waves and analyse the echo which is received from the sensor. The sensors measure the time interval between transmitted and received echoes so that the distance to the target is known.

Ultrasonic Sensor Specifications

Knowing the specifications of an ultrasonic sensor helps in understanding the reliable approximations of distance measurements.

- The sensing range lies between 40 cm to 300 cm.
- The response time is between 50 milliseconds to 200 milliseconds.
- The Beam angle is around 50.
- It operates within the voltage range of 20 VDC to 30 VDC
- Preciseness is ±5%
- The frequency of the ultrasound wave is 120 kHz
- Resolution is 1mm.
- The voltage of sensor output is between 0 VDC – 10 VDC
- The ultrasonic sensor weight nearly 150 grams
- Ambient temperature is -250C to +700C
- The target dimensions to measure maximum distance is 5 cm × 5 cm

Working

In general, an ultrasonic sensor has two sections which are the transmitter and receiver. These sections are closely placed so that the sound travel in a straight line from the transmitter to the target and travels back to the receiver. Making sure to have minimal distance between transmitter and receiver section delivers minimal errors while calculations.

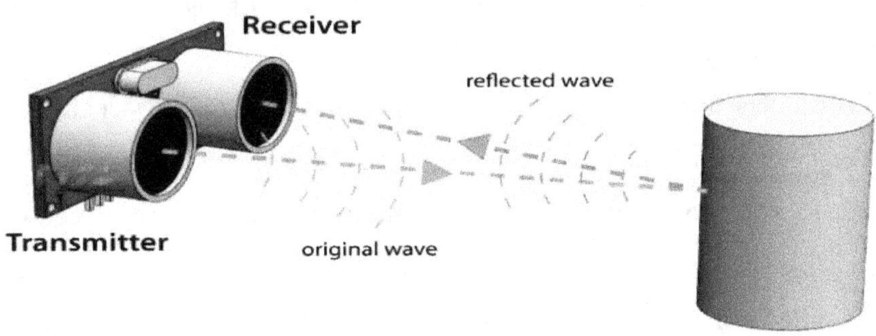

Fig 3.13 Operation principle of Ultrasonic Transducer

These devices are also termed ultrasonic transceivers if both the transmitter and receiver sections are combined in a single unit which considerably minimizes the PCB footprint. Here, the sensor operates as a burst signal, and it is transmitted for some period. Later the transmission, there exists a **silent period** and this period is termed **response time**. The response time indicates that it is waiting for the reflected waves.

The shape of the acoustic waves that leave the transmitter section resembles the same shape of the light emitted from a laser so beam angle and spread must be measured. When the sound waves move away from the transmitter, the detection area increases vertically and sideways too. Because of the varying detection area, the coverage specification is considered either as beam angle/beam width other than the standard area of detection.

It is more recommended to observe the beam angle pattern for the sensor whether it is the complete angle of the beam or the angle of variation corresponding to the straight line that forms a transducer. Mostly, a thin beam angle results in a higher detection range, and a broader beam angle corresponds to a lesser detection range.

The transmitted/acoustic signals might find a hindrance or not. When there is any hindrance, the acoustic wave bounces back from the hindrance. This bounced signal is termed ECHO. This echo travels to the receiver.

Then the received signal is either filtered or amplified and then transformed into a digital signal. With the time between transmission and reception of acoustic waves, the distance between the ultrasonic system and hindrance can be known.

Calculating displacement using an ultrasonic sensor involves measuring the time it takes for an ultrasonic pulse to travel to an object and back, and then using this time to determine the distance the object is from the sensor. Here's the basic equation and steps for calculating displacement using an ultrasonic sensor:

Basic Equation:

The equation used to calculate displacement (distance) based on the time-of-flight of an ultrasonic pulse is

Distance = (Speed of Sound × Time-of-Flight) / 2

Where:

Distance is the calculated displacement or distance to the object.

Speed of Sound is the speed at which sound waves travel through the medium (typically air, at around 343 meters per second or 1125 feet per second at room temperature).

Time-of-Flight is the time it takes for the ultrasonic pulse to travel to the object and back to the sensor.

Steps to Calculate Displacement:

- **Emit Ultrasonic Pulse:** The ultrasonic sensor emits a short burst of ultrasonic waves.

- **Measure Time-of-Flight:** The sensor measures the time it takes for the ultrasonic pulse to travel to the object, reflect off it, and return to the sensor. This time is typically measured in microseconds (μs) or milliseconds (ms).

- **Calculate Distance:** Plug the measured time-of-flight and the speed of sound into the equation to calculate the displacement (distance) to the object. Divide the product of the speed of sound and time-of-flight by 2 to get the one-way distance.

Example (in meters):

Speed of Sound = 343 m/s (at room temperature)

Time-of-Flight = 0.01 seconds (10 milliseconds)

Distance = (343 m/s × 0.01 s) / 2 = 1.715 meters (one-way distance)

Account for Two-Way Distance: The calculated distance is the one-way distance travelled by the ultrasonic pulse. Since the pulse travelled to the object and back, you need to double the calculated distance to get the total round-trip distance (displacement).

Example (total round-trip distance):

Total Displacement = 2 × 1.715 m = 3.43 meters

It's important to note that the speed of sound can vary with changes in temperature, humidity, and pressure. Therefore, for more accurate measurements, it's recommended to calibrate the sensor or incorporate compensation for environmental conditions.

Additionally, consider the sensor's response time, accuracy, and resolution when using ultrasonic displacement measurements for specific applications.

3.7 References & Further Reading

1. "Optical Sensors: Basics and Applications"by Pavel Ripka, Alois Tipek, Springer, 1st Edition (2004).

2. Instrumentation for Engineers and scientists by John Turner, Oxford University Press 2014.

Unit – IV Embedded Strain and Pressure Sensors

4.0 Objectives.

4.1 Introduction.

4.2. Foil strain gauge

4.3 Semiconductor strain Gauge

4.4 Bridge circuits for strain gauge Transducer

4.5 Elastic Pressure sensors

> 4.5.1 Bourdon Type
>
> 4.5.2 Bellow Type
>
> 4.5.3 Diaphragm Transducer

4.6 Capacitive pressure sensor

References and Further Reading

4.0 Objectives

Embedded strain and pressure sensors serve various purposes across different industries and applications. The objectives for these sensors can vary based on the specific use case and industry, but here are some common objectives.

- Embedded strain and pressure sensors are used to accurately measure and monitor strain and pressure levels in each system, structure, or environment. This data helps in understanding real-time conditions and detecting any deviations from normal operating parameters.

- To assess the structural integrity of components, buildings, bridges, aircraft, and vehicles. Continuous monitoring helps identify potential defects, fatigue, and stress-related issues before they lead to catastrophic failures.

- Strain and pressure sensors embedded within manufacturing equipment or machinery provide valuable data for process optimization. By monitoring strain and pressure levels during production processes, manufacturers can adjust enhance efficiency, reduce waste, and improve product quality.

- One of the key objectives of embedded sensors is to ensure the safety and reliability of critical systems and structures. For example, pressure sensors in pipelines can detect leaks, preventing environmental disasters. Strain sensors in bridges can help assess load-bearing capacity and detect potential weaknesses.

- Embedded sensors are used in material testing and research to study the behavior of different materials under various strain and pressure conditions. This helps researchers understand material properties, durability, and performance characteristics.

- By analyzing strain and pressure data over time, predictive maintenance strategies can be developed. Equipment maintenance can be scheduled based on sensor data, reducing downtime, and minimizing costs.

- Embedded sensors are crucial for R&D purposes, allowing researchers and engineers to test new designs, materials, and technologies under controlled strain and pressure conditions.

4.1 Introduction

Embedded strain and pressure sensors have emerged as essential components in a wide range of industries and applications, revolutionizing the way we monitor, analyze, and optimize various systems and structures. These sensors are designed to accurately measure and quantify the strain and pressure levels experienced by objects, machinery, and environments. By seamlessly integrating into the very fabric of the systems they serve, these sensors provide invaluable insights that drive efficiency, safety, and innovation. In recent years, the demand for real-time data and precise measurements has led to the rapid development and adoption of embedded strain and pressure sensors. These sensors have found their way into critical sectors such as aerospace, automotive, civil engineering, healthcare, and manufacturing, each with its own unique set of objectives and challenges. The ability to monitor structural health, ensure operational safety, and optimize processes has propelled these sensors into the spotlight of technological advancement. Embedded strain sensors are designed to detect and quantify deformation within materials and structures, allowing engineers and researchers to assess structural integrity, predict potential failures, and implement preventive measures. This capability has a profound impact on industries where safety and reliability are paramount, as it enables proactive maintenance strategies and safeguards against catastrophic events. On the other hand, embedded pressure sensors play a crucial role in monitoring the forces exerted by liquids or gases on various surfaces. From medical devices that measure blood pressure to industrial applications that gauge pipeline integrity, these sensors provide invaluable data for decision-making, performance enhancement, and risk mitigation.

This introduction sets the stage for exploring the diverse objectives and applications of embedded strain and pressure sensors across industries. As we delve deeper into their specific roles in different sectors, we will uncover the transformative potential of these sensors in shaping the way we design, build, and interact with the world around us. Through a comprehensive exploration of their functionalities and applications, we aim to gain a holistic understanding of how embedded strain and pressure sensors are contributing to innovation and progress across various domains.

4.2. Foil strain gauge

Foil strain gauge is an extension of resistance wire strain gauge. Here this gauge also uses a resistance material foil deposited over an insulating material such as Bakelite rather than winding a wire. The metals and alloys used for foil are like wire material used in wire wounded strain gauge.

Foil type gauges are having more advantages over wire strain gauge as given below-

- They have a much higher dissipation capacity than wire wound gauges due to their larger surface area for the same volume. So, they can be used for higher operating temperature ranges.
- In addition, the larger surface is of foil gauge leading to better bonding.
- No stress concentration exists on terminals.
- These gauge transducers can be fabricated on a large scale and in any shape.
- These gauge transducers have similar properties to wire strain gauges. Their gauge factors are usually the same.
- These gauges are manufactured using diffusion process. So as a resistance foil, semiconductor materials can be used. Thus, we can achieve high gauge factor / strain sensitivity to detect a very small change in length.

Construction

The foil is achieved by etching and deposition technique on a carrier. Etched foil gauge manufacturing involves first attaching a layer of stress sensitive material to a thin sheet of paper or Bakelite. The metal part used as the wire element is covered with a suitable masking material, and an etching solution is applied to the unit. The solution removes the part of the metal that is not masked, leaving the desired grid structure intact.

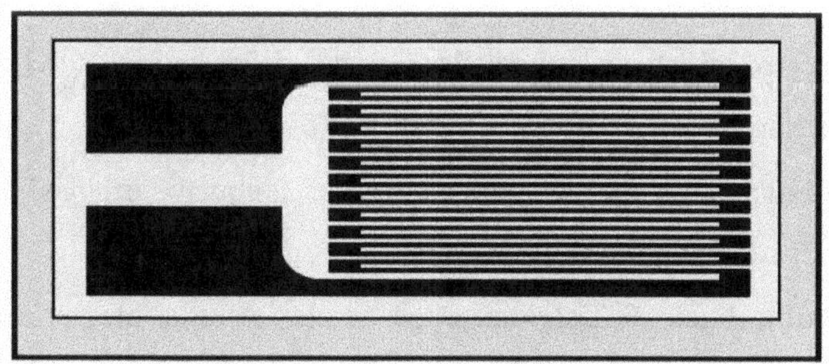

Fig 4.1Diagram of foil type strain gauge

Strain Gauge foil material

There are various resistance materials available to construct strain gauge. Gauge wires are made up of metals, or alloys. Some of them are as follows-

- Constantan (Copper nickel alloy)
- Nichrome (Nickel Chromium alloy)
- Isoelastic (Fe + Ni + Cr)
- Platinum alloy, etc.

The Measuring Principles of Foil Strain Gauges

Foil strain gauges are used to determine the value and direction of strain. This is achieved by a measuring grid that is usually installed on a material surface to acquire applied strain as a factor of changes in electrical resistance against the foil strain gauge's nominal resistance and its sensitivity factor. It registers compression as a decrease in electrical resistance and elongation as an increase. To calculate material stresses (Experimental stress analysis) the strain values are coupled with a material's physical properties such as its Young's modulus (Hooke's law). Alternate applications for strain gauges are transducers such as load cells, force-, torque- and pressure transducers. There are thousands of distinct foil strain gauges available from HBM including linear, rosette, torsion/shear, full bridge, and chain formats.

- **Linear strain gauges** are preferable for measuring strain across a single plane of direction.
- **Rosette foil strain gauges** feature dual measuring grids to offset strain measurements at a 90° angle to measure biaxial stress.
- **Torsion/shear strain gauges** feature uniquely arranged measuring grids for determining the shear stress of torsion bars.
- **Double linear foil strain gauges** feature parallel measuring grids for acquiring perpendicular stress in bending beams.

- **Full bridge strain gauges** feature 4 integrated measuring grids for robust strain measurements of shear stresses in tension and compression bars.

- **Chain foil strain gauges** are equipped with several smaller measuring grids to acquire shear force gradients across the measuring bridge.

A foil strain gauge is a specialized sensor widely used in engineering and scientific applications to measure mechanical strain in various materials and structures. Its design and functionality make it an indispensable tool for stress analysis, structural monitoring, and material testing.

At its core, a foil strain gauge consists of a thin, flexible strip of metal (often made of materials like constantan or nickel-chromium alloy) that is precisely adhered to the surface of the object being monitored. As the object undergoes mechanical deformation or strain, the foil also stretches or compresses, causing a change in its electrical resistance. This change in resistance is directly proportional to the strain experienced by the object, allowing for accurate strain measurement.

One of the notable advantages of foil strain gauges is their sensitivity and ability to detect even small changes in strain. This sensitivity makes them suitable for applications where precise measurements are essential, such as in the aerospace and automotive industries, where structural integrity and safety are paramount.

The installation of a foil strain gauge requires careful surface preparation, adhesive application, and electrical connections. The gauge's electrical resistance change is typically very small, necessitating the use of precision signal conditioning and amplification to obtain meaningful data. Modern advancements have led to the development of self-temperature-compensated strain gauges, which mitigate the effects of temperature variations on the measurements.

Foil strain gauges find applications in a wide array of scenarios. In civil engineering, they monitor the structural health of bridges and buildings, helping engineers assess potential weaknesses and prevent structural failures. In the automotive industry, these gauges play a critical role in crash testing, ensuring that vehicles meet safety standards. Additionally, they aid in the design and testing of mechanical components, materials, and products across industries.

In conclusion, the foil strain gauge's fundamental principle of measuring mechanical strain by monitoring changes in electrical resistance underscores its significance in various sectors. Its sensitivity, precision, and adaptability make it an invaluable tool for engineers and researchers, enabling them to analyze and enhance the performance, safety, and reliability of diverse structures and systems.

4.3 Semiconductor strain Gauge

When external forces are applied to a stationary object, stress and strain are the result. Stress is defined as the object's internal resisting forces, and strain is defined as the displacement and deformation that occur. For a uniform distribution of internal resisting forces, stress can be calculated by dividing the force (F) applied by the unit area (A):

$$Stress(\sigma) = F/A$$

Strain is defined as the amount of deformation per unit length of an object when a load is applied. Strain is calculated by dividing the total deformation of the original length by the original length (L):

$$Strain(\epsilon) = (\Delta L)/L$$

Typical values for strain are less than 0.005 inch/inch and are often expressed in micro-strain units:

$$Micro - strain = Strain \, x \, 10^6$$

Strain may be compressive or tensile and is typically measured by strain gages. It was Lord Kelvin who first reported in 1856 that metallic conductors subjected to mechanical strain exhibit a change in their electrical resistance. This phenomenon was first put to practical use in the 1930s.

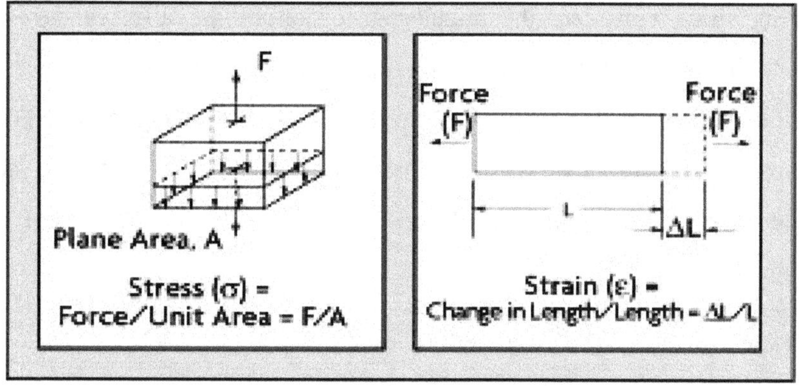

Fig 4.2 Definitions of Stress & Strain

Fundamentally, all strain gages are designed to convert mechanical motion into an electronic signal. A change in capacitance, inductance, or resistance is proportional to the strain experienced by the sensor. If a wire is held under tension, it gets slightly longer, and its cross-sectional area is reduced. This changes its resistance (R) in proportion to the strain sensitivity (S) of the wire's resistance. When a strain is introduced, the strain sensitivity, which is also called the gage factor (GF), is given by:

$$GF = \frac{\frac{\Delta R}{R}}{\frac{\Delta L}{L}} = (\Delta R/R)/Strain$$

The ideal strain gage would change resistance only due to the deformations of the surface to which the sensor is attached. However, in real applications, temperature, material properties, the adhesive that bonds the gage to the surface, and the stability of the metal all affect the detected resistance. Because most materials do not have the same properties in all directions, a knowledge of the axial strain alone is insufficient for a complete analysis. Poisson, bending, and torsional strains also need to be measured. Each requires a different strain gauge arrangement.

Shearing strain considers the angular distortion of an object under stress. Imagine that a horizontal force is acting on the top right corner of a thick book on a table, forcing the book to become somewhat trapezoidal Fig4.3. The shearing strain in this case can be expressed as the angular change in radians between the vertical y-axis and the new position. The shearing strain is the tangent of this angle.

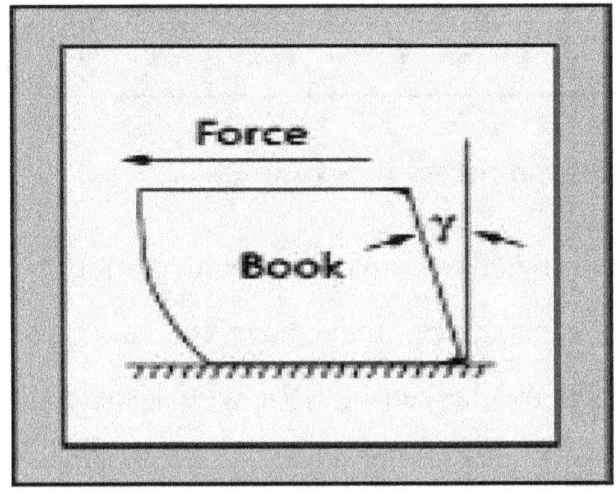

Fig 4.3 Shearing Strain

Poisson strain expresses both the thinning and elongation that occurs in a strained bar Fig 4.3. Poisson strain is defined as the negative ratio of the strain in the traverse direction (caused by the contraction of the bar's diameter) to the strain in the longitudinal direction. As the length increases and the cross-sectional area decreases, the electrical resistance of the wire also rises.

Bending strain, or moment strain, is calculated by determining the relationship between the force and the amount of bending which results from it. Although not as commonly detected as the other types of strain, torsional strain is measured when the strain produced by twisting is of interest. Torsional strain is calculated by dividing the torsional stress by the torsional modulus of elasticity.

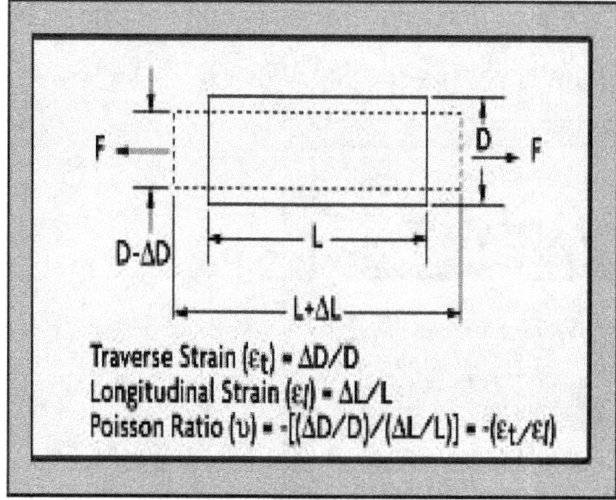

Fig 4.4 Poisson Strain

Sensor Design

The deformation of an object can be measured by mechanical, optical, acoustical, pneumatic, and electrical means. The earliest strain gages were mechanical devices that measured strain by measuring the change in length and comparing it to the original length of the object. For example, the extension meter (extensiometer) uses a series of levers to amplify strain to a readable value. In general, however, mechanical devices tend to provide low resolutions, and are bulky and difficult to use.

Optical sensors are sensitive and accurate but are delicate and not very popular in industrial applications. They use interference fringes produced by optical flats to measure strain. Optical sensors operate best, Under laboratory conditions.

The most widely used characteristic that varies in proportion to strain is electrical resistance. Although capacitance and inductance-based strain gages have been constructed, these devices' sensitivity to vibration, their mounting requirements, and circuit complexity have limited their application. The photoelectric gage uses a light beam, two fine gratings, and a photocell detector to generate an electrical current that is proportional to strain. The gage length of these devices can be as short as 1/16 inch, but they are costly and delicate. The first bonded, metallic wire-type strain gage was developed in 1938.

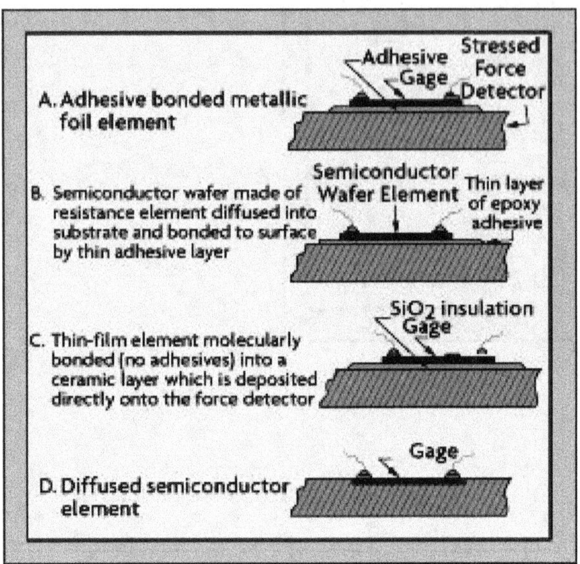

Fig4.5Strain Gage Designs

The metallic foil-type strain gage consists of a grid of wire filament (a resistor) of approximately 0.001 in. (0.025 mm) thickness, bonded directly to the strained surface by a thin layer of epoxy resin shown in **Fig4.5-A**. When a load is applied to the surface, the resulting change in surface length is communicated to the resistor and the corresponding strain is measured in terms of the electrical resistance of the foil wire, which varies linearly with strain. The foil diaphragm and the adhesive bonding agent must work together in transmitting the strain, while the adhesive must also serve as an electrical insulator between the foil Grid and the surface.

When selecting a strain gage, one must consider not only the strain characteristics of the sensor, but also its stability and temperature sensitivity. Unfortunately, the most desirable strain gage materials are also sensitive to temperature variations and tend to change resistance as they age. For tests of short duration, this may not be a serious concern, but for continuous industrial measurement, one must include temperature and drift compensation.

Each strain gage wire material has its characteristic gage factor, resistance, temperature coefficient of gage factor, thermal coefficient of resistivity, and stability. Typical materials include Constantan (copper-nickel alloy), Nichrome V (nickel-chrome alloy), platinum alloys (usually tungsten), Isoelastic (nickel-iron alloy), or Karma-type alloy wires (nickel-chrome alloy), foils, or semiconductor materials. The most popular alloys used for strain gages are copper-nickel alloys and nickel-chromium alloys.

In the mid-1950s, scientists at Bell Laboratories discovered the piezoresistive characteristics of germanium and silicon. Although the materials exhibited substantial nonlinearity and temperature sensitivity, they had gage factors more than fifty times, and sensitivity more than 100 times, that of metallic wire or foil strain gages. Silicon wafers are also more elastic than metallic ones. After being strained they return more readily to their original shapes.

Around 1970, the first semiconductor (silicon) strain gages were developed for the automotive industry. As opposed to other types of strain gages, semiconductor strain gages depend on the piezoresistive effects of silicon or germanium and measure the change in resistance with stress as opposed to strain. The semiconductor bonded strain gage is a wafer with a resistance element diffused into a substrate of silicon. The wafer element usually is not provided with a backing and bonding it to the strained surface requires great care as only a thin layer of epoxy is used to attach it **Fig4.5-B** The size is much smaller and the cost much lower than for a metallic foil sensor. The same epoxies that are used to attach foil gages also are used to bond semiconductor gages.

While the higher unit resistance and sensitivity of semiconductor wafer sensors are definite advantages, their greater sensitivity to temperature variations and tendency to drift are disadvantages in comparison to metallic foil sensors. Another disadvantage of semiconductor strain gages is that the resistance-to-strain relationship is nonlinear, varying 10-20% from a straight-line equation. With computer-controlled Instrumentation, these limitations can be overcome through software compensation. A further improvement is the thin-film strain gage that eliminates the need for adhesive bonding **Fig4.5-C** The gage is produced by first depositing an electrical insulation (typically a ceramic) onto the stressed metal surface, and then depositing the strain gage onto this insulation layer. Vacuum deposition Or sputtering techniques are used to bond the materials molecularly. Because the thin-film gage is molecularly bonded to the specimen, the installation is much more stable, and the resistance values experience less drift. Another advantage is that the stressed force detector can be a metallic diaphragm Or beam with a deposited layer of ceramic insulation. Diffused semiconductor strain gages represent a further improvement in strain gage technology because they eliminate the need for bonding agents. By eliminating bonding agents, errors due to creep and hysteresis are also eliminated. The diffused semiconductor strain gage uses photolithography masking techniques and solid-state diffusion of boron to molecularly bond the resistance elements. Electrical Leads are directly attached to the pattern shown in the **Fig4.5-D.** The diffused gage is limited to moderate-temperature applications and requires temperature compensation. Diffused semiconductors often are used as sensing elements in pressure transducers. They are small, inexpensive, accurate and repeatable, provide a wide pressure range, and generate a strong output signal. Their limitations include sensitivity to ambient temperature variations, which can be compensated for in intelligent transmitter designs.

In summary, the ideal strain gage is small in size and mass, low in cost, easily attached, and highly sensitive to strain but insensitive to ambient or process temperature variations.

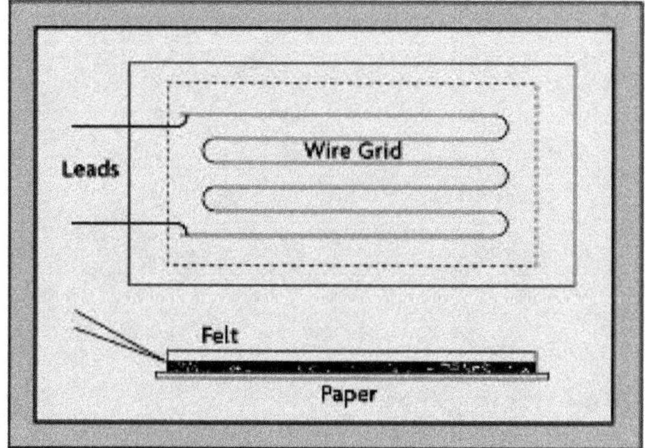

Fig 4.6 Bonded resistance strain gauge construction

Bonded Resistance Gages

The bonded semiconductor strain gage was schematically described in **Fig4.6** These devices represent a popular method of measuring strain. The gage consists of a grid of very fine metallic wire, foil, or semiconductor material bonded to the strained surface or carrier matrix by a thin insulated layer of epoxy. When the carrier matrix is strained, the strain is transmitted to the grid material through the adhesive. The variations in the electrical resistance of the grid are measured as an indication of strain. The grid shape is designed to provide maximum gage resistance while keeping both.

The length and width of the gage to a minimum. Bonded resistance strain gages have a good reputation. They are relatively inexpensive, can achieve overall accuracy of better than +/-0.10%, are available in a short gage length, are only moderately affected by temperature changes, have small physical size and low mass, and are highly sensitive. Bonded resistance strain gages can be used to measure both static and dynamic strain.

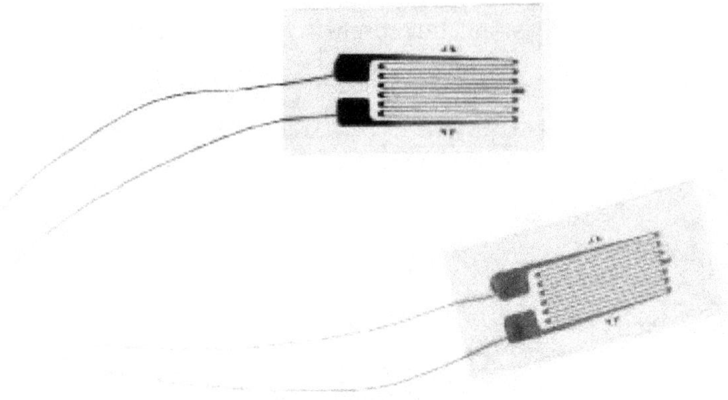

Fig 4.7Typical metal-foil strain gages.

In bonding strain gage elements to a strained surface, it is important that the gage experience the same strain as the object. With an adhesive material inserted between the sensors and the strained surface, the installation is sensitive to creep due to degradation of the bond, temperature influences, and hysteresis caused by thermoelastic strain. Because many glues and epoxy resins are prone to creep, it is important. To use resins designed specifically for strain gages. The bonded resistance strain gage is suitable for a wide variety of environmental conditions. It can measure strain in jet engine turbines operating at very high temperatures and in cryogenic fluid applications at temperatures as low as -452*F (-269*C). It has low mass and size, high sensitivity, and is suitable for static and dynamic applications. Foil elements are available with unit resistances from 120 to 5,000 ohms. Gage lengths from 0.008 in. to 4 in. are available commercially. The three primary considerations in gage selection are: operating temperature, the nature of the strain to be detected, and stability requirements. In addition, selecting the right carrier material, grid alloy, adhesive, and protective coating will guarantee the success of the application.

4.4 Bridge circuits for strain gauge Transducer

Different physical phenomena can cause changes in the electrical resistance of a conductor. For example, temperature, strain, and photo illumination are known factors that affect electrical resistance. Force transducers, such as load cells, use strain gauges to take advantage of the relationship between mechanical strain and the electrical resistance of a conductor. All components experience some form of loading when motion or forces are applied. Understanding the properties of mechanical stress and strain is important for deciding if a component can withstand the loading forces for an application. Strain gauges are devices that provide accurate and precise readings that make it possible to observe and monitor the amount of stress a component may be enduring. They assist in predicting potential failure of or damage to an application.

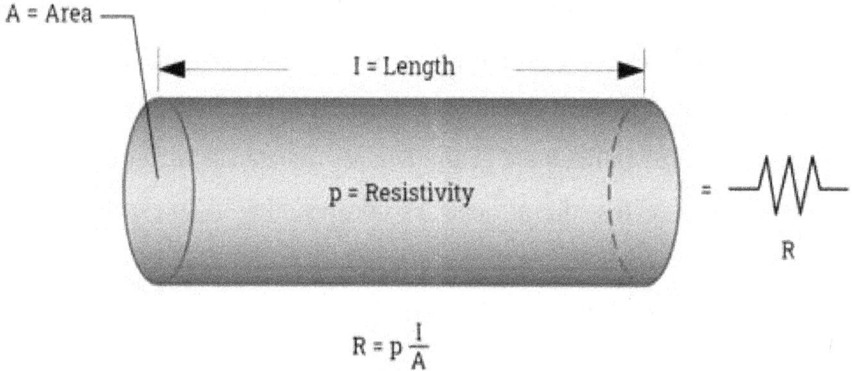

Fig 4.8 Relationship between Conductor Geometry to Resistivity

The electrical resistance of a wire is directly proportional to its length and inversely proportional to its cross-sectional area. When stretching a strain gauge, the length of its wire increases while the cross-section decreases. Thus, the electrical resistance of the wire is increased. Conversely, compressing the strain gauge without buckling its wires causes the electrical resistance to decrease. The strain gauge is an application of the Wheatstone bridge circuit. A

Wheatstone bridge circuit is composed of four resistors and an electrical energy source. Among the four resistors, one is variable while the rest are fixed. This variable resistor is the strain gauge. Regarding the energy source, a direct current (DC) supply is fed across the bridge circuit. This is called the excitation source.

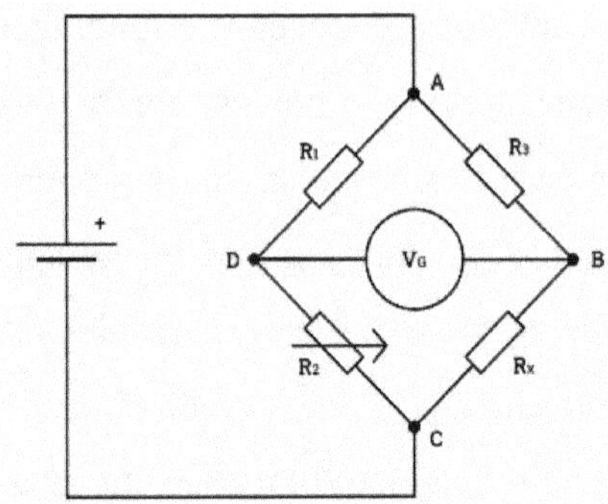

Fig 4.9 Wheatstone bridge circuit

The Wheatstone bridge output is the gap voltage measured at Vg indicated in the figure below. The bridge is said to be balanced when the gap voltage is zero. This is typically the initial state of the device. Imbalance is caused when the resistance changes across the variable resistor, resulting in an electric potential present across the gap.

Strain Gauge Bridge Configurations

One way strain gauges are classified is by their bridge configuration. A simple load cell or force transducer uses only one strain gauge. They use a circuit called quarter-bridge configuration. To achieve better performance, most designs use two or four strain gauges. Those that use two strain gauges are called half bridges, while those that use four are called full bridge circuits.

Quarter Bridge

The previously described Wheatstone bridge is called a quarter bridge circuit. A single active strain gauge takes the place of the variable resistor. Since only one strain gauge is used, it can only measure of strain. For the same reason, they are also the least sensitive.

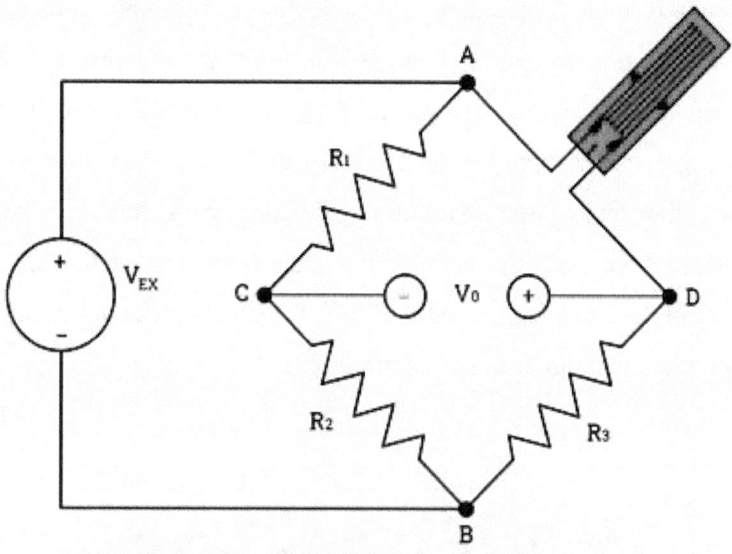

Fig 4.10 Quarter Bridge

Quarter bridge circuits are further divided into two configurations.

Simple Quarter Bridge: This is the simplest among the strain gauge types in this category. It is composed of one active gauge and three completion resistors. The completion resistor paired with the strain gauge is called a dummy resistor. This type is the least sensitive and is prone to errors caused by temperature variations.

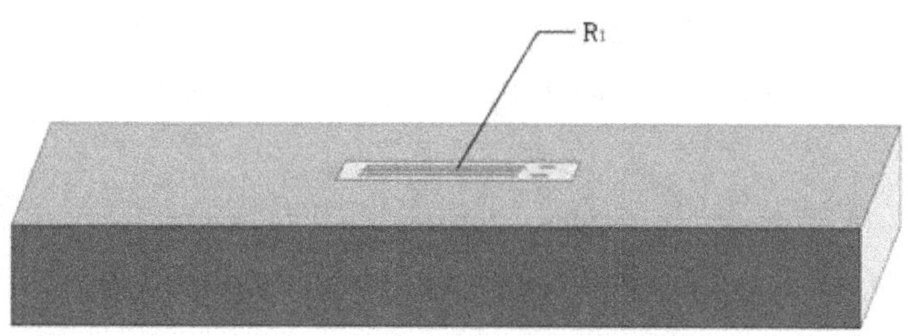

Fig 4.11 Simple Quarter Bridge

Quarter Bridge with Dummy Gauge: In this circuit, two strain gauges are employed. One strain gauge is active, while the other is used as a dummy. The active gauge is aligned according to the direction of the strain to be measured. In contrast, the dummy gauge is oriented in the transverse direction. When a mechanical load is applied, the active gauge experiences greater strain and, therefore, greater change in electrical resistance than the dummy gauge. Regarding the temperature variations, the change is felt with the same magnitude by both the active and dummy gauges. Since the active and dummy gauges are in the same leg, the ratio of their resistances does not change. Thus, the effect of temperature is nulled or minimized.

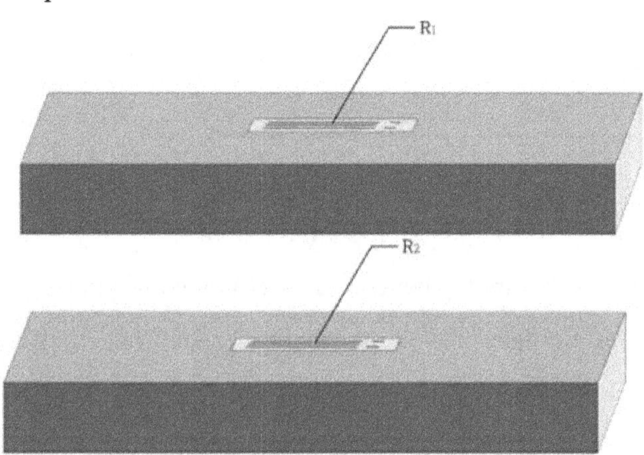

Fig 4.12 Double Quarter Bridge or Diagonal Bridge

This type has two active strain gauges. One strain gauge is placed on one leg of the circuit, while the other gauge is on the second leg. On the elastic element or structure, the gauges are mounted on opposite sides parallel to the loading direction.

There are two known advantages when using a diagonal bridge design. The first is the increased sensitivity. Since two strain gauges experience the same amount of deformation, a larger output can be obtained. The increase is approximately twice that of a simple quarter bridge circuit. Another advantage is its ability to reject bending strain. Diagonal bridge strain gauges only measure tensile and compressive strains.

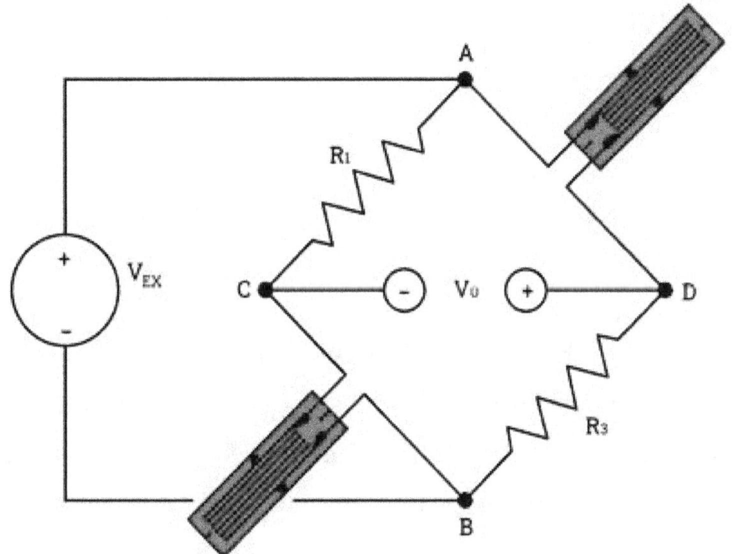

Fig 4.13 Diagonal Bridge Configuration

When the gauges detect oppositely directed strains, the effect is negated. The strains experienced by the gauges must be in the same direction. However, the downside of using this type is the large effect of temperature variation. This configuration doubles the error. To counter this, dummy gauges must be paired with each active gauge.

Half Bridge

Half bridge circuits feature two strain gauges used as active gauges. They are more sensitive than the quarter bridge types since there are two strain measuring elements. The strain gauges in a half bridge circuit can be configured in two ways.

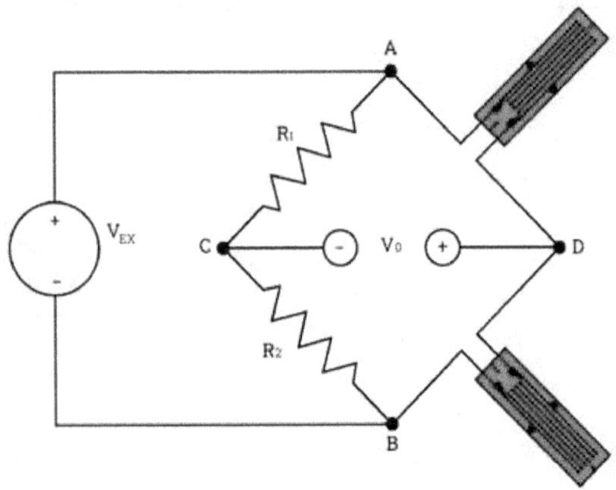

Fig 4.14 Half Bridge Configuration

Half Bridge with Poisson Gauge: In this design, one strain gauge is oriented in the longitudinal or axial direction while the other is in transverse. It can measure tensile, compressive, and bending strains with higher sensitivity.

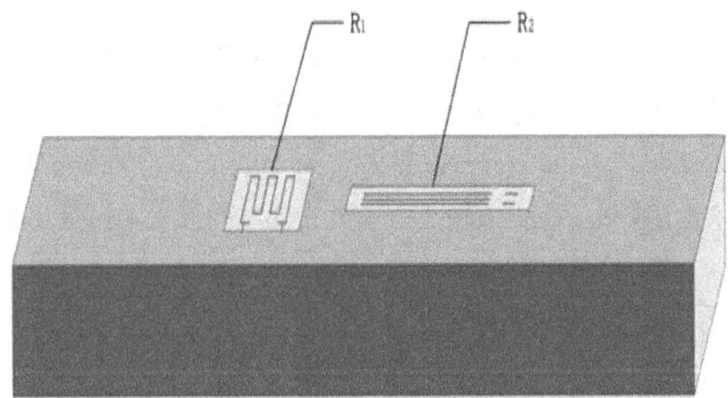

Fig 4.15 Half Bridge with Poisson Gauge

This half bridge configuration operates on the Poisson effect. The Poisson effect is the tendency of a material to change its cross-section in the direction perpendicular to the load. Most materials experience opposite strains in perpendicular directions. Since both strain gauges are used to measure the change in dimension of both axes, the effect on the varying resistances is increased. This, in turn, improves the magnitude of the output voltage. The additional output depends on the Poisson ratio of the material. Moreover, by having both strain gauges at the same leg of the bridge circuit, they cancel out the effect of temperature. This is like the advantage seen in the quarter bridge with a dummy gauge circuit.

Bending Half Bridge: The second type of the half bridge configuration features two parallel strain gauges mounted on opposite sides of the transducer's elastic element. The strain gauges are not coplanar with each other, unlike the previous type.

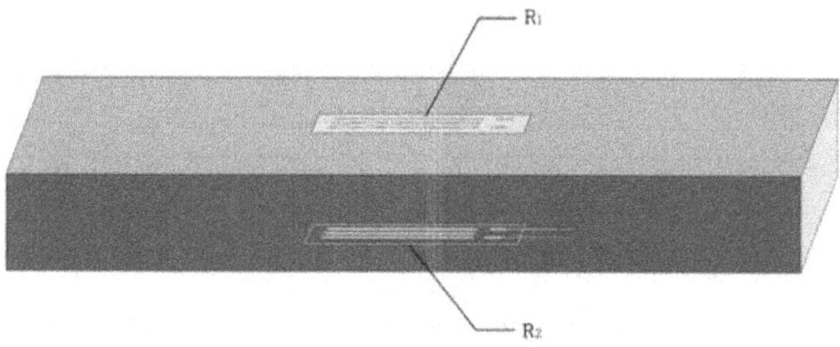

Fig 4.16 Bending Half Bridge

This configuration is only applicable for measuring bending strain. When the elastic element is bent, the sides normal to the direction of the applied force experience either tension or compression. The two strain gauges measure the deflection of the elastic element. A unique feature of this design is its ability to eliminate the measured axial strain. The transducer interprets the voltage reading such that one strain gauge is in tension while the other is in compression. When both strain gauges are in either tension or compression, the resistance change of one strain gauge is negated by the other. Similarly, this ability also negates the effect of temperature.

Full Bridge

A full bridge circuit replaces all resistors with active gauges. They are the most versatile due to the many different configurations possible using four strain gauges. Since all resistances vary, temperature effects are negated throughout the circuit, regardless of the configuration. Enumerated below are the subtypes of full bridge circuits.

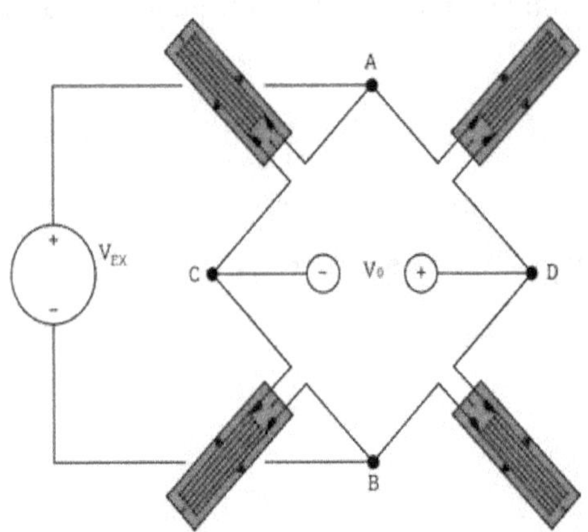

Fig 4.17 Full Bridge Configuration

Axial and Bending Full Bridge: In this configuration, all four strain gauges are mounted on one side of the structure. As much as possible, the gauges are coplanar with each other. The gauge pairs on one leg of the bridge are oriented such that one is perpendicular to the other.

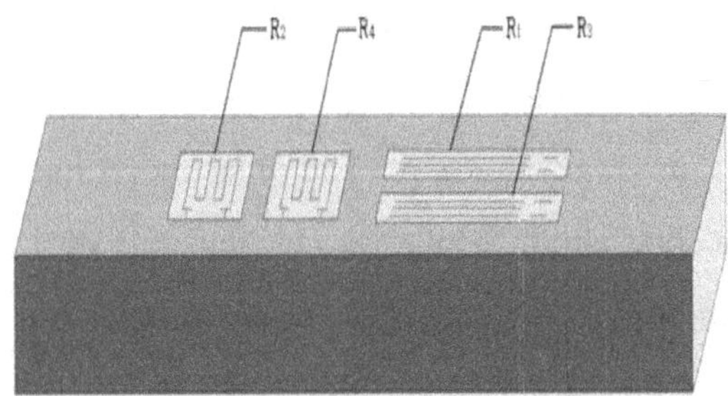

Fig 4.18 Full Bridge Circuit

An axial and bending full bridge circuit is regarded as two Poisson half bridge circuits working in tandem. The result is an output signal with twice the magnitude of its half bridge counterpart.

Axial Full Bridge: In this design, two strain gauges are mounted on one side of the structure while the other two are mounted on the opposite side. The coplanar gauges are aligned perpendicularly with their pair. Similar to the previous type, this configuration works like two Poisson half bridge circuits. This results in an extremely sensitive sensor.

Axial full bridge circuits eliminate bending strain readings like that to diagonal bridge circuits. The strain gauges on opposite sides of the structure are assumed to have the same strain direction. When these strain gauges are inversely directed strains, the effect on the resistance ratio is nulled.

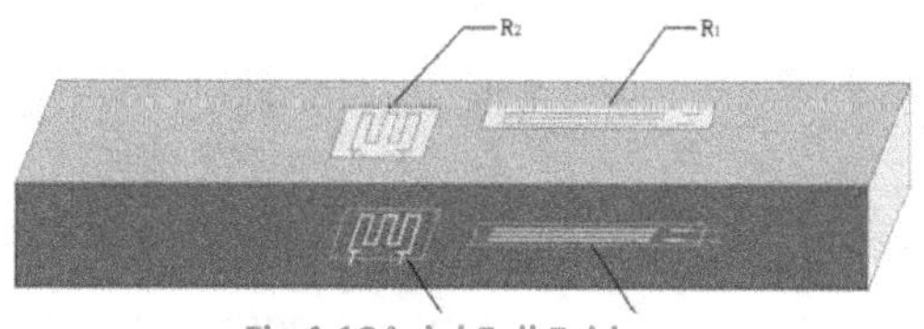

Fig 4.19 Axial Full Bridge

Bending Full Bridge: This circuit is created by placing the strain gauge pairs on the opposite sides of the structure and parallel with each other.

The arrangement may seem like that of the axial type. However, both Poisson gauges are placed on one leg of the circuit. This version of the bending full bridge circuit combines the characteristics of the Poisson half bridge and bending half bridge circuits.

Not only is the axial strain

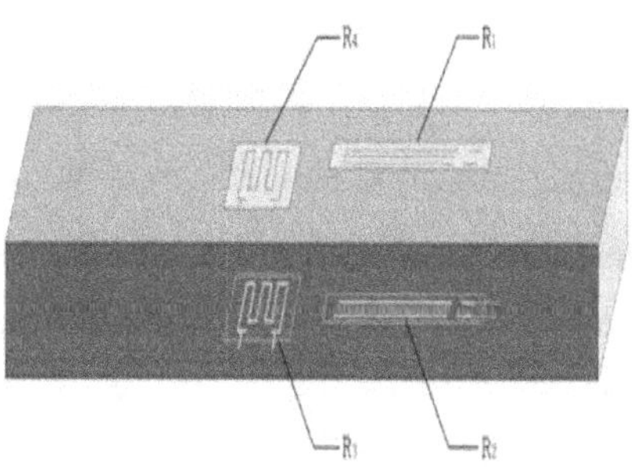

Fig 4.20 Bending Full Bridge

eliminated, but the signal sensitivity is increased. The output signal produced is twice that of a Poisson half bridge.

Bending Full Bridge without Poisson Gauge: This bending full bridge circuit has all four strain gauges aligned in one direction. Thus, this type does not have a Poisson gauge. Strain gauge pairs are placed on opposing sides of the structure.

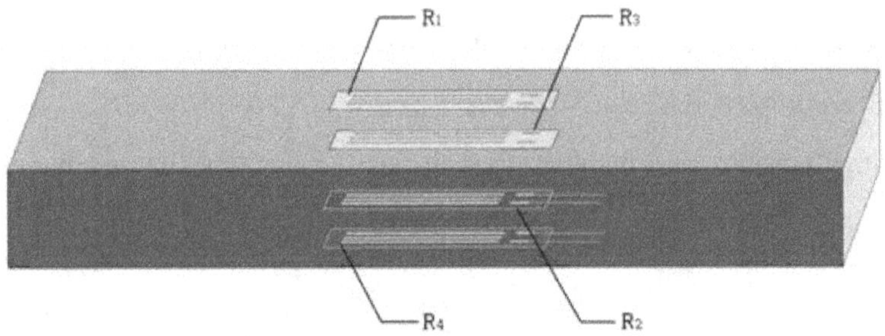

Fig 4.21 Bending Full Bridge without Poisson Gauge

This type functions like two bending half bridge circuits. The strain gauge pairs on one leg of the circuit experience tension and compression. It also eliminates the effect of axial strain when the pairs detect deflection in a single direction. Since there are four strain measuring conductors, this configuration's sensitivity is quadrupled compared to the simple quarter bridge type.

4.5 Elastic Pressure sensors

Elastic pressure sensors have emerged as a vital innovation in the field of sensing technology, offering a sophisticated and versatile approach to measuring pressure changes in a wide range of applications. These sensors, based on the principles of elasticity and deformation, have redefined our ability to monitor and quantify pressure variations with exceptional accuracy and sensitivity.

At their core, elastic pressure sensors leverage the inherent properties of elastic materials to detect and convert applied pressure into measurable signals. These sensors consist of carefully engineered materials that undergo deformation when subjected to external pressure. The resulting mechanical strain is then transduced into an electrical response, providing valuable insights into pressure changes.

One of the remarkable attributes of elastic pressure sensors is their adaptability to different environments and pressure ranges. Their ability to accurately capture minute pressure fluctuations as well as handle high-pressure scenarios positions them as indispensable tools across various industries. From medical devices monitoring physiological pressure in the human body to industrial applications gauging fluid pressure in complex systems, elastic pressure sensors demonstrate unparalleled versatility.

The design and construction of elastic pressure sensors require a delicate balance of material selection, sensor geometry, and signal processing techniques. As these sensors operate on the principles of elasticity, they are inherently sensitive to mechanical changes. Consequently, meticulous attention is given to factors such as material resilience, sensor robustness, and calibration procedures to ensure reliable and repeatable measurements.

In the subsequent exploration of elastic pressure sensors, we will delve into their underlying mechanisms, discuss the intricacies of their design and fabrication, and examine their diverse applications across industries. By delving into the nuances of how these sensors convert physical pressure into actionable data, we aim to gain a comprehensive understanding of the pivotal role elastic pressure sensors play in modern sensing technology.

Elastic pressure elements or mechanical type of transducers are used for measurement of very high pressures up to about 700MN/m^2. There are three main types of pressure elements. These are:

(i.) Bourdon tube

(ii.) Bellows

(iii.) Diaphragm

Most pressure measuring devices use elastic members for sensing pressure at the primary stage. These elastic members are of many types and convert the pressure into mechanical displacement which is later converted into an electrical form using a secondary transducer.

4.5.1 Bourdon Type

A bourdon pressure gauge is the most common type of pressure gauge, and it uses a curved tube that straightens under pressure and shows the reading on a dial. Key features of them are high accuracy, high precision, resistance to vibration, and easy maintenance. A **Bourdon gauge** is a mechanical device used to **measure** and **display pressure**. The gauge can be used for measuring pressure in both gas and liquid state systems.

The bourdon gauge may appear like one of the least interesting pieces of equipment out there, but it is still one of the most widely spread. Indeed it's difficult to imagine most engineering processes without these gauges. The bourdon pressure gauge is attached to the pipeline of the system's inlet pipe. The socket block holds the inlet pipe in place, allowing the pressure to flow into the stationary end of the tube. This pressure is distributed throughout the elastic C-shaped tube between the fixed and the moving ends. As the inlet pressure increases, the C-shape tube straightens. The pivot and pivot pin attached to the moving end of the tube connects this movement with the sector gear. This leads to an amplified motion which causes a deflection of the indicator needle for every small change in inlet pressure. When the inlet pressure increases, the indicator moves clockwise (from left to right) over a calibrated scale. Once the pressure drops, the tube regains its helix shape, and the indicator moves in an anticlockwise direction (from right to left).

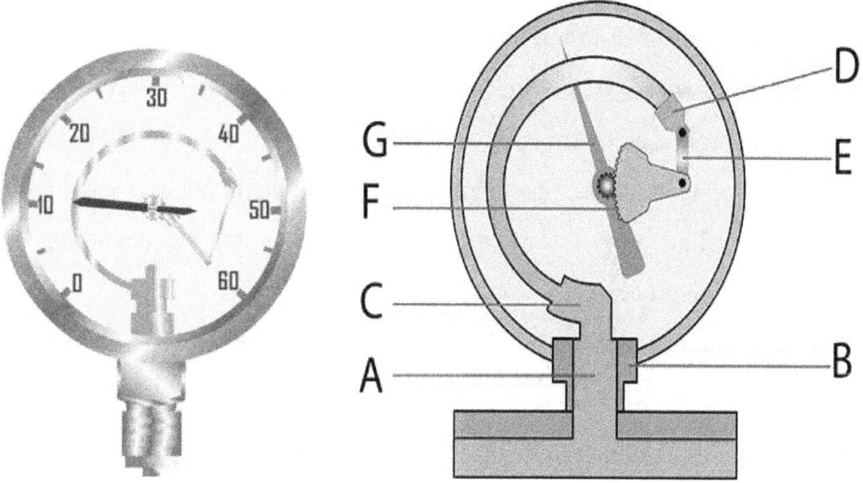

Fig 4.22(i) Bourdon Pressure Gauge; (ii) parts of Bourdon Pressure gauge A) Inlet pipe, (B) socket block, (C) stationary end, (D) moving end, (E) pivot and pivot pin, (F) sector gear, (G) indicator needle.

Due to its design, the bourdon tube is sensitive to pressure changes, making it suitable for high-precision applications. It is also resistant to corrosion and vibration.

The heart of the Bourdon gauge is the **Bourdon tube**. The tube is manufactured in a semi-circular C-shape, or coiled shape. The tube is open to atmosphere at one end and sealed closed at the other. Any increase in system pressure within the tube causes the tube to expand and straighten; the change is small but magnified due to the shape of the tube. The change in C-shape or coil radius is transferred to the indicator needle and this movement allows personnel to visually view the pressure within the system.

Applications

The Bourdon tube is a fundamental component in pressure measurement technology and finds various applications across industries where accurate pressure measurement is essential. Its ingenious design, characterized by a curved, flattened tube, allows it to convert pressure changes into mechanical motion, which is then translated into readable pressure values. Here are some notable applications of Bourdon tubes:

- **Industrial Process Control:** Bourdon tubes are extensively used in industrial processes to monitor and control pressure levels. They can be found in applications such as monitoring hydraulic and pneumatic systems, regulating fluid flow, and ensuring optimal operating conditions in manufacturing processes.

- **Oil and Gas Industry:** In the oil and gas sector, Bourdon tubes are employed to measure pressure in pipelines, storage tanks, and refining processes. They play a crucial role in ensuring the safe and efficient extraction, transportation, and processing of oil and gas.

- **Aerospace:** In aviation and aerospace industries, Bourdon tubes are used for pressure measurement in aircraft hydraulic systems, fuel lines, and cabin pressurization systems. Accurate pressure data is vital for safe and reliable flight operations.

- **HVAC Systems:** Heating, ventilation, and air conditioning (HVAC) systems utilize Bourdon tubes to maintain optimal pressure levels in various components, such as compressors, condensers, and evaporators. Proper pressure control contributes to efficient HVAC performance.

- **Automotive:** Bourdon tubes play a role in automotive applications, including monitoring tire pressure, brake systems, and fuel lines. Tire pressure monitoring systems (TPMS) use Bourdon tubes or similar technology to ensure vehicle safety and fuel efficiency.

- **Medical Equipment:** Bourdon tubes are used in medical devices like blood pressure monitors (sphygmomanometers) to measure and display blood pressure readings. They are also used in ventilators, anesthesia machines, and other medical equipment where pressure control is critical.

- **Marine Industry:** In marine applications, Bourdon tubes are utilized to measure pressure in ship systems, including water supply networks, engine rooms, and hydraulic systems. They contribute to the proper functioning and safety of marine vessels.

- **Water Treatment:** Bourdon tubes are used in water treatment plants to monitor pressure in various stages of the water treatment process. They help regulate water flow, pressure, and distribution.

- **Test and Measurement Equipment:** In laboratories and industrial testing environments, Bourdon tubes are integrated into pressure gauges and sensors for precise pressure measurements during research, quality control, and testing processes.

- **Energy Production**: In power generation facilities, Bourdon tubes are employed to monitor pressure in steam boilers, turbines, and other equipment. Accurate pressure measurement ensures safe and efficient energy production.

- **Chemical Processing:** Bourdon tubes are used in chemical processing plants to measure pressure in pipelines, reactors, and storage vessels. They contribute to process control and safety in these demanding environments.

- **Railway Systems:** Bourdon tubes are used in railway applications to monitor and regulate pressure in pneumatic systems, such as brake systems and suspension components.

These applications showcase the versatility and significance of Bourdon tubes in a wide range of industries, where precise pressure measurement is essential for operational efficiency, safety, and quality assurance.

4.5.2 Bellow Type

The pressure measuring elements are formed by the series combination of capsules. The working principle of bellows is same as that of diaphragms i.e., the applied displacement is converted into proportionate mechanical displacement. The materials used to construct bellows are beryllium copper, brass, Monel, stainless steel and nickel. Whenever the pressure to be measured is applied the sealed end of bellow suffers displacement. The generated displacement can be known by attaching a pointer scale arrangement to the sealed end or by transmitting the displacement to the secondary transducer. Bellow-type pressure gauge is a type of mechanical pressure measuring instrument that utilizes the elastic deformation of a bellow (bellows) to measure the pressure of gases or liquids in a system. This design offers certain advantages over other pressure gauge types. Here's construction and working along with its applications.

Construction:

A bellow-type pressure gauge consists of the following components:

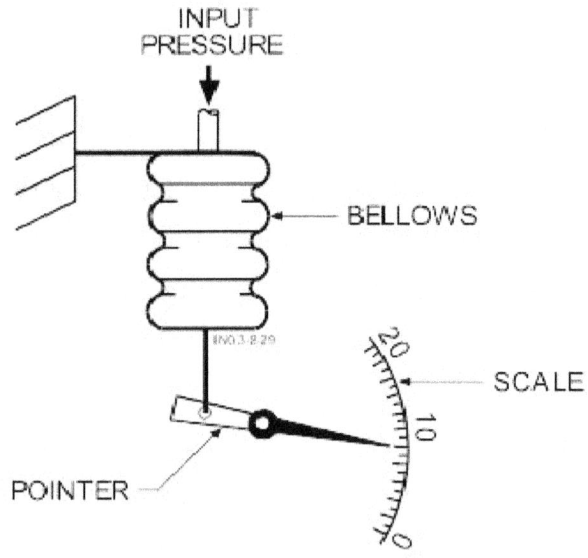

Fig 4.23 Bellow Pressure Gauge

Bellow: The bellow is typically a cylindrical or accordion-like flexible metallic tube sealed at both ends. It is often made of materials like stainless steel, brass, or other alloys that can withstand the pressure and temperature conditions of the application.

Connection Ports: The bellow is connected to the pressure source and the gauge housing through appropriate connection points or ports.

Mechanical Linkage: A mechanical linkage system is used to transfer the movement of the bellow to the pointer. This system usually involves levers and gears that amplify the bellow's movement.

Pointer and Scale: The pointer indicates the pressure on a circular scale that is calibrated with pressure units. The scale is typically marked in units like psi, kPa, bar, etc.

Working Principle:

Bellow Deformation: The core principle of a bellow-type pressure gauge is similar to that of a diaphragm pressure gauge. When the pressure of the fluid being measured changes, it exerts force on the bellow, causing it to deform either outward or inward.

Linkage Mechanism: The deformation of the bellow is connected to a mechanical linkage system, which converts the movement of the bellow into a corresponding movement of a pointer on a calibrated scale.

Pointer and Scale: The pointer moves along a circular scale that is calibrated with pressure units. As the bellow deforms due to pressure changes, the pointer's position on the scale changes, indicating the pressure of the fluid being measured.

Applications:

Bellow-type pressure gauges are well-suited for various applications due to their design and construction. Some common applications include:

Hydraulic Systems: Bellow-type pressure gauges can be used to measure pressure in hydraulic systems, where accurate pressure readings are crucial for system performance.

Pneumatic Systems: These gauges are also used in pneumatic systems to monitor air pressure, ensuring proper operation and safety.

Industrial Processes: Bellow-type gauges find applications in industries such as manufacturing, chemical processing, and petrochemicals, where pressure monitoring is important for quality control and safety.

HVAC Systems: Heating, ventilation, and air conditioning (HVAC) systems often use bellow-type pressure gauges to monitor air and fluid pressures.

4.5.3 Diaphragm Transducer

A diaphragm pressure gauge is a type of pressure-measuring instrument used to determine the pressure of gases or liquids in a system. It operates based on the principle of elastic deformation of a flexible diaphragm under the influence of pressure changes.

Construction

Diaphragm: The diaphragm is a thin, flexible, circular or domed membrane typically made of metal (such as stainless steel) or other suitable materials. It is installed in the pressure gauge and is in direct contact with the fluid whose pressure is being measured.

Connecting Mechanism: The diaphragm is connected to the pressure source through a port or connection point. When the pressure of the fluid changes, it exerts force on the diaphragm.

Deformation: As the pressure increases, the diaphragm experiences elastic deformation, causing it to deflect or bulge outward. The amount of deflection is directly proportional to the pressure applied. Conversely, as the pressure decreases, the diaphragm returns to its original position.

Linkage Mechanism: The diaphragm's deflection is transferred to a mechanical linkage system, which translates the diaphragm's movement into a corresponding movement of a pointer on a calibrated scale.

Pointer and Scale: The pointer is attached to the linkage system and moves along a circular scale that is marked with pressure units (such as psi, kPa, bar, etc.). The scale is calibrated during the manufacturing process to ensure accurate pressure readings.

Reading the Pressure: As the diaphragm deflects due to the pressure change, the pointer moves along the scale, indicating the pressure of the fluid being measured. The user can then read the pressure value from the scale where the pointer aligns.

Operation

The diaphragm pressure gauge consists of a circular membrane, made from sheet metal of precise dimensions, which can either be flat or corrugated. The diaphragm is mechanically connected to the transmission mechanism which will amplify the small deflections of the diaphragm and transfer them to the pointer. The fig below shows the pressure gauge working principle. We can see the movement of the diaphragm and the functioning of the transmission mechanism.

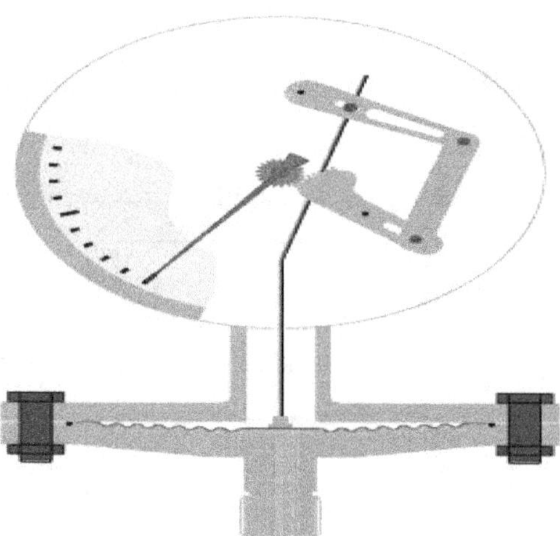

Fig 4.24 Diaphragm Pressure gauge working principle.

The process pressure is applied to the lower side of the diaphragm, while the upper side is at atmospheric pressure. The differential pressure arising across the diaphragm lifts the diaphragm and puts the pointer in motion. The deflection of the diaphragm is very small (+/- 1 mm) making it necessary to use a high-ratio multiplying movement to rotate the pointer along the full length of the scale. The actuation of such a high-ratio transmission mechanism is possible because diaphragm deflection can generate large forces.

Diaphragm pressure gauges are commonly used in applications where the pressure range is relatively low and where isolation from the process fluid is necessary. They are suitable for measuring pressures of gases and non-corrosive liquids. However, it's important to note that diaphragm pressure gauges might not be suitable for highly corrosive or abrasive media, as they can affect the durability and accuracy of the diaphragm over time.

4.6 Capacitive pressure sensor

Capacitive pressure sensors measure pressure by detecting changes in electrical capacitance caused by the movement of a diaphragm.

Working principle.

A capacitor consists of two parallel conducting plates separated by a small gap. The capacitance is defined by: $C = \epsilon_r \epsilon_0 \dfrac{A}{d}$

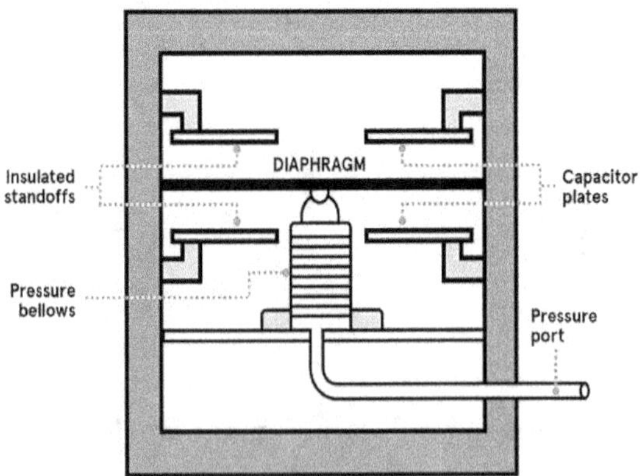

Fig 4.25 Working principle of Capacitive pressure Sensor.

Where : **εr** is the dielectric constant of the material between the plates (this is 1 for a vacuum)

ε0 is the electric constant (equal to 8.854x1012 F/m),

A is the area of the plates.

d is the distance between the plates

Changing any of the variables will cause a corresponding change in the capacitance. The easiest one to control is the spacing. This can be done by making one or both plates a diaphragm that is deflected by changes in pressure. Typically, one electrode is a pressure sensitive diaphragm and the other is fixed. An example of a capacitive pressure sensor is shown to the right. An easy way of measuring the change in capacitance is to make it part of a tuned circuit, typically consisting of the capacitive sensor plus an inductor. This can either change the frequency of an oscillator or the AC coupling of a resonant Circuit.

Construction

The diaphragm can be constructed from a variety of materials, such as plastic, glass, silicon, or Ceramic, to suit different applications. The capacitance of the sensor is typically around 50 to 100 pF, with the change being a few picofarads. The stiffness and strength of the material can be chosen to provide a range of sensitivities and operating pressures. To get a large signal, the sensor may need to be fairly large, which can limit the frequency range of operation. However, smaller diaphragms are more sensitive and have a faster response time.A large thin diaphragm may be sensitive to noise from vibration (after all, the same basic principle is used to make condenser microphones) particularly at low pressures. Thicker diaphragms are used in high-pressure sensors and to ensure mechanical strength. Sensors with full-scale pressure up to 5,000 psi can readily be constructed by controlling the diaphragm thickness.

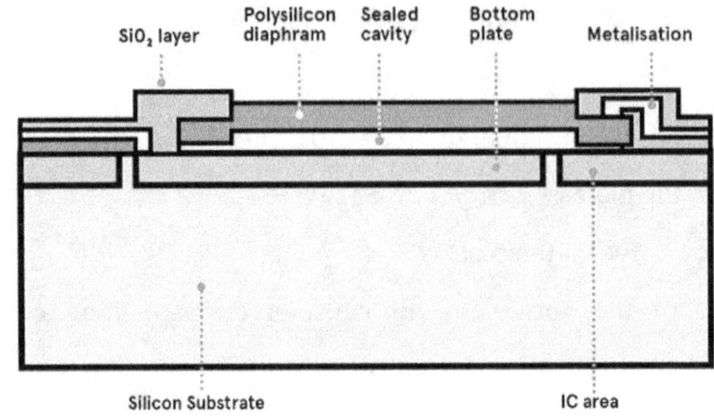

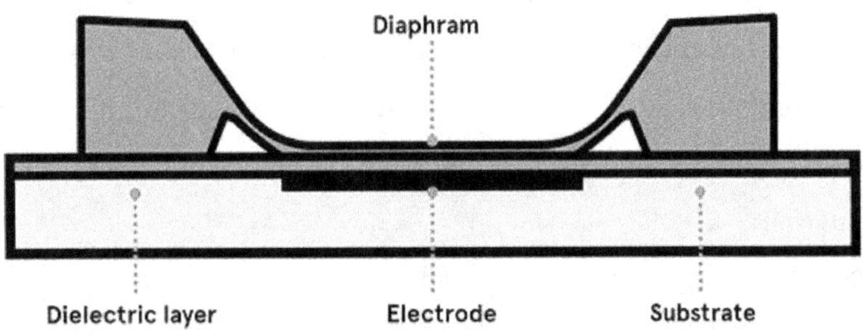

Fig 4.26 A cross section of capacitive sensor construction.

By choosing materials for the capacitor plates that have a low coefficient of thermal expansion, it's possible to make sensors with very low sensitivity to temperature change. The structure also needs to have low hysteresis to ensure accuracy and repeatability of measurements. Because the diaphragm itself is the sensing element, there are no issues with extra components being bonded to the diaphragm, so capacitive sensors can operate at higher temperatures than some other types of sensors. Capacitive pressure sensors can also be constructed directly on a silicon chip with the same fabrication techniques that are used in manufacturing semiconductor electronic devices shown in Fig 4.26 This allows very small sensing elements to be constructed and combined with the electronics for signal conditioning and reporting.

Function

The change in capacitance can be measured by connecting the sensor in a frequency-dependent circuit such as an oscillator or an LC tank circuit. In both cases, the resonant frequency of the circuit will change as the capacitance changes with pressure. An oscillator requires some extra electronic components and a power supply. A resonant LC circuit can be used as a passive sensor, without its own source of power. The dielectric constant of the material between the plates may change with pressure or temperature and this can also be a source of errors. The relative permittivity of air, and most other gasses, increases with pressure so this will slightly increase the capacitance change with pressure. Absolute pressure sensors, which have a vacuum between the plates, behave ideally in this respect. A more linear sensor can be constructed by using 'touch mode' where the diaphragm contacts the opposite plate (with a thin insulating layer in between) throughout the normal operating range The geometry of this structure results in a more linear output signal. This type of sensor is also more robust and able to cope with a larger over-pressure. This makes it more suited to industrial environments. However, this structure is more prone to hysteresis because of friction between the two surfaces.

Applications

Capacitive pressure sensors are often used to measure gas or liquid pressures in jet engines, car tyres, the human body, and many other places. But they can also be used as tactile sensors in wearable devices or to measure the pressure applied to a switch or keyboard. They are particularly versatile, in part due to their mechanical simplicity, so can be used in demanding environments. Capacitive sensors can be used for absolute, gauge, relative or differential pressure measurements.

Advantages and disadvantages: Capacitive pressure sensors have several advantages over other types of pressure sensors. They can have very low power consumption because there is no DC current through the sensor element. Current only flows when a signal is passed through the circuit to measure the capacitance. Passive sensors, where an external reader provides a signal to the circuit, do not require a power supply .These attributes make them ideal for low power applications such as remote or IoT sensors. The sensors are mechanically simple, so they can be made rugged with stable output, making them suitable for use in harsh environments. Capacitive sensors are usually tolerant of temporary over-pressure conditions. They have low hysteresis with good repeatability and are not very sensitive to temperature changes. On the other hand, capacitive sensors have non-linear output, although this can be reduced in touch-mode devices. However, this may come at the cost of greater hysteresis. Finally, careful circuit design is required for the interface electronics because of the high output impedance of the sensor and to minimise the effects of parasitic capacitance.

References and Further Reading

1. Embedded Sensor Systems" by Oliver Am ft, Paul Lukowicz, Gerhard Tröster, Springer,2006.

2.Modern Instrumentation by Neelapala Anil Kumar ManTech Publications Pvt. Ltd Aug 2020.

Unit –V Flow and Optical sensors

Unit Structure

5.0 Objectives

Flow sensors and optical sensors serve various purposes across different industries and applications. Here are some general objectives for both types of sensors:

Flow Sensors:

Measurement and Monitoring: Flow sensors are designed to accurately measure and monitor the flow rate of liquids or gases in pipelines, tubes, or channels.

Process Control: They are used to control and regulate the flow of fluids within industrial processes to maintain desired levels or meet specific operational requirements.

Energy Efficiency: Flow sensors help optimize energy consumption by ensuring that fluids are transported or distributed at the right rates, reducing waste and energy costs.

Safety: Flow sensors play a crucial role in ensuring the safe operation of systems by detecting abnormal flow conditions and triggering alarms or shutdowns when necessary.

Leak Detection: Detecting unexpected variations in flow rates allows for early detection of leaks or blockages in pipelines, minimizing potential damage and loss.

Quality Assurance: In manufacturing and production environments, flow sensors help maintain product quality by ensuring precise ingredient or material flow rates.

Data Collection and Analysis: Flow sensor data is often collected and analysed to improve processes, identify trends, and implement predictive maintenance strategies.

Optical Sensors:

Detection and Sensing: Optical sensors are designed to detect and measure various physical properties, including light intensity, color, distance, motion, and more.

Automation and Control: They enable automation and control systems to make decisions based on real-time data, such as object detection, presence, or position.

Environmental Monitoring: Optical sensors are used for monitoring environmental conditions, including pollution levels, air quality, and weather patterns.

Biomedical and Healthcare: In the healthcare sector, optical sensors play a vital role in non-invasive patient monitoring, blood oxygen measurement, and diagnostics.

Consumer Electronics: Optical sensors are integrated into consumer electronics devices for functions like ambient light sensing, proximity detection, and fingerprint recognition.

Security and Surveillance: Optical sensors are used in security systems for motion detection, facial recognition, and imaging in surveillance cameras.

Scientific Research: Optical sensors are essential tools in scientific research for experiments involving spectroscopy, microscopy, and other optical measurements.

Communication: Optical sensors are used in optical communication systems, such as fiber optics, to transmit and receive data using light signals.

Quality Control: Optical sensors help ensure product quality in manufacturing processes by inspecting items for defects, color consistency, and more.

Robotics: Optical sensors are employed in robotics for tasks like obstacle avoidance, object tracking, and precise positioning.

These general objectives demonstrate the versatility and importance of flow and optical sensors in various industries and applications, ranging from industrial automation and environmental monitoring to healthcare and consumer electronics. Specific applications may have additional, context-specific objectives.

5.1 Introduction

Flow sensors and optical sensors are integral components of modern technology, facilitating a wide range of applications across diverse industries. These sensors are designed to gather critical data about the physical world, providing valuable insights, enabling automation, and ensuring safety and efficiency in various processes.

Flow Sensors are engineered to measure and monitor the flow rates of liquids and gases. They play a pivotal role in industries such as manufacturing, energy, and healthcare, where precise control of fluid flow is essential. Flow sensors enable us to optimize processes, reduce waste, enhance energy efficiency, and ensure the safety and reliability of fluid systems. Whether it's measuring the flow of water in a municipal water supply network, monitoring oil flow in an industrial pipeline, or regulating the flow of medical gases in a hospital, flow sensors are fundamental in countless applications.

Optical Sensors, on the other hand, encompass a diverse range of sensors that interact with light and use its properties to detect and measure various phenomena. These sensors are ubiquitous in our daily lives, from the cameras and touchscreens on our smartphones to the automatic doors that sense our presence. Optical sensors are indispensable in industries like healthcare, telecommunications, environmental monitoring, and beyond. They enable us to capture images, measure distances, assess environmental conditions, and even monitor the vital signs of patients in real-time. As technology advances, optical sensors continue to evolve, offering increasingly sophisticated capabilities for applications in research, industry, and consumer products.

In this exploration of flow and optical sensors, we will delve deeper into their principles of operation, common applications, and the pivotal roles they play in shaping the world around us. These sensors are not just components; they are the eyes and ears of modern technology, helping us gather information, make informed decisions, and create a safer, more efficient, and interconnected world.

5.2. Vector flow transducers

Vector flow transducers are specialized sensors used to measure the velocity and direction of fluid flow in various applications, such as medical imaging, environmental monitoring, and industrial processes. These sensors provide valuable information about the flow patterns of liquids or gases, which can be crucial for optimizing processes, diagnosing medical conditions, and ensuring the efficient operation of systems. Here's an overview of vector flow transducers:

Key Features:

Directional Information: The primary advantage of vector flow transducers is their ability to provide both the speed and direction of fluid flow. This is essential in applications where understanding flow direction is critical, such as in medical imaging for blood flow visualization.

Accuracy: Vector flow transducers are designed for high accuracy in measuring fluid velocity in multiple directions. This accuracy is crucial in applications where precision is paramount.

Non-Invasive: In medical applications, vector flow transducers are often used non-invasively, meaning they can measure blood flow without the need for catheters or invasive procedures, reducing patient discomfort and risks.

A basic vector flow transducer is a device used to measure the velocity and direction of fluid flow. While there are various types of vector flow transducers with different operational principles, we will describe the operation of a basic electromagnetic-based vector flow transducer. This type of transducer is often used in industrial applications to measure fluid flow in pipes. Here's how it works:

Construction:

A basic electromagnetic vector flow transducer typically consists of the following components:

Electromagnetic Coils: There are two coils, typically positioned perpendicular to each other. One coil generates a magnetic field in the horizontal direction (X-axis), and the other generates a magnetic field in the vertical direction (Y-axis).

Electrodes or Sensors: Electrodes or sensors are placed to detect the voltage induced by the magnetic field. There are typically four electrodes or sensors: two for each coil, positioned to measure voltage in both the X and Y directions. Piping or Flow Tube: The transducer is installed in a pipe or flow tube through which the fluid (liquid or gas) flows.

Operation:

Generation of Magnetic Field: An alternating current (AC) is applied to the X-axis coil, creating a magnetic field in the horizontal direction. Simultaneously, another alternating current is applied to the Y-axis coil, creating a magnetic field in the vertical direction.

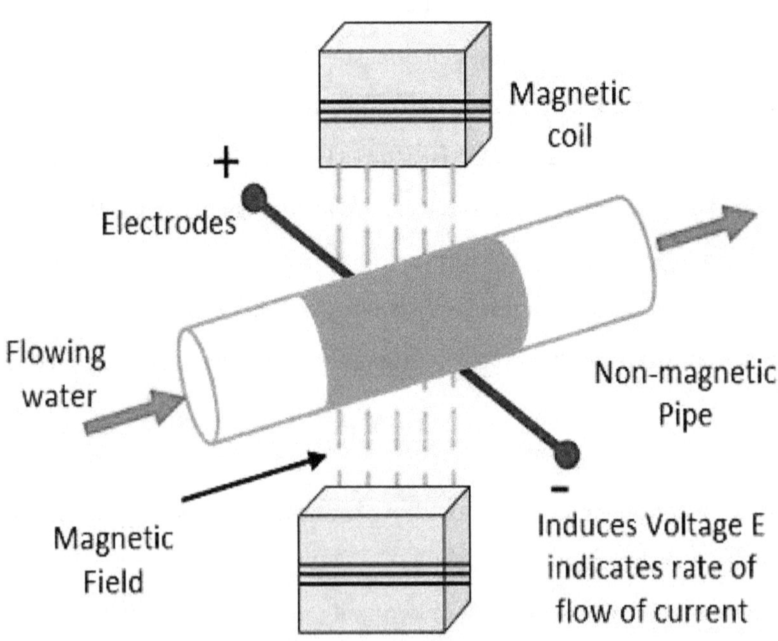

Fig 5.1Electromagnetic flow meter

Interaction with the Fluid Flow: As the fluid flows through the pipe, it cuts through the magnetic fields generated by the coils. According to Faraday's law of electromagnetic induction, the movement of the conductive fluid through the magnetic fields induces a voltage in the fluid. This induced voltage is directly proportional to the fluid's velocity in the respective coil's direction (X or Y).

Voltage Sensing:

The four electrodes or sensors are positioned to measure the induced voltages in both the X and Y directions. Each electrode is connected to a measurement circuit.

Direction Calculation: By comparing the voltages induced in the X and Y directions, the transducer can determine both the magnitude and direction of the fluid flow. The phase difference between the induced voltages in the X and Y directions provides information about the flow direction.

Data Processing: The transducer's electronics process the voltage measurements and calculate the fluid's velocity components in both the horizontal and vertical directions.

Output:

The transducer typically provides an output signal that represents both the speed and direction of the fluid flow. Basic electromagnetic vector flow transducers are known for their reliability and accuracy in measuring fluid flow in pipes. They are used in various industrial applications, including monitoring and controlling fluid processes in industries such as water treatment, oil and gas, and chemical processing. The ability to determine both the magnitude and direction of fluid flow makes them valuable tools for optimizing and managing fluid systems.

Applications:

Medical Imaging: Vector flow transducers are commonly used in medical ultrasound imaging to visualize blood flow patterns in vessels and the heart. This information is vital for diagnosing cardiovascular conditions and assessing blood flow in real-time.

Environmental Monitoring: Vector flow transducers are used in environmental monitoring systems to study and manage water and air flow patterns in natural ecosystems, aiding in the understanding of environmental changes and pollution control.

Industrial Processes: In industrial settings, these transducers are employed to monitor and control fluid flow in complex pipelines, ensuring efficient and safe operation.

Aeronautics and Aerospace: Vector flow transducers are used in wind tunnels and aircraft design to study and optimize airflow around aircraft and aerospace vehicles.

Automotive Engineering: These transducers are used in automotive design and testing to analyse air and fuel flow within engines and optimize combustion processes.

Marine Engineering: In the maritime industry, vector flow transducers can be used to study water flow patterns around ships and underwater structures for efficient design and navigation.

Hydrodynamics Research: They play a vital role in hydrodynamics research, helping scientists understand and model fluid flow in rivers, oceans, and other natural water bodies.

Vector flow transducers are critical tools in various fields, providing valuable insights into fluid flow dynamics. Their ability to capture both magnitude and direction information makes them invaluable in applications where understanding flow patterns is essential for safety, efficiency, and research purposes.

5.2.1 Hot-Wire and hot-film flow transducer.

Hot-wire and hot-film anemometers are types of velocity sensors used to measure fluid flow, particularly in gases like air. They operate based on the principle of convective heat transfer, where a heated element is exposed to the fluid flow, and changes in temperature are used to determine the fluid velocity. Here's an overview of both types:

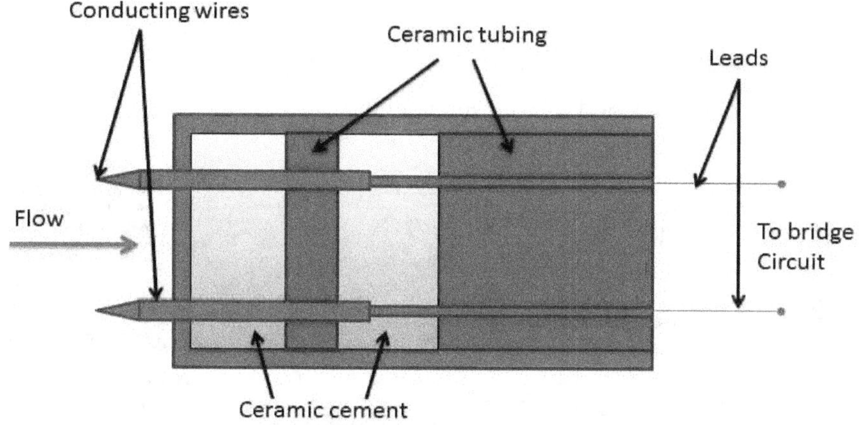

Fig 5.2 Hot-Wire Anemometer

Construction:

A hot-wire anemometer consists of a very thin, fine wire typically made of platinum, tungsten, or nickel-chromium alloy. The wire is mounted within a probe or sensor assembly, often referred to as a probe head. The probe is exposed to the fluid flow being measured.

Operation:

The wire is heated to a constant temperature above that of the surrounding fluid using electrical current. As the fluid flows over the wire, it carries away heat from the wire, causing a change in its resistance. The electrical resistance of the wire increases or decreases proportionally to the fluid velocity. This change in resistance is used to calculate the flow velocity.

Output:

The hot-wire anemometer provides an output signal that correlates with the velocity of the fluid. This signal can be processed and displayed as a measure of flow velocity.

Hot-Film Anemometer:

Construction:

A hot-film anemometer uses a thin film made of a conductive material (commonly platinum or nickel) that is deposited onto a substrate. The film is typically mounted on a probe or sensor assembly.

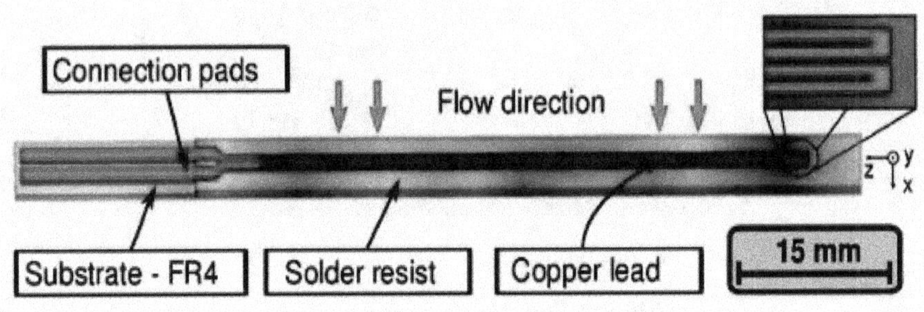

Fig 5.3 Hot-film Anemometer

Operation:

Similar to the hot-wire anemometer, the film is heated to a constant temperature above the fluid temperature using electrical current. As the fluid flows over the film, it carries away heat, leading to a change in temperature of the film. The film's resistance changes as a result of this temperature change, and this change in resistance is proportional to the fluid velocity.

Output:

The hot-film anemometer provides an output signal corresponding to the fluid velocity, similar to the hot-wire anemometer.

Advantages:

- Hot-wire and hot-film anemometers offer high sensitivity and quick response times.
- They are suitable for measuring low to high fluid velocities, depending on the sensor's design.

- These anemometers can measure both steady-state and fluctuating flow velocities.

Applications:

- Hot-wire and hot-film anemometers are used in various applications, including aerodynamics research, environmental monitoring (e.g., wind speed measurement), HVAC (Heating, Ventilation, and Air Conditioning) systems, and fluid mechanics experiments.

- They are commonly used in wind tunnels to measure airflow around objects and in industrial settings to monitor and control air and gas flow in ducts and pipelines.

- Hot-film anemometers are often preferred in applications with particulate-laden or dirty flows because they are less prone to clogging than hot-wire anemometers.

- These anemometers are valuable tools for researchers and engineers to measure fluid flow velocities accurately, making them widely used in scientific research and various industries.

5.2.2 Pitot tube flow sensor(https://instrumentationtools.com/pitot-tube-working-principle/)

The **Pitot tube** is named after Henri Pitot who used a bent glass tube to measure velocities in a river in France in the 1700s. Pitot tubes can be very simple devices with no moving parts used to measure flow velocities. Pitot tubes are a common type of insertion flow meter. Where a pressure is generated in a tube facing the flow, by the velocity of the fluid. This 'velocity' pressure is compared against the reference pressure (or static pressure) in the pipe.

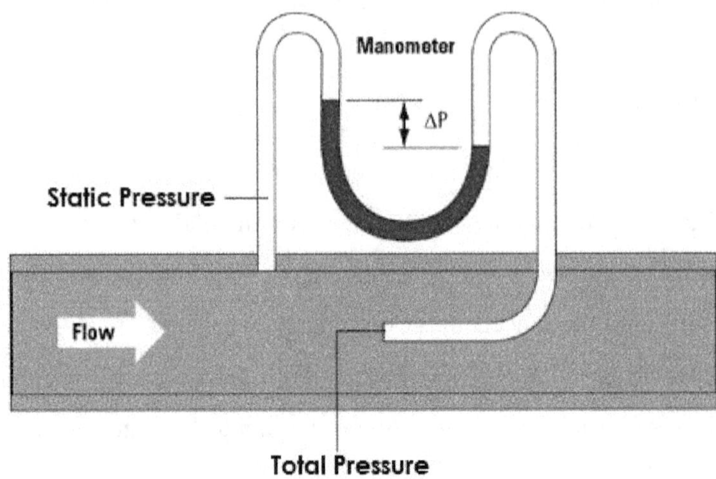

Fig 5.4 Pitot tube with Manometer differential pressure measurement

When the flow rate through the pipe changes, the pressures at the total pressure tube and static pressure tube varies with respect to the flow velocities. The difference between the total pressure and static pressure is used to measure the proportional flow rate passing through the pipe. A Differential Pressure type transmitter is used to measure the difference between total pressure and static pressure, and it is converted into proportional flow rate.

A Pitot tube is a commonly used device for measuring fluid flow velocity, such as in gases or liquids. It operates based on the principle of Bernoulli's equation, which relates the pressure in a fluid to its velocity. Pitot tubes are often used in aviation to measure the airspeed of aircraft, but they are also used in various industrial applications to measure fluid flow.

Here's how a Pitot tube flow sensor works and its construction:

Construction:

A Pitot tube typically consists of two tubes, one inside the other. The outer tube has an opening (often at a 90-degree angle) that faces into the fluid stream, while the inner tube is sealed at one end and connects to a pressure sensor at the other end. The open end of the outer tube is called the "impact" or "total pressure" port, while the open end of the inner tube is called the "static pressure" port.

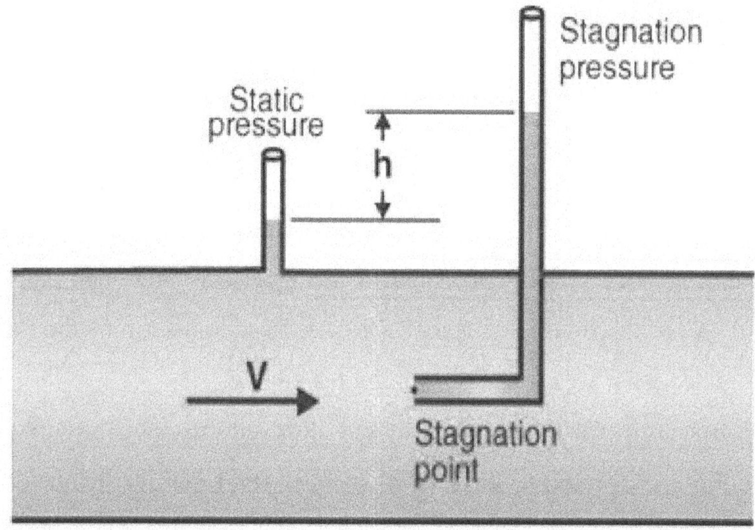

Fig 5.5 Construction and working of Pitot tube.

The construction may vary depending on the specific application and design, but the basic concept remains the same: it measures the difference between the total pressure and static pressure of the fluid to determine its velocity.

Working Principle:

Total Pressure: As the fluid flows into the open end of the outer tube, it creates a stagnation point. At this point, the fluid's kinetic energy is converted into pressure energy, resulting in a higher pressure inside the tube compared to the surrounding fluid. This pressure is known as "total pressure" or "stagnation pressure" and is represented as **Pt.**

Static Pressure: The inner tube is sealed at one end, and it measures the pressure of the fluid at this point, which is called the "static pressure" (Ps). The static pressure represents the pressure of the fluid at rest.

Dynamic Pressure: The difference between the total pressure (Pt) and static pressure (Ps) is called the "dynamic pressure" (Pd), which is directly related to the velocity of the fluid according to Bernoulli's equation.

$$Pd = Pt - Ps$$

Velocity Calculation: The dynamic pressure (Pd) can be used to calculate the velocity (V) of the fluid using the Bernoulli equation:

$$Pd = 0.5 * \rho * V^2$$

Where:

ρ (rho) is the density of the fluid. By measuring the dynamic pressure (Pd) using the pressure sensor connected to the inner tube, one can calculate the velocity (V) of the fluid. This velocity is often used to determine the flow rate if the cross-sectional area of the pipe or duct is known.

Pitot tubes are reliable and widely used flow sensors, but they may require calibration and correction for factors such as fluid density, temperature, and pressure variations to ensure accurate flow measurements in different conditions.

5.3 Volume flow sensors

Volume flow sensors are essential devices used in various industries to measure and monitor the rate of fluid flow through pipes, ducts, or channels. They play a crucial role in ensuring the efficient operation of fluid systems and are employed in applications ranging from industrial processes to environmental monitoring and HVAC (Heating, Ventilation, and Air Conditioning) systems. Volume flow sensors provide valuable data that enables engineers, technicians, and researchers to optimize processes, control systems, and maintain desired flow rates. In this introduction, we will explore the fundamental principles behind volume flow sensors and their significance in diverse fields.

Principle of Operation: Volume flow sensors operate on different principles depending on the specific design and application. Some common methods include measuring the speed of fluid (velocity) and the cross-sectional area of the flow. These sensors can be broadly categorized into two types.

Velocity-Based Sensors: These sensors determine the flow rate by measuring the speed of the fluid at a particular point within the conduit. Examples include Pitot tubes, electromagnetic flow meters, and ultrasonic flow meters. By analysing the fluid's velocity, these sensors calculate the volume flow rate using the cross-sectional area of the pipe or duct.

Differential Pressure-Based Sensors: These sensors rely on the principle of pressure drop across a constriction or an obstruction in the flow path. The pressure difference between two points is used to infer the flow rate. Orifice plates, Venturi tubes, and flow nozzles are common examples of differential pressure-based volume flow sensor.

Significance and Applications

Volume flow sensors are integral to various industries for several reasons:

Process Control: In manufacturing and industrial processes, maintaining precise flow rates of liquids or gases is critical for product quality and consistency. Volume flow sensors ensure that the desired flow rates are achieved and maintained, contributing to process efficiency and cost-effectiveness .

Energy Efficiency: In HVAC systems and building automation, volume flow sensors help optimize air and fluid distribution. By adjusting flow rates based on demand, these sensors enhance energy efficiency, reduce operational costs, and improve occupant comfort.

Environmental Monitoring: Volume flow sensors are used in environmental monitoring applications, such as water management and pollution control. They aid in measuring the flow of liquids in rivers, wastewater treatment plants, and industrial discharges, enabling authorities to assess and regulate environmental impacts.

Research and Development: Scientists and researchers rely on volume flow sensors to conduct experiments, study fluid dynamics, and develop innovative technologies. These sensors provide accurate data for research in fields like aerodynamics, hydrodynamics, and fluid mechanic.

volume flow sensors are indispensable tools for measuring and controlling fluid flow rates across a wide range of applications. Their ability to provide real-time data on fluid movement allows industries to optimize processes, enhance energy efficiency, and ensure compliance with environmental regulations. As technology continues to advance, volume flow sensors are expected to play an increasingly vital role in improving the efficiency and sustainability of various systems and processes.

5.3.1 Orifice plates

Construction of Orifice Plates

Orifice plates are simple, yet effective devices used to measure the flow rate of fluids (liquids or gases) within pipelines or ducts. They consist of a flat, circular plate with a precisely machined hole (or orifice) at its center. The key components and construction of an orifice plate include:

Plate Material: Orifice plates are typically made from materials such as stainless steel, carbon steel, or other suitable materials depending on the fluid being measured and the environmental conditions.

Orifice Hole: The orifice itself is the central feature of the plate. It is carefully machined to have a specific diameter (d) and shape, usually circular. The diameter of the orifice is crucial in determining the accuracy of flow measurement.

Upstream and Downstream Pipe Sections: Orifice plates are installed within a pipeline or duct. Upstream and downstream pipe sections are required to ensure that the fluid approaches the orifice with a uniform velocity profile. These sections are usually long enough to meet the necessary flow conditioning requirements.

Tapping's: On either side of the orifice plate, pressure tapping's or ports are installed. These tapping's allow for the measurement of pressure both upstream and downstream of the orifice. They are usually connected to pressure transmitters or manometers to obtain pressure differentials for flow rate calculations.

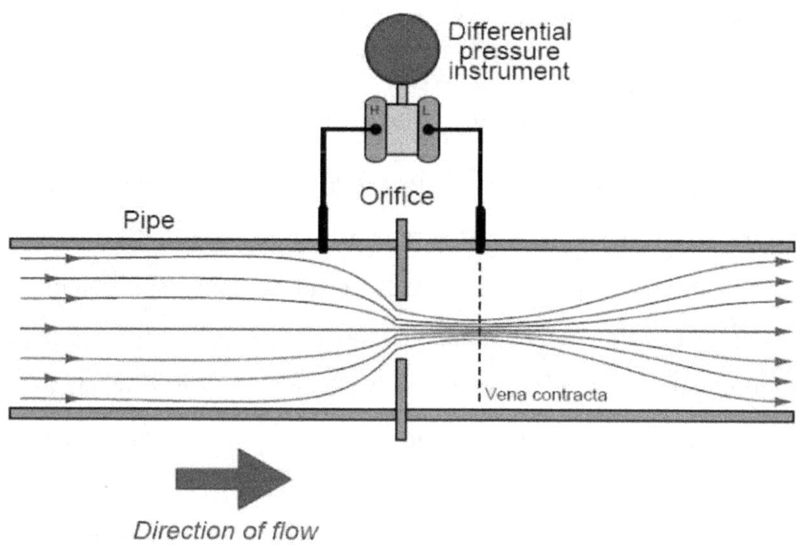

Fig 5.6 Construction and working of Orifice flow meter.

Working Principle:

The operation of an orifice plate is based on the principle of Bernoulli's equation, which relates the pressure drop across an orifice to the flow rate of a fluid. Here's how it works:

Flow Restriction: When fluid flows through the orifice, it encounters a restriction due to the smaller cross-sectional area of the orifice compared to the pipe or duct. This constriction causes an increase in the fluid's velocity as it passes through the orifice.

Pressure Drop: According to Bernoulli's equation, as the fluid's velocity increases, its pressure decreases. Therefore, there is a pressure drop (ΔP) between the upstream and downstream sides of the orifice.

Flow Calculation The pressure drop (ΔP) across the orifice is proportional to the square of the flow rate (Q) through it. This relationship is described by the following equation, known as the orifice equation:

$$\Delta P = K * \rho * (Q^2) / 2$$

Where:

- ΔP is the pressure drop across the orifice.
- K is a discharge coefficient that depends on the orifice's size and shape.
- ρ is the fluid density.
- Q is the volumetric flow rate.

By measuring the pressure drop (ΔP) and knowing the fluid properties (ρ) and the orifice characteristics (K), it is possible to calculate the flow rate (Q). The orifice plate is a primary element, meaning that it provides a direct measurement of flow rate, but this measurement is differential and requires the use of pressure instrumentation to determine the flow rate accurately.

Orifice plates are widely used due to their simplicity, reliability, and low cost. However, their accuracy can be affected by factors such as pipe conditions, fluid properties, and the accuracy of pressure measurements, so proper calibration and consideration of these factors are essential for precise flow measurements. Orifice plates are accurate within their specified flow range but may have limitations at extremely low or high flow rates. They can also be more affected by changes in fluid properties (e.g., density and viscosity) compared to Venturi tubes.

Venturi tubes and orifice plates are both flow measurement devices, but they have different characteristics and advantages. Here's a merits of venturi tube.

Venturi Tube:

Accuracy: Venturi tubes are generally considered more accurate than orifice plates. This is because they offer a smoother and less turbulent flow profile due to their gradual tapering design, which results in less energy loss.

Pressure Recovery: Venturi tubes have better pressure recovery compared to orifice plates. After the fluid passes through the throat of the Venturi tube, it partially recovers its pressure, which can be important in applications where energy conservation is a concern.

Flow Range: Venturi tubes can handle a broader range of flow rates compared to orifice plates. They are suitable for both low and high-flow applications.

Maintenance: Venturi tubes are less prone to clogging and fouling compared to orifice plates because of their smoother internal surface.

Installation: Venturi tubes require a longer section of straight pipe upstream to ensure accurate measurements. This can be a disadvantage in tight or limited space installations.

Construction and Working

A Venturi pipe, often referred to as a Venturi tube, is a device used to measure fluid flow rates by taking advantage of the Venturi effect, which is a phenomenon related to fluid dynamics. It consists of three main sections: the inlet section, throat, and outlet section.

Construction:

Inlet Section (Converging Section): This is the first part of the Venturi pipe, where the fluid enters. It has a gradually tapering shape, which reduces the cross-sectional area as the fluid moves from the wider pipe into the Venturi tube.

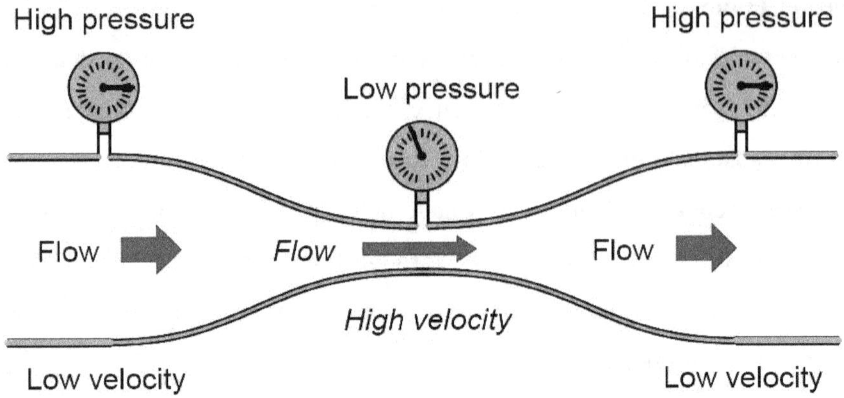

Fig 5.7 Pressure measurements taken in a venturi pipe.

Throat: The throat is the narrowest part of the Venturi pipe, located between the inlet and outlet sections. It is precisely designed and machined to create a constriction in the flow path, which accelerates the fluid and reduces its pressure.

Outlet Section (Diverging Section): After passing through the throat, the fluid enters the outlet section, which gradually widens to match the original pipe diameter. This section allows the fluid to

Working Principle:

The operation of a Venturi pipe is based on Bernoulli's equation and the Venturi effect:

Flow Constriction: As fluid enters the Venturi pipe through the inlet section, it encounters a gradual reduction in cross-sectional area as it approaches the throat. This constriction causes the fluid's velocity to increase according to Bernoulli's equation.

Pressure Difference: According to Bernoulli's equation, as the fluid's velocity increases, its pressure decreases. Therefore, the pressure at the throat is lower than at the inlet. This pressure difference between the inlet and throat is proportional to the flow rate of the fluid.

Pressure Measurement: Pressure taps or ports are installed at the inlet and throat sections to measure.

Flow Rate Calculation: By measuring the pressure difference between the inlet and throat sections and knowing the fluid properties, you can calculate the flow rate through the Venturi pipe using the following equation:

$$Q = A * \sqrt{(2 * \Delta P) / \rho}$$

Where:

Q is the flow rate.

A is the cross-sectional area of the throat.

ΔP is the pressure difference between the inlet and throat.

ρ is the density of the fluid.

Venturi pipes are widely used for their accuracy in measuring fluid flow rates, especially in applications where precise measurements are required. They are used in various industries, including water treatment, chemical processing, and HVAC systems, to ensure efficient and controlled fluid flow.

5.3.2 Turbine flow meter

Turbine flow meters are widely used in various industries to measure the flow rate of liquids, particularly in applications where high accuracy and reliability are essential. They operate based on the principle of a rotating turbine, which interacts with the flowing liquid to provide a measurement of the flow rate.

Construction of Turbine Flow Meter:

Turbine Rotor: The central component of the turbine flow meter is the rotor, which is typically a bladed wheel or impeller. This rotor is mounted on a shaft and placed inside the flow stream. The blades of the rotor are designed to capture the kinetic energy of the flowing liquid.

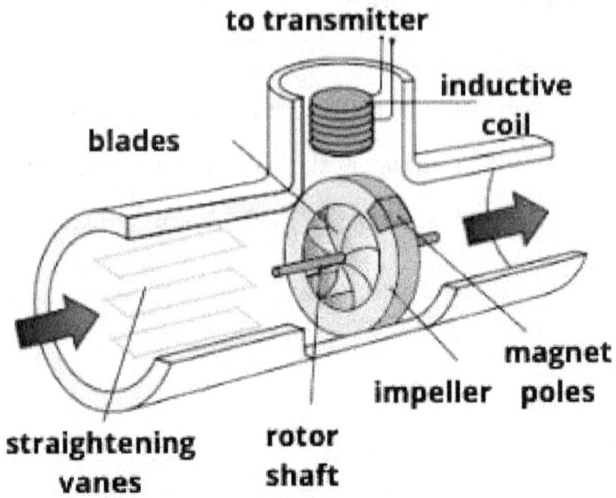

Fig 5.8 Turbine Flow Meter

Housing: The rotor and shaft assembly is housed within a pipe or casing, allowing the liquid to flow through. The housing is designed to guide the liquid flow and ensure that it passes through the rotor in a controlled manner.

Magnetic Pickup: A magnetic pickup is placed near the rotor, and the rotor itself is often equipped with magnets. As the rotor spins in response to the flowing liquid, it generates a magnetic field that is detected by the pickup.

Signal Processing Unit: The magnetic pickup's output is processed by a signal processing unit, which converts the electrical signals into flow rate measurements. This unit may also include a display or output for reading and recording the flow data.

Operation Principle of Turbine Flow Meter:

The operation of a turbine flow meter is based on the principle that when a fluid flows through the meter, it imparts kinetic energy to the blades of the rotor. This kinetic energy causes the rotor to spin at a rate directly proportional to the fluid's flow velocity.

Working of Turbine Flow Meter:

As the liquid flows through the turbine flow meter, it encounters the rotor. The liquid's kinetic energy causes the rotor to rotate. The rotation of the rotor generates a series of electrical pulses due to the interaction of the magnets on the rotor and the magnetic pickup sensor. The signal processing unit counts the pulses over a specific period, which is used to calculate the flow rate. The flow rate is typically displayed on a digital readout or transmitted as an electrical signal for further processing or recording. The larger volume of substance passing through pipeline, the more mechanical energy created, and the higher the angular (rotational) speed of the blades. Blades with magnets on its edge pass near an electrical pickoff sensor at a certain speed and cause changes in magnetic fields. If the device has an induction coil, then an electric pulse is induced in it. If a Hall sensor is installed, it simply captures those changes. This method is like the meter. Value of frequency with which these changes occur is monitored and sent to the transmitter. The frequency of such signals is directly proportional to the flow velocity. Here is a turbine flow meter equation about dependence between volume flow and pulse frequency:

$$F = k * Q$$

Where:

F - The indicator that displays how many pulses the pickup sensor detects per minute or second

Q - Volumetric flow (m^3, gallons, Liters / s)

k - Special coefficient, also known as k-factor (for example, the number of pulses per m^3). We consider it in more detail below.

Further, the transmitter analyses the received data and converts them into an analog or digital signal.

K-factor is a key coefficient that displays the number of pulses per unit volume or mass of the medium. This constant value includes main characteristics of substance and pipe (viscosity, temperature, diameter, etc.)It is necessary for the correct display of values in measuring systems. After calibration, this coefficient is indicated in product certificate.

Applications of Turbine Flow Meters:

Turbine flow meters find applications in various industries, including:

- Oil and gas production
- Chemical processing
- Water treatment and distribution
- Food and beverage production
- Pharmaceutical manufacturing
- Aerospace and aviation
- HVAC (Heating, Ventilation, and Air Conditioning) systems
- Automotive and transportation

Merits of Turbine Flow Meters:

- High accuracy and repeatability.
- Suitable for measuring a wide range of flow rates.
- Can handle both clean and mildly corrosive liquids.
- Compact design and easy installation.
- Low pressure drop compared to some other flow measurement devices.
- Digital output for easy integration into control and monitoring systems.

Demerits of Turbine Flow Meters:

- Susceptible to damage by abrasive or viscous fluids.
- Not ideal for gas flow measurement.
- Limited suitability for highly corrosive or abrasive liquids.
- Requires a clean and debris-free fluid to maintain accuracy.
- Calibration may be required for different fluid types and conditions.

In summary, turbine flow meters are versatile and widely used instruments for measuring liquid flow rates accurately. Their construction, based on the rotation of a turbine rotor, makes them well-suited for a variety of industrial applications, but their performance can be affected by factors like fluid properties and the presence of contaminants. Proper maintenance and calibration are essential to ensure reliable and precise measurements.

5.3.3 Rotameters

Rotameters, also known as variable area flow meters or float meters, are widely used instruments for measuring and controlling the flow rate of fluids, both gases and liquids. They operate on a simple and visual principle, making them valuable in various industrial applications.

Construction:

Tube: The core component of a rotameter is a tapered, transparent tube typically made of glass or plastic. This tube has a larger diameter at the top (inlet) and narrows down towards the bottom (outlet).

Float: Inside the tube, there's a float, which can be a ball, needle, or similar shape. The float is buoyant in the fluid and moves up and down freely within the tube.

Scale: Adjacent to the tube, there's a calibrated scale marked with flow rate units like Liters per minute (LPM) or cubic feet per hour (CFH). This scale is used to read the flow rate based on the float's position.

Operation Principle:

The operation of a rotameter is based on the principles of buoyancy and fluid dynamics. It relies on the equilibrium between the upward buoyant force on the float and the downward gravitational force and drag force exerted by the flowing fluid.

Working:

- Fluid enters the rotameter at the bottom and flows upward through the tapered tube, lifting the float.
- The float's buoyancy increases with higher flow rates, causing it to rise. Simultaneously, the drag force on the float due to the flowing fluid also increases with higher flow rates.

- At a certain flow rate, an equilibrium is established between the buoyant force, gravitational force, and drag force. The float stabilizes at a specific position within the tube.

- The position of the float corresponds to the flow rate, which can be read directly from the calibrated scale.

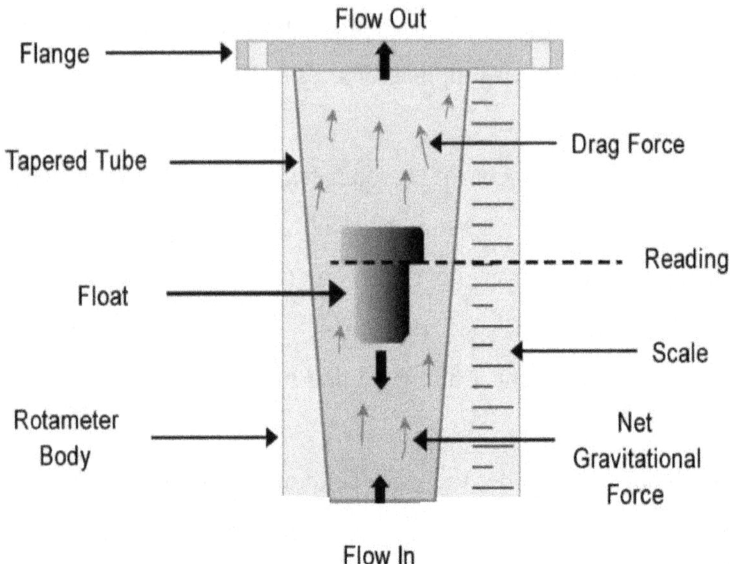

Fig 5.9 Working of Rotameter.

Merits:

Simplicity: Rotameters have a straightforward design, making them robust and reliable instruments.

Low Pressure Drop: They offer minimal pressure drop across the meter, making them suitable for applications where pressure loss must be minimized.

Wide Application Range: Rotameters are versatile and can be used to measure the flow of gases and liquids in various industries.

Visual Confirmation: The transparent tube allows for visual inspection of flow, ensuring the meter's proper functioning.

Low Maintenance: They require minimal maintenance and calibration.

Demerits:

Accuracy: Rotameters are generally less accurate than some other flow measurement methods, particularly at low flow rates.

Pressure Limitations: They are not suitable for high-pressure applications due to the risk of tube breakage.

Fluid Compatibility: The choice of materials for the tube and float limits their compatibility with corrosive or abrasive fluids.

Limited Turndown Ratio: Rotameters have a limited turndown ratio, restricting their range between the maximum and minimum flow rates they can measure.

In conclusion, rotameters are simple, reliable, and visually intuitive flow meters, suitable for applications where moderate accuracy and low-pressure drop are acceptable. Their operation is based on the position of a float in a tapered tube, and they provide visual confirmation of flow. However, their accuracy may decrease at low flow rates, and they have limitations for certain fluid types and high-pressure conditions.

5.4 Laser Doppler Flow meter

The Laser Doppler Flow Meter (LDF) is a non-invasive medical and scientific instrument used to measure blood flow or fluid flow in tissues and other applications. It is based on the principles of the Doppler effect, which involves the shift in frequency or wavelength of light as it interacts with moving objects.

Principle:

The Laser Doppler Flow Meter operates on the Doppler principle, which is based on the idea that when laser light interacts with moving red blood cells, the frequency of the scattered light shifts in proportion to the velocity of the moving blood cells. This shift is known as the Doppler shift.

Construction:

A typical Laser Doppler Flow Meter consists of the following components:

Laser Light Source: It includes a low-power laser diode that emits a coherent beam of light, usually in the red or near-infrared spectrum.

Optical Components: Lenses and mirrors are used to focus and direct the laser beam onto the tissue or area of interest.

Photo detector: A photo detector, such as a photodiode or photomultiplier tube (PMT), collects the scattered light after it interacts with the moving blood cells.

Signal Processing Electronics: Sophisticated electronics process the electrical signal generated by the photo detector. This process involves analyzing the frequency shift caused by the Doppler Effect.

Output Display: The flow velocity measurement is typically displayed on a monitor or recorded for further analysis.

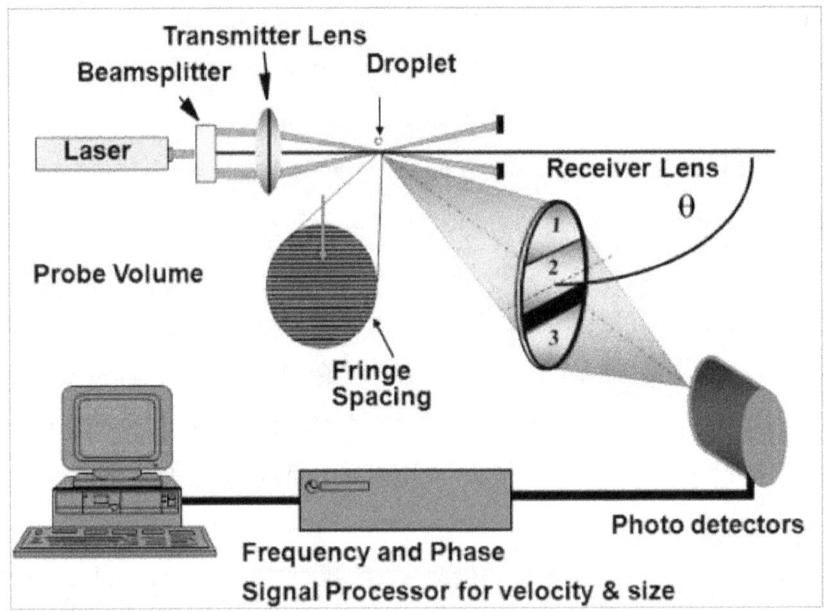

Fig 5.10 Working of Laser Doppler Flow meter.

Working:

- The laser beam is directed onto the tissue being studied, where it interacts with the moving blood cells.

- As the laser light interacts with the blood cells, the Doppler shift occurs, causing a change in the frequency of the scattered light.

- The scattered light is collected by the photodetector.

- The photodetector converts the changes in light frequency into an electrical signal.

- Signal processing electronics analyze this electrical signal to determine the flow velocity of the blood or fluid.

- The measured flow velocity is then displayed or recorded for analysis.

Merits (Advantages):

- **Non-invasive:** Laser Doppler Flow Meters are non-invasive, meaning they do not require penetration or damage to the tissue being studied.

- **Real-time Measurements:** They provide continuous, real-time blood or fluid flow measurements, making them suitable for dynamic studies.

- **High Resolution:** LDF can measure blood flow in small blood vessels and capillaries, providing high-resolution data.

- **Versatility:** They can be used in various applications, including medical research, clinical diagnostics, and scientific experiments.

Demerits (Disadvantages):

- Limited Depth: LDF is primarily suited for measuring flow close to the surface of tissues and may not be suitable for deep tissue measurements.

- Sensitivity to Motion: The measurements can be affected by the movement of the subject or tissue being studied.

- Calibration: Proper calibration is essential to obtain accurate measurements, and calibration can be complex.

- Cost: High-quality LDF instruments can be expensive.

- Limited Quantitative Information: LDF provides relative measurements of flow velocity but may not provide absolute blood flow values without additional calibration and assumptions.

In summary, Laser Doppler Flow Meters are valuable tools for studying blood and fluid flow in various applications. They offer non-invasive, real-time measurements with high resolution but have limitations related to depth, motion sensitivity, and calibration.

5.5. Ultrasonic Flow meters

The first ultrasonic flow meter was introduced by a Japanese inventor in 1959. It used doppler technology to measure blood flow. In the early 1960s, flow meters found use as industrial instruments for measuring the flow of gasses and liquids. From their early beginnings, they have become the main product for many instrument manufacturing companies. A flow meter aims to measure the volume of flow of liquids and gases to provide accurate readings for flow control. Many industrial applications, such as chemical companies, require exact readings for production processes.

Ultrasonic flow sensors are devices used to measure the flow rate of fluids (liquids or gases) by utilizing the principles of ultrasonic sound waves. These sensors are commonly used in various industrial applications due to their non-invasive nature and ability to provide accurate flow measurements. Here's a principle of operation, construction, merits, and demerits:

Principle of Operation:

Ultrasonic flow sensors operate based on the principle of the Doppler effect and the transit-time difference. The theory behind an ultrasonic flow meter's operation rest on the concept that there is a change in velocity of ultrasonic wave pulses when there is a change in the flow rate of a fluid.

Doppler Shift Principle In this method, the sensor emits ultrasonic waves (sound waves with frequencies above the audible range) into the flowing fluid. Particles or bubbles in the fluid act as reflectors and scatter the sound waves back to the sensor. The sensor then analyzes the frequency shift (Doppler shift) between the transmitted and received waves to determine the flow velocity. This method is suitable for fluids with suspended particles or bubbles.

Transit-Time Difference Principle: In this method, the sensor uses two ultrasonic transducers, one as a transmitter and the other as a receiver. Ultrasonic pulses are alternately transmitted upstream and downstream in the direction of flow. The time it takes for the pulse to travel upstream and downstream is measured. The flow velocity is calculated by comparing the difference in transit times for the two pulses. This method is applicable to clean and homogeneous fluids.

Construction

Ultrasonic flow sensors typically consist of the following components:

One transmitter, the preferred transmitter, sends sound waves along the direction of the flow. It is preferred because it happens in the direction of the flow. The other transmitter sends sound waves in the opposite direction of the flow. The signal from the first transmitter increases as the speed of the fluid increases. The signal from the second transmitter decreases since it is sent in the opposite direction of the flow.

Transducers These are piezoelectric crystals that convert electrical energy into ultrasonic waves and vice versa. One transducer emits ultrasonic waves, while the other receives them.

Signal Processing Unit This unit processes the received signals, calculates flow parameters, and provides an output signal (usually in the form of flow rate).

Housing or Pipe Attachment The sensors are designed to be mounted externally on the pipe or inserted into the fluid-carrying pipe. The housing ensures proper alignment of the transducers with the fluid flow.

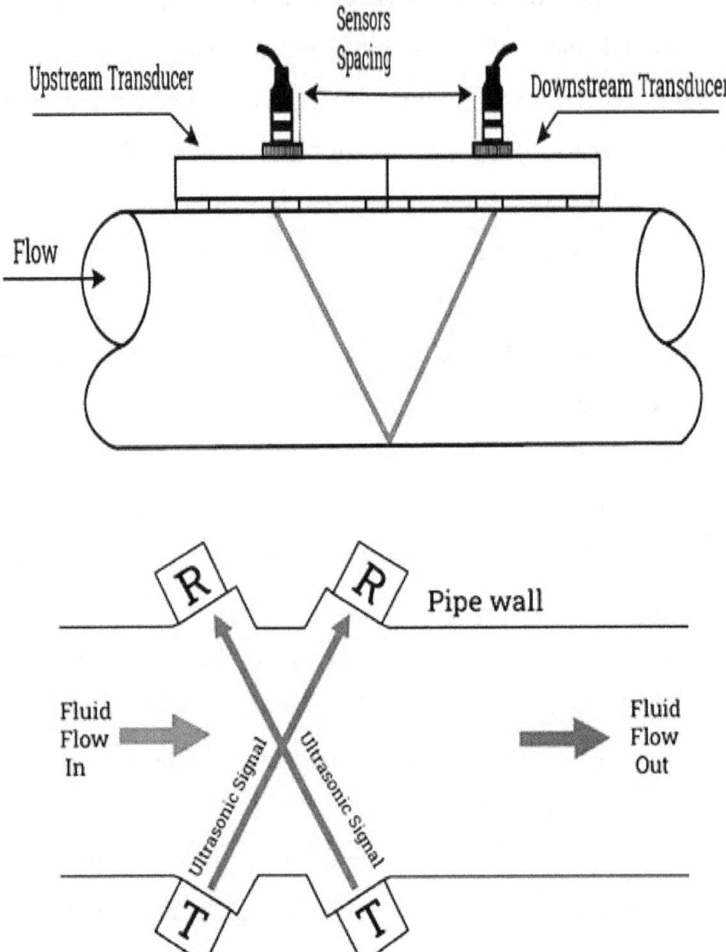

Fig 5.13 a) Construction and b) Working of Ultrasonic Flow meter.

Working

The transducer, the device that calculates the flow rate, can be mounted parallel or at an angle to the side of the pipe. Ultrasonic flow meters have two transmitters that send the sound and two receivers that receive the sound. The transmitters send out short bursts of ultrasonic signals or pulses through the flow of the fluid. The ultrasonic flow sensor uses two ultrasonic transducers:

one serves as a transmitter, and the other as a receiver. The basic working steps are as follows:

The transmitter sends ultrasonic pulses diagonally across the pipe, at an angle to the direction of flow.

These pulses travel through the fluid, and their speed is influenced by the flow velocity of the fluid.

The receiver, placed at a known distance from the transmitter, measures the time it takes for the ultrasonic pulses to travel upstream and downstream. The flow sensor calculates the transit-time difference between the upstream and downstream pulses. Flow velocity is then determined using the formula: Flow Velocity = Distance / (Transit-Time Difference).By knowing the pipe's cross-sectional area, the flow rate of the fluid can be calculated.

Key points to note about ultrasonic flow sensors:

They are non-invasive and do not require direct contact with the fluid.

The accuracy of measurements may be affected by factors such as fluid properties (e.g., temperature, viscosity), pipe conditions, and sensor placement and alignment.

Ultrasonic flow sensors can measure flow in both directions (bi-directional), making them suitable for various applications.

Some sensors can provide additional data, such as fluid temperature and pressure, depending on their design and capabilities.

Overall, ultrasonic flow sensors are commonly used for their accuracy, versatility, and non-invasive nature in a wide range of industries, including water management, industrial processes, and HVAC systems. Proper installation and calibration are essential to ensure accurate flow rate measurements.

Merits

Non-invasive Ultrasonic flow sensors do not require direct contact with the fluid, making them suitable for applications involving corrosive or hazardous materials.

High accuracy They offer precise flow rate measurements with minimal pressure drop.

Wide application range Suitable for a variety of fluids, including liquids and gases.

No moving parts This reduces the need for maintenance and minimizes wear and tear.

Bi-directional measurement Most ultrasonic flow sensors can measure flow in both directions.

Demerits

Cost Ultrasonic flow sensors can be more expensive than some other flow measurement techniques.

Installation complexity Proper installation and alignment are crucial for accurate measurements, which can be challenging in some cases.

Fluid propertiesthe accuracy of ultrasonic flow sensors can be affected by the fluid's properties, such as temperature, viscosity, and the presence of bubbles or particles.

Limited pipe size in very large pipes, ultrasonic sensors may not be practical or may require specialized designs.

ultrasonic flow sensors are versatile instruments that offer accurate and non-invasive flow measurements for a wide range of applications. However, they have some limitations related to cost, installation complexity, and sensitivity to certain fluid properties. Careful consideration of these factors is essential when choosing an appropriate flow measurement technology.

5.6 Optical Sensors

Optical sensors, also known as optoelectronic sensors, are devices that use light to detect and measure various physical properties or environmental conditions. These sensors rely on the interaction between light and matter to generate electrical signals that can be processed and analyzed for a wide range of applications. Optical sensors have gained significant importance in various industries due to their versatility and precision. Optical sensors operate based on the principles of optics, which involve the behavior of light when it interacts with materials. The fundamental components of an optical sensor include a light source, a sensing element, and the medium or substance being measured.

Types of Optical Sensors

There are various types of optical sensors designed for specific applications. Some common types include:

5.6.1 Light-dependent resistors

LDR (Light Dependent Resistor) optical sensor, also known as a photoresistor, is a type of optical sensor that changes its electrical resistance in response to changes in incident light intensity. LDRs are passive electronic components whose resistance decreases as the light intensity on their surface increases. They are widely used in various applications for light sensing and control. Here's an overview of LDR optical sensors:

Working Principle:

LDRs are made of semiconductor materials whose electrical properties change when exposed to light. The key principle behind LDRs is the photoconductivity effect. When photons (light particles) strike the semiconductor material of the LDR, they excite electrons within the material, allowing them to move more freely. This increased mobility of electrons reduces the resistance of the LDR, allowing more current to flow through it.

Construction:

LDRs typically consist of a cylindrical or flat disk-shaped package with two electrical leads. The semiconductor material is often cadmium sulfide (CdS) or cadmium selenide (CdSe), and it is deposited onto a ceramic substrate. The leads are connected to the semiconductor material, allowing it to be integrated into electronic circuits.

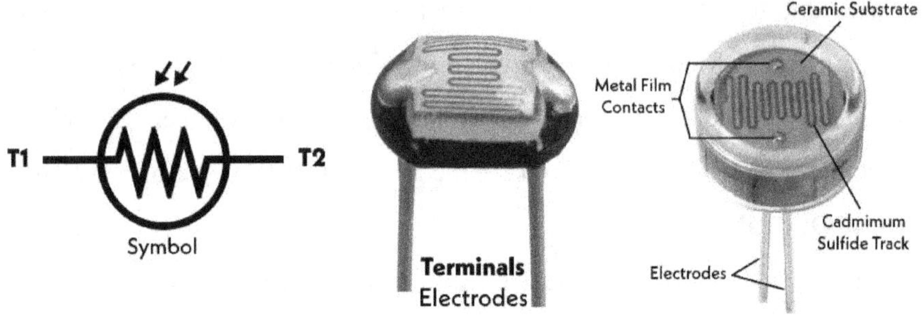

Fig 5.14 a) Construction of Light depending resistors.

An LDR is made of an N-type semiconductor material that is sensitive to light and possesses less or no free electrons in no light conductions such as cadmium selenide CdSe or cadmium sulfide CdS. It has very high resistance in the range of mega Ohms under no light conditions. A strip of photoconductive material is placed on top of an insulating substrate in a zigzag pattern to acquire desired resistance and power ratings. Ohmic contacts are made on either side of the strip to form the terminals. The resistance of the ohmic contacts is designed to be as low as possible so that the resistance of LDR only varies with the incident light. The whole structure is encapsulated inside a transparent resin that protects the photoconductive material from contamination and also allows light through it. When constructing LDR it is necessary to select a semiconductor material that has excellent light sensitivity and it can handle the current.

Operation:

LDR works on the principle of photoconductivity. According to photoconductivity the conductivity of a material is increased when the intensity of incident light is increased. There are certain semiconductor materials that exhibit such property known as photoconductive material. There is an energy band gap between the valance band and the conduction band of the semiconductor material. The electrons residing in the valance band cannot participate in the conduction unless energy equal to the amount of the band gap energy is provided. The incident light containing photons had enough energy to excite electrons into the conduction band. The number of electrons passing into the conduction band depends on the amount of light energy. Since these electrons contribute to the current flow, the resistance of the material decreases. Therefore, increasing the intensity of light increases the number of free electrons and decreases the resistance of the LDR.

When exposed to light, an LDR's resistance decreases, and this change in resistance is used to sense and measure light intensity. The amount of change in resistance depends on factors such as the wavelength of the light and the properties of the semiconductor material.

Characteristics of LDR

There are certain characteristics of LDR that determine its performance.

Photocurrent and Bright Resistance

The photocurrent is the current flowing through the LDR with the application of voltage when there is light. And the resistance which is the ratio between applied voltage and the photocurrent is called bright Resistance. The bright resistance is denoted by "100lux".

Dark Current and Dark Resistance

Dark current is the current flowing through LDR with the application of voltage when there is no light. And the resistance is called dark resistance denoted by "0lux"

Max Power Dissipation

The maximum power the LDR dissipates operating in a given range of temperature. LDR is temperature sensitive therefore it is mostly given at room temperature around 25°C.

Maximum Operating Voltage

This is the maximum applied voltage the LDR can tolerate as it is a semiconductor-based device. This is taken at no light conditions as LDR exhibits maximum resistance in darkness.

Wavelength

LDR is made from different photoconductive materials having different sensitivity to different wavelengths. It specifies the wavelength range for the specific LDR to show maximum sensitivity. Even its sensitivity varies over a range of wavelengths. It will show no change in resistance to light having wavelength out of this range.

Sensitivity

Sensitivity is the relative change in resistance under no light conditions and full light conditions. It has lower sensitivity as compared to phototransistors and photodiodes due to a lack of PN junctions. Its sensitivity is greatly affected by temperature. They should not be used for the measurement of light intensity.

Spectral Response

Spectral response refers to the sensitivity of LDR with respect to the different wavelengths of monochromatic light. It is a graph of LDR sensitivity at different wavelengths showing a curve. **Temperature Coefficient**

The temperature coefficient describes the temperature relationship with the resistance of LDR and its sensitivity. The LDR sensitivity greatly depends on the temperature. Its sensitivity reduces with an increase in temperature.

Rated Power

It refers to the max power that the LDR can consume at a certain temperature. It decreases with an increase in temperature.

Illumination Characteristics

This is a graph between the resistance of the LDR and with change in the intensity of the incident light called illumination. As LDR is not linear, the relationship forms a curve as shown in the figure below 5.15 . The x-axis represents illumination in lux while the y-axis represents the resistance of LDR in ohms.

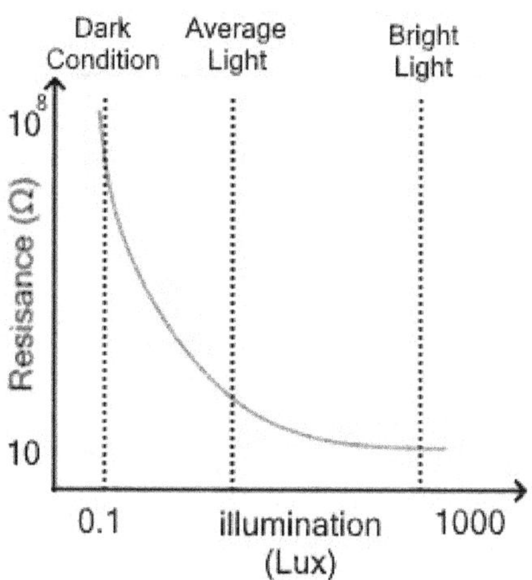

Fig 5.15 Illumination Curve of LDR

Under no light or dark conditions, the resistance of LDR is very high in the range of mega ohms. It reduces with an increase in light intensity. Initially, the resistance decreases drastically but with a gradual increase in intensity, the change in resistance becomes small to form a curve and eventually becomes straight with the x-axis showing no more change in resistance.

VI Characteristics

The VI characteristics show the relationship between the applied voltage and the current flowing through the LDR. It has a linear relationship between them. The current increases with an increase in the applied voltage. However, the resistance decreases with the intensity of light. Therefore, the slope of the VI increases and the current increase more steeply as shown in the graph below.

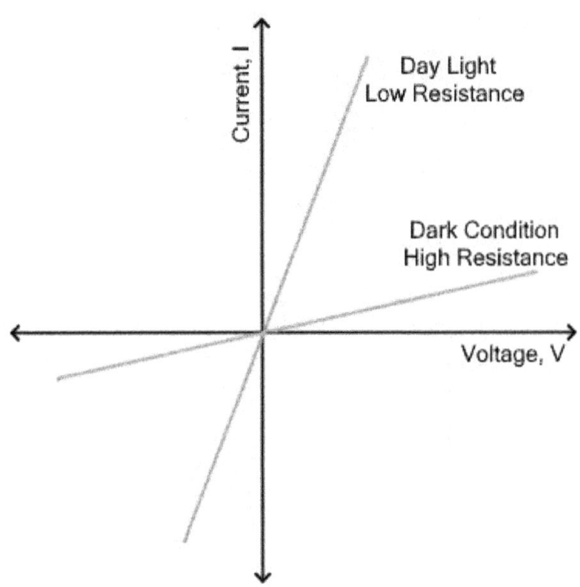

Fig 5.16 VI characteristics of LDR

Advantages and Disadvantages of LDR

Advantages

- Here are some advantages of LDR.

- It consumes very low power.

- It is high sensitivity.

- It is small and low cost.

- It has a simple design and is easily available in many shapes and sizes in the market.

- It is easier to connect to a circuit and does not require biasing.

Disadvantages

- Here are some disadvantages of LDR.

- Its sensitivity is greatly affected by temperature change.

- It has a very slow response time and cannot keep up with sudden changes in light intensity.

- LDR has a narrow spectral response i.e., a specific material is used for a narrow range of wavelengths of light.

- It is also affected by the hysteresis effect.

5.6.2 Photodiode

Photodiodes are a class of diodes that converts light energy to electricity. Their working is exactly the opposite of LEDs which are also diodes, but they convert electricity to light energy. Photodiodes can also be used in detecting the brightness of the light.

A photodiode is a PN-junction diode that consumes light energy to produce an electric current. They are also called a photo detector, a light detector, and a photo-sensor. Photodiodes are designed to work in reverse bias condition. Typical photodiode materials are Silicon, Germanium, and Indium gallium arsenide.

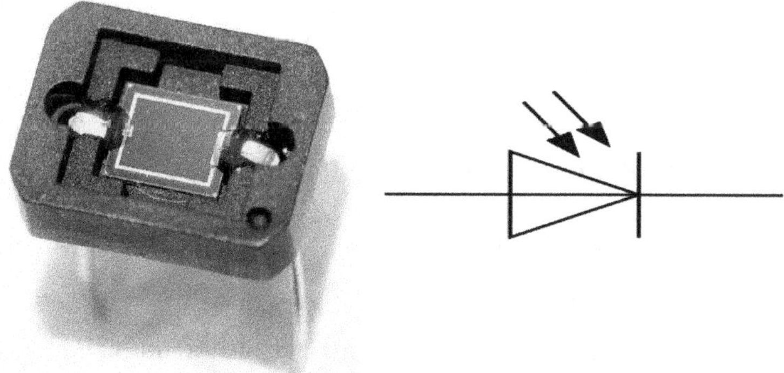

Fig 5.17 Symbol of Photodiode

The following image shows the symbol of the photodiode:

The symbol of the photodiode is like that of an LED, but here the arrow points inwards.

Construction

The photodiode is made up of two layers of P-type and N-type semiconductor. In this, the P-type material is formed from diffusion of the lightly doped P-type substrate. Thus, the layer of P+ ions is formed due to the diffusion process. And N-type epitaxial layer is grown on N-type substrate. The P+ diffusion layer is developed on N-type heavily doped epitaxial layer. The contacts are made up of metals to form two terminal cathode and anode.

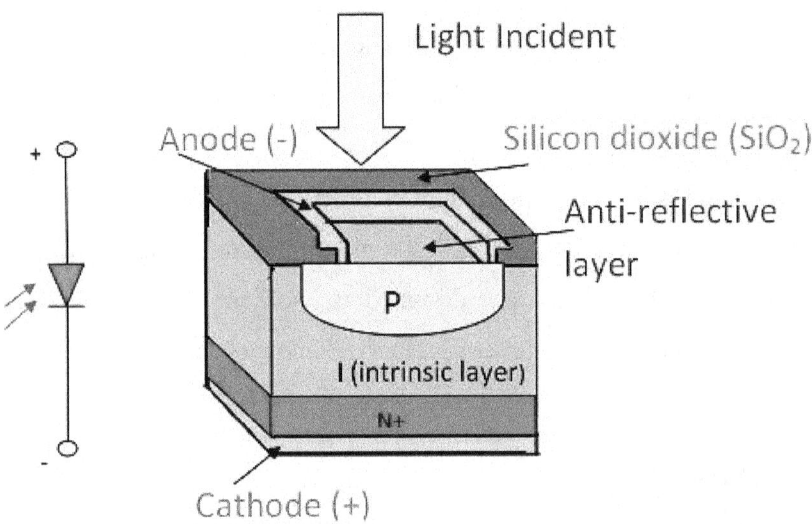

Fig 5.18 Construction of Photodiode

The front area of the diode is divided into two types that are active surface and non-active surface. The non-active surface is made up of **SiO2 (Silicon di Oxide)** and the active surface is coated with **anti-reflection material**. The active surface is called so because the light rays are incident on it. While on the non-active surface the light rays do not strike. The active layer is coated with anti-reflection material so that the light energy is not lost and the maximum of it can be converted into current. The entire unit has dimensions of the order of **2.5 mm.**

Photodiode Working

A photodiode is subjected to photons in the form of light which affects the generation of electron-hole pairs. If the energy of the falling photons (hv) is greater than the energy gap (Eg) of the semiconductor material, electron-hole pairs are created near the depletion region of the diode. The electron-hole pairs created are separated from each other before recombining due to the electric field of the junction. The direction of the electric field in the diode forces the electrons to move towards the n-side and consequently the holes move towards the p-side. As a result of the increase in the number of electrons on the n-side and holes on the p-side, a rise in the electromotive force is observed. Now when an external load is connected to the system, a current flow is observed through it. The more electromotive force created, the greater the current flow. The magnitude of the electromotive force created depends directly upon the intensity of the incident light. This effect of the proportional change in photocurrent with the change in light intensity can be easily observed by applying a reverse bias. Since photodiodes generate current flow directly depending upon the light intensity received, they can be used as photodetectors to detect optical signals. Built-in lenses and optical filters may be used to enhance the power and productivity of a photodiode.

5.6.3 Phototransistor

When the conventional diode is reverse biased, the depletion region starts expanding and the current starts flowing due to minority charge carriers. With the increase of reverse voltage, the reverse current also starts increasing. The same condition can be obtained in Photodiode without applying reverse voltage.

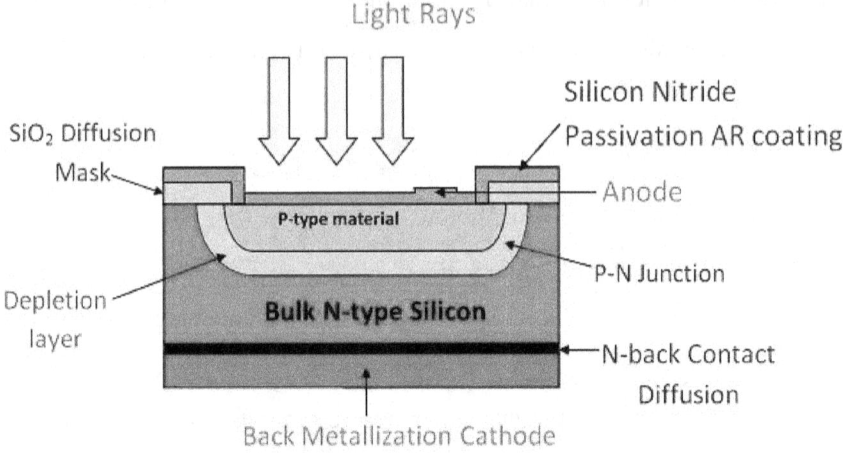

Fig 5.19 Cross-sectional view of Photo Diode

The junction of Photodiode is illuminated by the light source, the photons strike the junction surface. The photons impart their energy in the form of light to the junction. Due to which electrons from valence band get the energy to jump into the conduction band and contribute to current. In this way, the photodiode converts light energy into electrical energy.

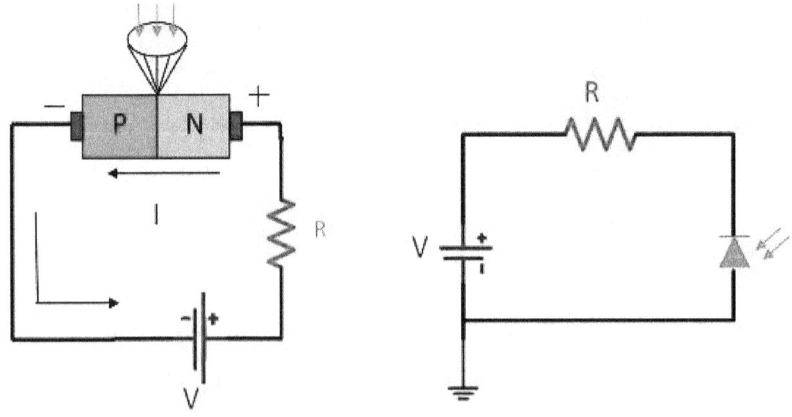

Fig 5.20 Basic Biasing arrangement of Photo Diode

The current which flows in photodiode before light rays are incident on it is called dark current. As leakage current flows in the conventional diode, similarly the dark current flows in the photodiode.

Modes of Operation of Photodiode

It operates in two modes, Photo-conductive and Photo-voltaic.

Photo-Conductive: When the Photo diode operates in reverse biased mode it is called Photoconductive mode. In this, the current flowing in diode varies linearly with the intensity of light incident on it. To turn-off the diode, it should be provided with forward voltage.

Photo-Voltaic: When the diode is operated without reverse biased it is said to be operated in photovoltaic mode. When the reverse biased is removed, the charge carriers are swept across the junction. The barrier potential is negative on the N-side and positive on P-side.

When an external circuit is connected to photodiode after removal of reverse biasing, the minority carriers in both P, as well as N-region, return to their original region. It means the electrons which crossed the junction from N-type to P-type again move to N-side with the help of external circuit.

And the holes which crossed the junction and moved from P-type to N-type during junction fabrication will now again move to P-side with the help of external circuit.

Thus, the electrons can now flow out from N-type and holes can flow out from P-type thus in this condition they behave as voltage cell having N-type as the negative terminal and P-type as a positive terminal. Thus, the photodiode can be used as a photoconductive device or a photovoltaic device.

V-I Characteristics of Photodiode

The characteristics curve of the photodiode can be understood with the help of the below diagram. The characteristics are shown in the negative region because the photodiode can be operated in reverse biased mode only.

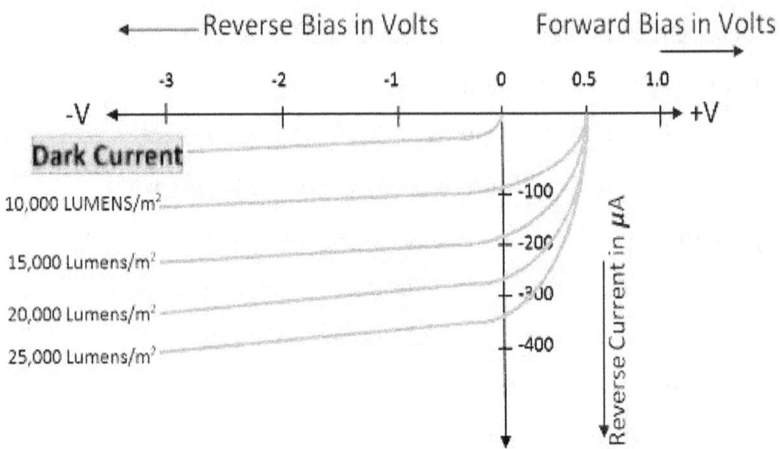

Fig 5.21Characteristics of Photo Diode

The reverse saturation current in the photodiode is denoted by I0. It varies linearly with the intensity of photons striking the diode surface. The current under large reverse bias is the summation of reverse saturation current and short circuit current.

$$I = I_{sc} + I_0 (1 - e^{V/\eta Vt})$$

Where Isc is the short circuit current, V is positive for forward voltage and negative for reverse bias, Vt is volt equivalent for temperature, η is unity for germanium and 2 for silicon.

Advantages of Photodiodes

The reverse current is low in the tens of microamperes.

The rise and fall times in case of photodiodes is very small making it suitable for high-speed counting and switching applications.

Disadvantages of Photodiodes

Photodiodes have lower light sensitivity than cadmium sulphide LDRs (Light dependent resistors), thus they CdS LDRs are considered more suitable for some applications.

Applications of Photodiodes

It is used for detection of both visible as well as invisible light rays. Photodiodes are used for the communication system for encoding & demodulation purpose. It is also used for digital and logic circuits which require fast switching and high-speed operation. These diodes also find application in character recognition techniques and IR remote control circuits. Photodiodes are considered as one of the significant optoelectronics devices which is extensively used in the optical fibre communication system.

5.6.3 Phototransistor

Phototransistors resemble normal transistors except for the fact that the base terminal is not present in the case of the phototransistor. Phototransistors convert the incident light into photocurrent. Instead of providing the base current for triggering the transistor, light rays are used to illuminate the base region. The base terminal is made up of material which shows sensitivity towards the light. The circuit symbol of the phototransistor is like that of the conventional transistor, but the base terminal can be omitted. The two arrows pointing towards phototransistor indicates that the phototransistor is triggered by the light incident on it.The circuit symbol of the **phototransistor** is described in the diagram below.

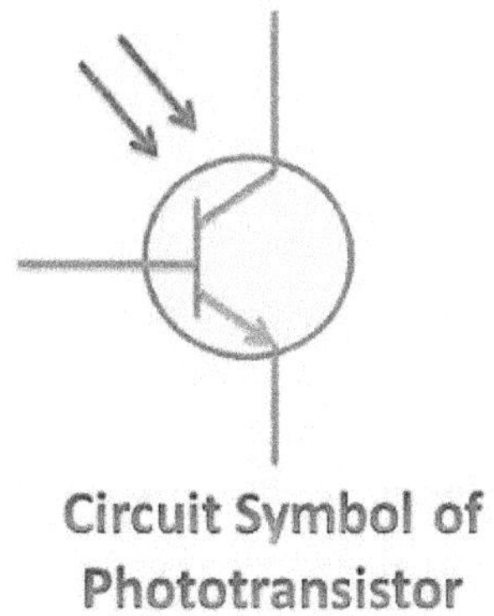

Fig 5.22 Symbol of Photo Transistor

Construction of the Phototransistor

Phototransistors are manufactured in the similar way by which normal transistor is manufactured, the only difference is the area of the base and collector region in case of phototransistors is quite large as compared to the normal transistor. This is because the more the light falls on the phototransistor the more current it will generate.

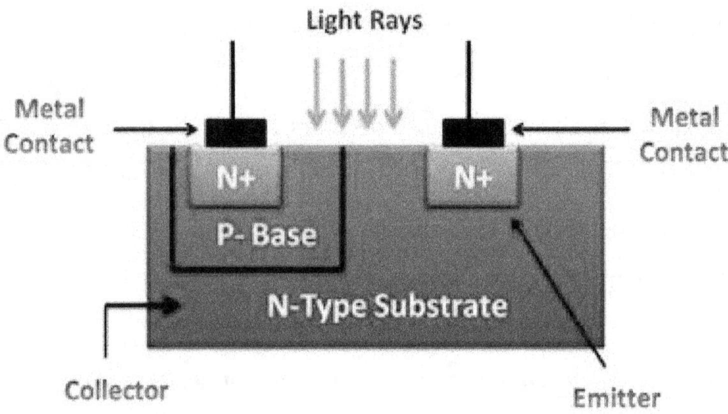

Fig 5.23 Homo-Junction Structure of Phototransistor

The collector and base region are formed by the techniques of ion-implantation and diffusion. The transistor which were used earlier was made of semiconductor material such as Germanium and Silicon and the resulting structure becomes a homogeneous material consist of either Silicon or Germanium. On the contrary, contemporarily, phototransistors are made up of Group-III and Group-V materials such as GaAs (Gallium Arsenide) in such a way that gallium and arsenide, each of these are used on either side of the transistor. The resulting structure becomes heterogeneous in nature. This type of structure is used widely because the conversion efficiency increases several times as compared to the conversion efficiency of the homogenous transistor.

Working of the Phototransistor

The output of the phototransistor is taken from the emitter terminal and the light rays are allowed to enter the base region. The magnitude of the photocurrent generated by the phototransistor depends on the light intensity of the light falling on the transistor.

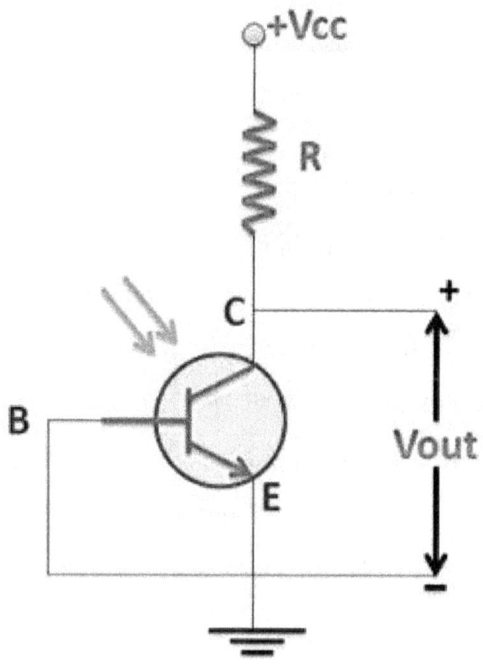

Fig 5.24 Phototransistor used as a Photodiode

It can be of three terminals or two terminals we can omit base as per our requirement. The phototransistor can be operated in three regions that are the cut-off region, active region, and the saturation region. The cut-off region and saturation region can be used to operate the transistor as the switch.

The active region is used for generating current. The current generated from phototransistor depends on several factors apart from luminous intensity such as

1. **DC current gain of the transistor:** The higher the DC current gain of the transistor, the higher will be the intensity of photocurrent generated.

2. **Time constant:** Response time of the transistor also effects the efficiency of phototransistor to generate photocurrent.

3. **Luminous Sensitivity:** The luminous sensitivity can be determined by the ratio between the photoelectric current and incident luminous flux.

4. **Area of the collector-base junction:** The area of the collector-base junction is crucial for the generation of photocurrent, the higher the area of the collector-base junction the higher will be the magnitude of photocurrent generated by the phototransistor.

5. **Wavelength of the incident light:** The wavelength of the light incident on phototransistor controls the amount of photocurrent generated. The higher the wavelength the lower will be the frequency.

Output Characteristics of Phototransistor

The output characteristics of phototransistor can be understood with the help of the diagram below. It shows the variation of collector current with respect to the variation in the emitter-collector voltage.

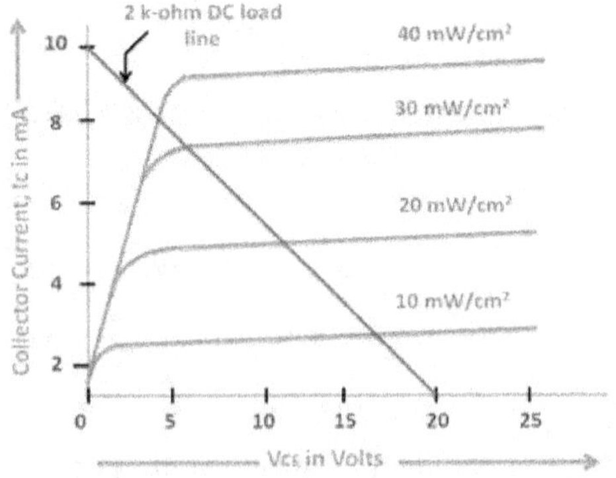

Fig 5.25 V$_{CE}$- Ic Characteristics of a Phototransistor

Advantages of Phototransistor

Higher Efficiency in Comparison to Photodiode: The efficiency of the phototransistor is higher than that of the photodiode. This is because the current gain in case of the phototransistor is more than that of the photodiode, thus, even if the amount of light incident on both is same the phototransistor will generate more photocurrent than the photodiode.

Faster Response: The response time of phototransistor is more than that of the photodiode, this provides the advantage of using the phototransistor in our circuit.

Less Noise interference: The major drawback of photodiodes especially that of avalanche photodiodes is that it is not immune to noise interference. On the contrary, the phototransistors are immune to noise interference.

Economical: Phototransistor is less costly than other light sensitive device, thus it is economical to use phototransistors in light-sensitive applications.

Less Complex: The designing of phototransistors is simple and less complex as compared to LDRs and photodiodes.

Disadvantages of Phototransistors

Effect of Electromagnetic energy: The efficiency of phototransistors decreases when electromagnetic field interferes within the operation region. This results in poor conversion efficiency of phototransistors.

Poor Performance at high frequency: Due to the large area of the collector-base region, the capacitance increases. Due to this it cannot convert light into photocurrent effectively at higher frequency ranges.

Electric spikes: It arises in phototransistors more frequently as compared to photodiodes.

Applications of Phototransistors

Counting Systems: The phototransistors are commonly used in counting systems. As this device works with the help of incident light, it is much easy to utilize such device in the computing system, as we don't need to worry about power supply.

Encoder sensing and object detection: The phototransistors can be used to detect the object or for encoding.

Printers and Optical control remotes: Due to its high light to current conversion efficiency, it is commonly used in optical devices such as remotes, printers etc.

Light detector: The most crucial application of phototransistor is to use it as the light detector. This is because it can detect even a small amount of light because it is highly efficient.

Level Indication and Relays: The phototransistors are also used to indicate the level in the various system. They also play a vital role in relays and punch cards. Phototransistors are crucial optoelectronics devices; they are also used in optical fibers. Due to its several advantages over photodiodes, it is more preferred over photodiodes.

References and Further reading

1.Modern Instrumentation" By Neelapala Anil Kumar-ManTech Publications Pvt. Ltd Aug 2020.

2. Sensors and Actuators, D. Patra Nabis, 2nd Ed., PHI, 2013.

Unit-VI Smart Sensors

Unit Structure

6.0 Objectives.

6.1 Introduction.

6.2 Block diagram

6.3 Types of smart sensors

6.4 Difference between Normal Sensor & Smart Sensor

6.5 Applications

References & Further Reading

6.0 Objectives

- To provide a thorough and easily understandable explanation of the principles and technologies behind smart sensors.

- Understand how smart sensors are used in various industries and applications, with practical examples.

- To keep updated with the latest advancements and trends in smart sensor technology and applications.

- To bridge the gap between different fields (by showcasing how smart sensors are applied across disciplines.

- To equip with the knowledge and tools needed to solve real-world problems using smart sensor technology.

- To guide readers through the design and development process of smart sensor systems, from concept to deployment.

6.1 Introduction.

In today's technologically infused landscape, we find ourselves standing at the intersection of innovation and possibility. The world as we know it is rapidly evolving, driven by a relentless quest for efficiency, precision, and connectivity.

At the heart of this transformation lies a silent revolution orchestrated by an unassuming yet indispensable hero—the smart sensor. In this chapter, we embark on a journey into the remarkable world of smart sensors and their multifaceted applications. These compact, intelligent devices serve as the senses of the modern world, capable of perceiving, analyzing, and communicating a vast array of data about our physical environment. From monitoring the structural integrity of bridges and skyscrapers to tracking the movement of wildlife in remote forests, from enabling precise agricultural practices to enhancing the safety of our cities, smart sensors have become the linchpin of innovation across diverse industries' we delve into the world of smart sensors, we will uncover the inner workings of these ingenious devices, demystifying the science and technology that powers them. We will explore their ability to sense a myriad of parameters, from temperature and pressure to light and motion, and their role in translating these measurements into actionable insights. Moreover, this chapter is more than a technical exposition. It is a testament to the transformative power of smart sensors, as we journey through a tapestry of real-world applications that illustrate their profound impact on our lives, industries, and the world at large. Whether you are an engineer seeking to optimize manufacturing processes, a healthcare professional striving to enhance patient care, or an environmental scientist dedicated to safeguarding our planet, the possibilities afforded by smart sensors are boundless. The chapter is structured to provide a holistic understanding of smart sensors, from their fundamental principles. We will explore case studies that highlight how these sensors are being leveraged to solve complex problems and improve decision-making in a variety of fields. In instrumentation systems, sensors are essential devices. At present, most of the types of sensors are smart. So, in these sensors, the sensing elements & electronics are integrated on the same chip. So, the integration of electronics and sensors to make an intelligent sensor is known as a smart sensor. This sensor can make some decisions. These sensors have many benefits like higher S/N ratio, fast signal conditioning, auto-calibration, self-testing, high reliability, small physical size, detection & prevention of failure. So, this article discusses an overview of a smart sensor, it's working, and its applications. A smart sensor is a device that uses a transducer to gather particular data from a physical environment to perform a predefined & programmed function on the particular type of gathered data then it transmits the data through a networked connection. The features of the smart sensor are self-identification, digital sensor data, smart calibration & compensation, multi-sensing capacity, sensor communication for configuration of remote & remote monitoring, etc.

Smart sensors work by capturing data from physical environments & changing their physical properties like speed, temperature, pressure, mass, or presence of humans into calculable electrical signals. These sensors include a Digital Motion Processor (DMP). Here a DMP is one type of microprocessor that allows the sensor to perform onboard processing of the smart sensor data like filtering noise otherwise performing different kinds of signal conditioning.

These sensors have 4 main functions measurement, configuration, verification & communication. Measurements are simply taken through detecting physical signals & changing them into electrical signals. So, this will help in monitoring and measuring things like temperature, traffic, & industrial applications. The configuration function is a significant feature as it allows the smart sensor to detect position otherwise installation errors. The verification function has different uses like nonstop supervision of sensor behavior, using a set of supervisory circuits or equipment executed within the sensor. Lastly, the communication feature allows the sensor to converse to the main microcontroller/ microprocessor.

6.2 Block diagram

Smart Sensor Block Diagram

The block diagram of the smart sensor is shown below. This block diagram includes different blocks like sensing unit, signal conditioning, analog to digital conversion, application algorithms, local user interface, memory, and communication unit or transceiver.

Sensing Unit

This unit detects the changes in physical parameters & generates electrical signals equivalent to it. Signal

Conditioning Unit: The signal conditioning unit controls the signal to meet the necessities of next-level operations without losing data.

Analog to Digital Converter: ADC converts the signal from analog to digital format & sends it to the microprocessor.

Local User Interface: The local user interface or LUI is a panel-mounted device used to allow building operators to monitor & control system equipment.

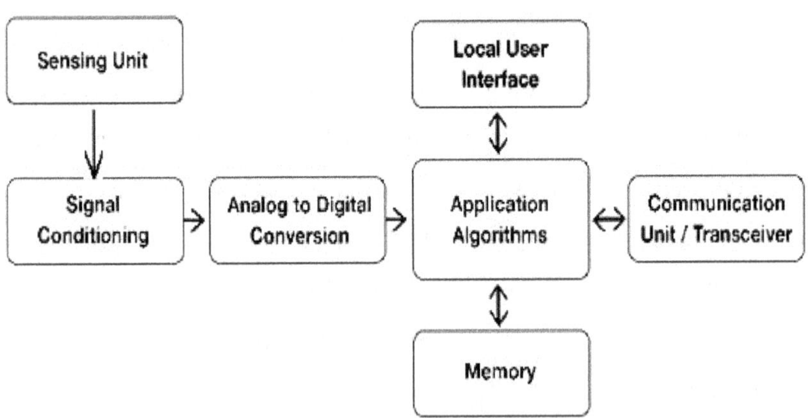

Fig 6.1 Smart Sensor Block Diagram

Application Algorithm

The signals from smart sensors reach here & process the received data based on the application programs previously loaded here & generate output signals.

Memory: It is used to store media for saving received & processed data.

Communication Unit: The output signals from the application algorithm or microprocessor are transmitted to the main station through the communication unit. This unit also gets command requirements from the key station to execute specific tasks.

6.3 Types of smart sensors

There are different types of smart sensor available in the market which is explained below.

Level Sensors: A level sensor is a type of device used to monitor, measure & maintain liquid levels. Whenever the level of liquid is sensed, this sensor changes the data into an electric signal. Levels are classified into two types point level & continuous level. A point level sensor is used to specify whether a liquid has achieved an exact point within a container whereas continuous level type sensors are used to provide precise measurements for liquid level. These sensors are mainly used in different industries like automotive, manufacturing, and in household applications. A level sensor can detect and communicate a change to a user. Level sensors are typically designed for a single application rather than a broad range of applications.

Types of Level Sensors

Level sensors can be split into two main categories.

Point Level Sensors:

Point level sensors mark a specific level and inform the user whether the media is above or below that level. In general, they are used as a high alarm or switch. These level sensors can also be combined in a single device to provide a low alarm or a stepped version of a continuous level. Examples of sensors for point-level indication include the following.

Capacitance Level Sensors: A capacitance level sensor is a proximity sensor that emits an electrical field and detects a level based on the effect on its electrical field. These sensors are small, less costly than other sensors, less intrusive to the product, accurate, and do not have any moving parts. They must, however, be calibrated and will only detect specific liquids. Capacitance sensors can be used in liquid storage tanks.

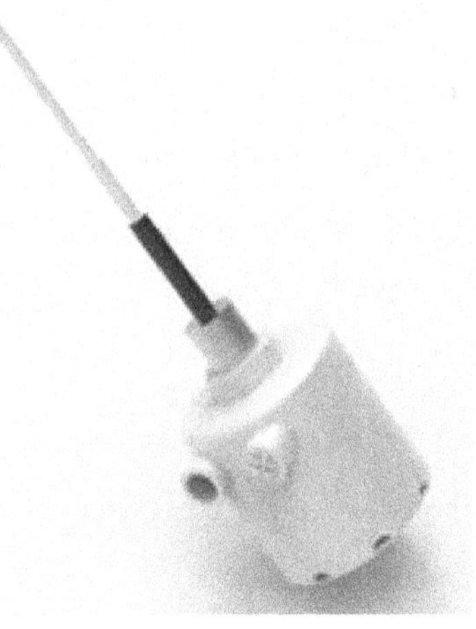

Fig 6.2 Capacitive level Sensor

Optical Sensors: Optical sensors convert light rays into electrical signals, translating the physical quantity of light into a measurement. These sensors contain no moving parts, are unaffected by high pressure or temperature, are compact, and can be used in liquid applications. However, they must be cleaned if their lens becomes coated or dirty. Oil, coolant, or hydraulics can be used as low-level indicators to prevent run-dry conditions.

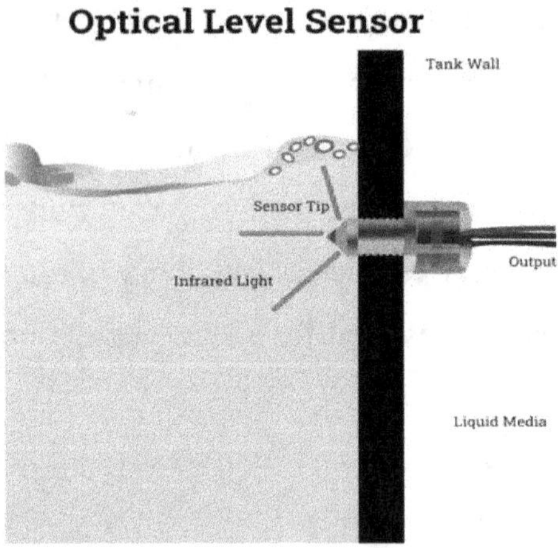

Fig 6.3 Optical level Sensor

Conductivity (Resistance) Sensors: A conductivity or resistance sensor reads conductivity with a probe. The probe has two electrodes and uses alternating currents to power them. When a liquid covers the probe, the electrodes connect to an electric circuit, causing current to flow and signalling a high or low level.

These conductivity level sensors have no moving parts, are inexpensive, and are simple to use. They are, however, invasive (they must touch the product being sensed), only detect conductive liquids, and the probe will rust over time. These sensors are useful for signalling high or low levels.

Vibrating (Tuning Fork) Sensors: They employ a sensing element in the shape of a fork with two tines. The fork vibrates at the frequency of its natural resonant frequency. Therefore, the frequency of the fork detecting the level will change as the level changes. These sensors are inexpensive and small, invasive to the product, meaning they must touch the material to determine the level. They are simple to install and virtually maintenance-free. These sensors are used in the mining, food and beverage, and chemical processing industries.

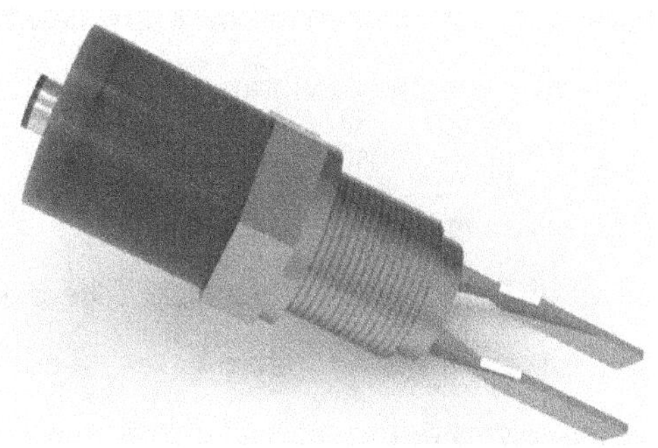

Fig 6.4 Tuning Fork point level Sensor

Float Switches: Float switches use a float, a device that raises or lowers when a product is applied or removed, opening or closing a circuit as the level rises or falls, moving the float. A float switch has many advantages. It does not require power, provides a direct indication, and is inexpensive. The disadvantages are that they are invasive to the product, have moving parts, and can be quite large. In addition, float switches can only indicate a high or low level and cannot measure a variable level. Float switches are commonly used in liquid storage tanks to indicate high or low levels.

Continuous Level Sensors:

They measure liquid or dry materials levels within a specified range and provide outputs that show the level continuously. They are more sophisticated than point-level sensors in that they measure over a range of levels rather than at a single point to provide the user with the exact amount of a substance. Continuous level measuring uses the following sensors.

Ultrasonic-Level Sensors: Ultrasonic-level sensors generate and receive ultrasonic waves using the time it takes to reflect and measure distance. Ultrasonic sensors have no moving parts, are compact, extremely reliable, non-invasive (non-contact), unaffected by the properties of the material they are sensing, and self-cleaning due to vibrations produced. They are, however, costly and may be affected by the environment.

Fig 6.5 Ultrasonic level Sensor

Radar (Microwave) Sensors: These sensors use an antenna on the radar sensor to transmit microwaves. The product being sensed reflects these microwaves to the antenna, and the time between signal emission and reception is proportional to the product level. Radar sensors offer many benefits. They are not affected by temperature, pressure, or dust and can measure liquids, pastes, powders, and solids. They are also very accurate and do not require calibration, and they are non-invasive because they do not have to touch the product. They are, however, expensive and have a limited detection range. Radar sensors, like ultrasonic sensors, are ideal for hot liquid storage tanks.

Fig 6.6 Radar Sensor

Applications of Level Sensors

- Level sensors are used in the following applications:
- automobiles in fuel tanks
- pharmaceutical processes
- power generation plants
- water treatment

Advantages of Level Sensors

- They give accurate values.
- They are robust.
- They have different configurations for different applications.
- Disadvantages of Level Sensors
- They are only used in specific liquids.
- Digital-level sensors are complex.

Temperature Sensors

Temperature sensors are used to measure temperatures like liquid temperature, air temperature, or solid matter temperature. These sensors are available in different types which use different principles to measure the temperature like RTDs, NTC thermistors, thermopiles & thermocouples. These sensors are mainly used in medical devices, computers, automobiles, cooking appliances & other types of machinery.

Fig 6.7 Temperature Sensor

Pressure Sensors

A pressure sensor is a transducer that changes the mechanical pressure input into an electrical output signal. There are different types of pressure sensors available based on capacity, size, sensing technology, measurement method

&output requirements. These sensors play a key role in monitoring pipelines & give an alert to overseers if there are any leaks otherwise irregularities so that they can repair or maintain pipelines.

Infrared Sensors

An infrared sensor is an electronic device used to emit light to detect some object in the surroundings and measures the object's heat & detects the motion. Generally, all the objects will emit some form of thermal radiation within the IR spectrum which is invisible but the IR sensor can sense this radiation.

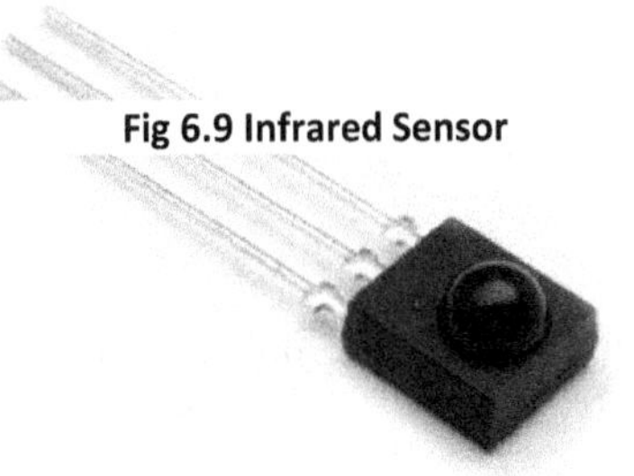

Fig 6.9 Infrared Sensor

IR sensor includes a transmitter like an IR LED and receiver as an IR photodiode. For infrared transmission, three types of media are used vacuum, atmosphere & optical fibers. These sensors are used in night vision devices, radiation thermometers, IR tracking, IR imaging, etc.

Proximity Sensors

A smart sensor like a proximity sensor is used to notice the existence of objects in its surrounding area without contacting them. These sensors are frequently used in collision avoidance systems & collision warnings. This sensor uses light, sound, IR radiation otherwise electromagnetic fields to notice an object. These sensors are applicable in consumer robotics, industrial applications and utilized in vehicles to detect the physical contact of other vehicles & also for parking-assist functions.

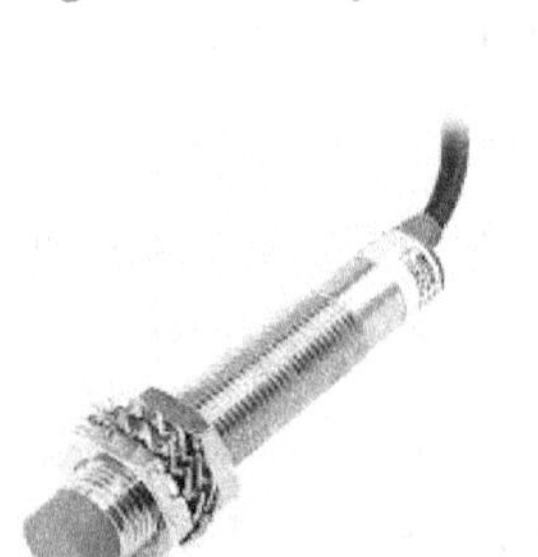

Fig 6.10 Proximity Sensor

Air Quality Detection Sensors

Air quality detection sensors are electronic devices that are used to detect & monitor the air pollution within the air in the nearby area. So, these sensors efficiently work for indoor & outdoor purposes. Air quality sensors can check the CO2 concentrations through VOC (volatile organic compounds) that have methane & ammonia as gases.

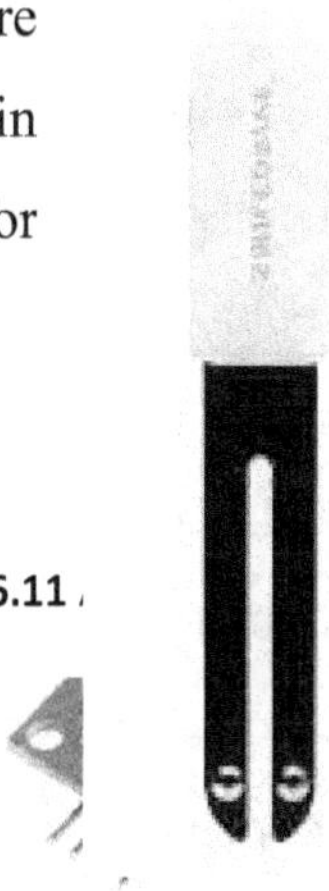

Motion Sensors

Motion sensors are electronic devices, used to detect movement inside and surroundings of your home and give an alert. For instance, this sensor can activate the lights once it detects you while entering a room otherwise, they can give an alert once an intruder is trying to enter your home. These types of sensors are mainly used in homes, security systems, paper towel dispensers, phones, virtual reality systems & game consoles.

Fig 6.11

Fig 6.12 Motion Sensor

Smart Plant Sensors

Plant sensors are advanced gardening sensors used to provide the data to the user from stem surface, leaf to root probes to feed the plants. They explain to us what nourishment and care are required for the plant. This sensor is very simple to use by placing it into the soil of the plant pot beside the potted plant. After that, it monitors the level of moisture, light intensity, and the temperature automatically to maintain the plant properly. The current plant sensors give an alert through smartphones to keep checking your plant's condition remotely and take appropriate action.

Smart Climate Sensors

Smart climate sensors are used to gather the data of barometric pressure, temperature & humidity that assist in evaluating the exact weather conditions & calculate as well. These sensors will assist you in setting your plan accordingly because these sensors are connected through your Smartphone to send alerts throughout the frequent changes within the weather. These sensors are essential for gardening and are connected to smart irrigation systems.

6.4 Difference between Normal Sensor & Smart Sensor

The difference between a normal sensor and a smart sensor includes the following.

Fig 6.14 Climate Sensor

Sensor	Smart Sensor
A sensor is a device used to detect the physical changing & chemical environment.	The part of a sensor is known as a smart sensor that is used for the computer.
A sensor doesn't include a DMP or digital motion processor.	A smart sensor includes a DMP or Digital Motion Processor.
The normal sensor includes three components like sensor element, packaging & connections, and also signals processing hardware.	Smart sensors include different components like amplifiers, transducers, analog filters, excitation control, and compensation sensors.

The different types of normal sensors are pressure, position, temperature, vibration, force, humidity & fluid property.	The different types of smart sensors are electric current, level, humidity, pressure, proximity, temperature, heat, flow, etc.
Normal sensor output cannot be used directly because we should convert it into a usable format.	The output of the smart sensor is ready to use.
Normal sensors are preferred when an engineer designing a device that requires complete control on sensor input.	Smart sensors are generally preferred over base sensors because they include native processing capabilities.
Normal sensors are not expensive because they contain fewer components.	Smart sensors are expensive as compared to normal sensors.

Advantages

- The advantages of the smart sensor include the following.
- These are small.
- These sensors are very easy to use, design &maintain.
- The performance level is higher.
- Speed of communication & reliability is higher due to the direct conversion with the processor.
- These sensors can perform self-calibration & self-assessments.
- These sensors can notice issues like switch failures, open coils & sensor contamination.
- These sensors optimize manufacturing processes easily that need changes.
- They can store many systems' data.

Disadvantages

- The disadvantages of the smart sensor include the following.
- Smart sensors' reliability is one of the major drawbacks because if they are stolen or get damaged then they can affect a lot of systems badly.

- It needs both sensors & actuators.

- Sensor calibration must be managed by an external processor.

- High complexity in wired smart sensors, so the cost is also very high.

6.5   Applications

The applications of the smart sensor include the following.

These sensors play a key role in monitoring different industrial processes like data collecting, measurement taking & transmitting the data to centralized cloud computing platforms wherever data is collected & analyzed for different patterns. So, this collected data can be simply monitored at any time by decision-makers.

Smart sensors are used mainly for monitoring & control mechanisms in different environments like water level & food monitoring systems, smart grids, traffic monitoring & control, environmental monitoring, conserving energy in artificial lighting, monitoring of the remote system, and fault diagnostics of equipment, transport & logistics, agriculture, telecommunications, industrial applications, animal tracking, etc.

References & Further Reading

1.Jacob Fraden, "Hand Book of Modern Sensors: physics, Designs and Applications", 3rd ed., Springer, 2010.

2. Course sensors and sensors circuit design:

(https://www.coursera.org/learn/sensors-circuit-interface#modules)

Unit-VII Smart Sensors Applications

Unit Structure

7.0 Objectives.

7.1 Introduction.

7.2 On-board Automobile Sensors (Automotive Sensors)

7.3 Home Appliance Sensors

7.4 Aerospace Sensors

7.5 Sensors for Manufacturing

7.6 Sensors for Environmental Monitoring

References & Further Reading

7.0 Objectives.

- Provide a comprehensive overview of smart sensors, their evolution, and their role in modern technology.

- Explore how smart sensors are a fundamental component of the Internet of Things (IoT) and how they enable connectivity and data sharing in IoT systems.

- Highlight how smart sensors are revolutionizing manufacturing processes, improving quality control, and enabling Industry 4.0 initiatives.

- Explore how smart sensors are used for environmental monitoring, pollution control, and sustainability initiatives.

- Discuss the use of smart sensors in precision agriculture, crop monitoring, and livestock management.

- Address the current challenges in smart sensor technology, such as power management, data security, and standardization, and explore future trends and innovations.

7.1 Introduction.

In a world increasingly driven by data and automation, the role of sensors has become pivotal. Smart sensors, equipped with advanced technologies and embedded intelligence, are at the forefront of this sensor revolution. This chapter serves as an introduction to the captivating realm of smart sensor applications, where we embark on a journey to explore how these miniature marvels are transforming industries, enhancing efficiency, and reshaping our daily lives. To understand the significance of smart sensors, it is essential to trace their evolution. We begin by delving into the historical development of sensors, from the rudimentary early designs to the cutting-edge smart sensors of today. This evolution not only showcases the impressive strides in sensor technology but also sets the stage for the transformative impact of smart sensors. The term 'smart' is not just a buzzword but a reflection of the remarkable capabilities that modern sensors possess. In this section, we demystify the components and features that differentiate smart sensors from their traditional counterparts. From integrated processing power to communication abilities, we dissect the anatomy of smart sensors. At the heart of every smart sensor is the generation of data. We explore the concept of data as the lifeblood of smart sensor applications. From real-time measurements to data analytics, we discuss how sensor-generated data drives decision-making, improves processes, and enables innovation.

Smart sensors are versatile and find application in an array of industries. We provide an overview of the diverse sectors benefiting from smart sensor technology, including manufacturing, healthcare, agriculture, transportation, and environmental monitoring. Real-world examples illustrate how these sensors are revolutionizing each domain.

One of the key enablers of smart sensor applications is their integration into the Internet of Things (IoT) ecosystem. We delve into how smart sensors play a pivotal role in the IoT landscape, facilitating seamless connectivity, data exchange, and remote monitoring.

These technologies not only optimize existing processes but also open doors to new possibilities. We set the stage for the subsequent chapters, where we'll explore specific applications, challenges, and trends in the world of smart sensors.

7.2   On-board Automobile Sensors (Automotive Sensors)

Sensors are the components of the system that provide the inputs that enable the computer **(ECM)** to carry out the operations that make the system function correctly. In the case of vehicle sensors, it is usually a voltage that is represented by a code at the computer's processor. If this voltage is incorrect the processor will probably take it as an invalid input and record a fault.

Types of Sensors

- Mass air flow(MAF)rate
- Exhaust gas oxygen concentration (possibly heated)
- Throttle plate angular position
- Crank shaft angular position/RPM
- Cool ant temperature
- Intake air temperature
- Man if old absolute pressure(MAP)
- Differential exhaust gas pressure
- Vehicle speed
- Transmission gear selector position

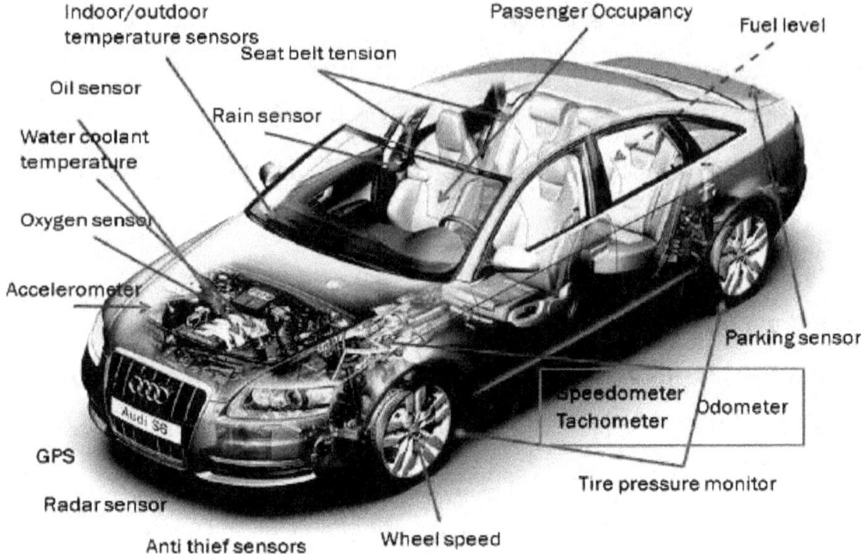

Fig 7.1 On-board Automobile Sensors

Mass air flow (MAF) rate sensor

Air flow sensors are used on engines with multi port electronic fuel injection. This is because the amount of fuel delivered by an EFI system is controlled by a computer (power train control module or PCM) which turns the fuels inject or son and off. The airflow sensor keeps the computer informed about how much air is being pulled into the engine past the throttle plates. This input along with information from other engine sensors allows the computer to calculate how much fuel is needed. The computer then increases or decreases injector duration(on time) to provide the correct air/fuel ratio.

Types: 1.Vane type Air Flow Rate Sensor

2. Hot Wire type Air Flow Rate Sensor

Vane type Air Flow Rate Sensor

An engine requires the correct air–fuel ratio to suit various conditions. With electronic fuel injection the ECM controls the air–fuel ratio and to do this it needs a constant flow of information about the amount of air flowing to the engine. With this information, and data stored in its memory, the ECM can then send out a signal to the injectors, so that they provide the correct amount of fuel. Airflow measurement is commonly performed by a 'flap'-type air flow sensor.

Hot Wire type Air Flow Rate Sensor

These sensors play a vital role in various industries and applications where precise airflow measurement is necessary for control, safety, or research purposes. Their ability to provide accurate and responsive airflow data makes them valuable in maintaining optimal performance in systems and processes. A hot wire air flow rate sensor is a type of airflow sensor that measures the rate of air flowing through a duct or pipe by using a heated wire as the sensing element.

Exhaust gas oxygen concentration (possibly heated)

Exhaust gas oxygen concentration sensors, commonly known as oxygen sensors or O2 sensors, are crucial components in modern vehicles' emissions control systems. These sensors are designed to measure the oxygen content in the exhaust gases, which provides valuable feedback to the engine control unit (ECU) for optimizing combustion efficiency and reducing emissions. Oxygen sensors play a pivotal role in reducing harmful emissions from vehicles. By ensuring that the air-fuel mixture is optimized, they contribute to lower levels of pollutants like carbon monoxide (CO), nitrogen oxides (NOx), and unburned hydrocarbons (HC). Maintaining the correct air-fuel ratio improves fuel efficiency, as it ensures that fuel is burned efficiently without wastage. Proper air-fuel ratio control not only reduces emissions but also contributes to smoother engine operation and overall performance. Oxygen sensors can degrade over time due to exposure to exhaust gases and high temperatures. When they fail, they can cause issues such as poor fuel economy, increased emissions, and engine performance problems. Routine maintenance and replacement, as specified by the vehicle manufacturer, are essential to ensure proper sensor function. Exhaust gas oxygen concentration sensors, whether heated or wideband, are critical on-board automobile sensors that enable precise control of the air-fuel mixture, reduce emissions, improve fuel efficiency, and enhance engine performance in modern vehicles. They are a key component of emissions control systems and contribute to cleaner and more efficient transportation.

Throttle plate angular position

The throttle plate angular position sensor, often referred to as the Throttle Position Sensor (TPS), is an essential component in an automobile's engine control system. It measures the position of the throttle plate in the throttle body or carburettor and provides this information to the Engine Control Unit (ECU) for various engine management functions. The primary function of the TPS is to measure the angular position of the throttle plate. This position corresponds to how open or closed the throttle is, which controls the amount of air entering the engine. The TPS generates an electrical signal (usually a voltage signal) that varies with the throttle plate's position. This signal is sent to the ECU, allowing the ECU to determine the driver's throttle input and the engine's load. The TPS is critical for engine control. It helps the ECU calculate the correct air-fuel mixture and ignition timing based on the driver's throttle input. This information is essential for optimizing engine performance, fuel efficiency, and emissions. The TPS data is crucial during acceleration and deceleration. It allows the ECU to adjust fuel injection and spark timing to provide the desired level of power and response. The TPS also plays a role in controlling engine idle speed. The ECU uses the TPS signal to adjust the throttle plate position during idle to maintain a stable and consistent engine speed. f the TPS malfunctions or provides erratic signals, it can trigger diagnostic trouble codes (DTCs) and illuminate the "Check Engine" light. Mechanics can use these codes to diagnose and repair throttle-related issues. The TPS is a wear-prone component due to its constant movement as the driver adjusts the throttle. Over time, it may wear out or develop electrical issues, leading to poor engine performance. Regular maintenance and periodic replacement, as recommended by the vehicle manufacturer, are important to ensure accurate throttle plate position sensing. The throttle plate angular position sensor, or Throttle Position Sensor (TPS), is a vital on-board automobile sensor that measures the position of the throttle plate. It provides crucial input to the ECU for engine control, optimizing performance, fuel efficiency, and emissions. Proper maintenance and replacement of the TPS are essential for ensuring the smooth operation of the vehicle's engine.

Crankshaft angular position/RPM

Measuring the crankshaft's angular position and RPM (Revolutions per Minute) is a critical function in an automobile's engine control system. This information is essential for managing engine performance, fuel injection, ignition timing, and various other engine-related functions. In some engines, especially those with variable valve timing systems, a Camshaft Position Sensor (CMP) is used in addition to the CPS. The CMP provides information about the camshaft's position, which the ECU uses in conjunction with the CPS data to optimize engine performance further. The data from the CPS is crucial for determining the optimal ignition timing. The ECU adjusts the spark timing based on the crankshaft's position and RPM to ensure efficient combustion. The CPS information is used to synchronize fuel injection. The ECU calculates the appropriate fuel injection timing and duration based on the crankshaft's position and RPM. The CPS helps the ECU maintain proper synchronization between the various engine components, including the crankshaft, camshaft (if applicable), and other auxiliary systems. If the CPS fails or provides erratic signals, it can trigger diagnostic trouble codes (DTCs) and illuminate the "Check Engine" light. Mechanics can use these codes to diagnose and repair crankshaft position sensor-related issues. Maintaining the crankshaft position sensor is crucial for reliable engine operation. These sensors can wear out over time or become contaminated with debris, leading to inaccurate readings and potential engine performance problems. Regular inspection, cleaning (if necessary), and replacement as recommended by the vehicle manufacturer are essential to ensure accurate crankshaft position and RPM sensing. the Crankshaft Position Sensor (CPS) is a critical on-board automobile sensor that monitors the crankshaft's angular position and RPM. This information is vital for precise engine control, including ignition timing, fuel injection, and overall engine performance. Proper maintenance and replacement of the CPS are essential to ensure the engine operates optimally.

Coolant temperature

Monitoring coolant temperature is a crucial aspect of an automobile's engine management system. This information helps the vehicle's engine control unit (ECU) optimize engine performance, ensure efficient combustion, and prevent overheating. The Coolant Temperature Sensor (CTS) is a vital component that measures the temperature of the engine coolant or antifreeze. It generates electrical signals that provide information to the ECU about the coolant's temperature. The CTS is typically located on or near the engine's cooling system components, such as the thermostat housing or the cylinder head. Its placement ensures it's in direct contact with the engine coolant. The CTS data plays a significant role in engine performance optimization. It helps the ECU determine the appropriate air-fuel mixture and ignition timing based on the coolant temperature. During a cold start, when the engine is cold, the CTS signals the ECU to enrich the air-fuel mixture to improve combustion and reduce emissions until the engine warms up. The CTS is crucial for monitoring the engine's temperature to prevent overheating. If the coolant temperature rises beyond a safe threshold, the ECU can trigger engine protection mechanisms, such as reducing power or activating the cooling fan. A malfunctioning CTS or erratic signals from the sensor can trigger diagnostic trouble codes (DTCs) and illuminate the "Check Engine" light. Mechanics can use these codes to diagnose and repair coolant temperature sensor-related issues. The coolant temperature sensor is exposed to the harsh environment of the engine compartment, and over time, it can become contaminated or fail. Routine maintenance includes inspecting the sensor for damage, checking its electrical connections, and replacing it as recommended by the vehicle manufacturer or if it's found to be faulty. In addition to the CTS and its role in engine control, many vehicles have a coolant temperature gauge on the instrument panel. This gauge provides a visual indication of the coolant temperature to the driver. It typically has a range indicating the optimal operating temperature range for the engine. If the temperature gauge shows an unusually high reading, it may signal a potential cooling system problem. he Coolant Temperature Sensor (CTS) is a critical on-board automobile sensor that measures the temperature of the engine coolant. This information is essential for engine control, including optimizing performance, preventing overheating, and ensuring efficient combustion. Proper maintenance and replacement of the CTS are important for the reliable operation of the vehicle's engine.

Intake air temperature

Monitoring the intake air temperature is an important aspect of an automobile's engine management system. It helps the vehicle's engine control unit (ECU) optimize the air-fuel mixture and ignition timing for efficient combustion and engine performance. The Intake Air Temperature Sensor (IAT) measures the temperature of the incoming air that enters the engine's intake manifold. It generates electrical signals that provide information to the ECU about the temperature of the intake air. The IAT sensor is typically located in the intake manifold or air intake tract, where it is exposed to the incoming air. The IAT data is used by the ECU to determine the optimal air-fuel mixture. Colder, denser air contains more oxygen and requires a different fuel mixture than warmer air. The IAT data helps adjust the mixture for efficient combustion. During a cold start, when the engine is cold, the IAT signals the ECU to enrich the air-fuel mixture to improve combustion and reduce emissions until the engine warms up. Accurate intake air temperature data helps prevent engine knock or detonation. High intake air temperatures can increase the likelihood of knocking, so the ECU may adjust timing and fuel delivery to prevent this. A malfunctioning IAT sensor or erratic signals from the sensor can trigger diagnostic trouble codes (DTCs) and illuminate the "Check Engine" light. Mechanics can use these codes to diagnose and repair IAT sensor-related issues. The IAT sensor is exposed to the elements and can become contaminated or fail over time. Routine maintenance includes inspecting the sensor for damage, checking its electrical connections, and replacing it as recommended by the vehicle manufacturer or if it's found to be faulty. In summary, the Intake Air Temperature Sensor (IAT) is a crucial on-board automobile sensor that measures the temperature of the incoming air. This information is essential for engine control, including optimizing the air-fuel mixture and ignition timing, preventing engine knock, and ensuring efficient combustion and engine performance. Proper maintenance and replacement of the IAT sensor are important for the reliable operation of the vehicle's engine.

Manifold absolute pressure (MAP)

The Manifold Absolute Pressure (MAP) sensor is a vital component of an automobile's engine control system, as it measures the absolute pressure inside the engine's intake manifold. The primary function of the MAP sensor is to measure the absolute pressure inside the intake manifold. This pressure is a combination of atmospheric pressure and the vacuum or boost created by the engine's operation. The MAP sensor generates an electrical signal (usually a voltage or frequency) that varies with the pressure it measures. This signal is sent to the Engine Control Unit (ECU), providing information about engine load and performance. he MAP sensor is typically mounted on or near the intake manifold of the engine, where it can directly sense the pressure conditions inside the manifold. he MAP sensor data is critical for the ECU to determine the engine's load and performance characteristics. It helps the ECU optimize various engine control parameters, including air-fuel mixture, ignition timing, and turbocharger (if equipped) operation. In turbocharged engines, the MAP sensor plays a key role in controlling the boost pressure generated by the turbocharger. It ensures that the engine operates within safe and efficient boost levels. A malfunctioning MAP sensor or erratic signals from the sensor can trigger diagnostic trouble codes (DTCs) and illuminate the "Check Engine" light. Mechanics can use these codes to diagnose and repair MAP sensor-related issues. The MAP sensor is exposed to the elements and can become contaminated or fail over time. Routine maintenance includes inspecting the sensor for damage, checking its electrical connections, and replacing it as recommended by the vehicle manufacturer or if it's found to be faulty. In some modern vehicles, the MAP sensor may be integrated with a barometric pressure sensor. This integrated sensor provides both manifold pressure and atmospheric pressure data to the ECU, allowing the ECU to compensate for changes in altitude and further optimize engine performance. In summary, the Manifold Absolute Pressure (MAP) sensor is a crucial on-board automobile sensor that measures the absolute pressure inside the engine's intake manifold. This information is vital for engine control, optimizing engine load and performance, boost control in turbocharged engines, and ensuring efficient combustion and engine operation. Proper maintenance and replacement of the MAP sensor are essential for reliable engine performance.

Differential exhaust gas pressure

Differential exhaust gas pressure sensors, often referred to as exhaust back pressure sensors, are sensors that measure the pressure difference between the exhaust gases before and after a component in the exhaust system, typically a Diesel Particulate Filter (DPF) or a diesel oxidation catalyst. These sensors play a crucial role in modern diesel engines equipped with emissions control systems. The primary function of a differential exhaust gas pressure sensor is to measure the pressure difference between the exhaust gases before and after a specific component in the exhaust system, such as a DPF or oxidation catalyst. The sensor generates an electrical signal (usually voltage or current) that corresponds to the pressure difference it measures. This signal is sent to the Engine Control Unit (ECU) or emissions control system, which uses the data for various purposes. Differential exhaust gas pressure sensors are typically located at strategic points in the exhaust system, before and after the component whose pressure difference needs to be monitored. Differential exhaust gas pressure sensors are critical for emissions control in modern diesel engines. They provide feedback to the ECU or emissions control system to monitor the condition and efficiency of emissions control components like DPFs and oxidation catalysts. Diesel engines equipped with DPFs periodically undergo a process called regeneration to remove accumulated particulate matter from the filter. The sensor data helps the ECU determine when regeneration is necessary and control the regeneration process to ensure efficient filter cleaning. A malfunctioning or clogged DPF or catalyst can be detected by the sensor. When there is a significant pressure difference, it can trigger diagnostic trouble codes (DTCs) and illuminate the "Check Engine" light. Mechanics can use these codes to diagnose and repair issues related to emissions control components. Differential exhaust gas pressure sensors require routine inspection to ensure they are functioning correctly. Additionally, regular maintenance of emissions control components like DPFs and oxidation catalysts is essential to prevent excessive pressure differences that could lead to sensor errors. n summary, differential exhaust gas pressure sensors are critical on-board automobile sensors that measure the pressure difference across emissions control components in the exhaust system. They play a pivotal role in emissions control, regeneration control, and diagnostic functions in modern diesel engines. Proper maintenance of these sensors and associated components is essential for efficient and compliant engine operation.

Vehicle speed

Measuring vehicle speed is a fundamental aspect of on-board automobile sensors. Various sensors and systems are employed to monitor and report a vehicle's speed accurately. Wheel speed sensors, also known as ABS (Anti-lock Braking System) sensors, are mounted at each wheel and measure the rotational speed of the wheel. By comparing the speeds of all four wheels, the ECU can calculate the vehicle's speed and detect wheel slippage. Typically, there is a wheel speed sensor at each wheel, positioned near the hub or wheel bearing. Wheel speed sensors play a crucial role in several vehicle systems, including ABS, traction control, and stability control. They help ensure safe braking and handling by preventing wheel lockup during hard braking or on slippery surfaces. The Vehicle Speed Sensor (VSS) is a sensor that directly measures the speed of the vehicle's driveshaft or transmission output. It generates an electrical signal that corresponds to the vehicle's speed. The VSS is typically located on or near the transmission, where it can monitor driveshaft or output shaft speed. The VSS provides essential speed data to various vehicle systems, including the transmission control module (TCM), cruise control, and the instrument cluster for speedometer readings. The vehicle speed data is displayed on the instrument cluster as the speedometer reading, allowing the driver to monitor the vehicle's speed. The speed sensor data is used by the cruise control system to maintain a constant speed set by the driver. In automatic transmissions, the VSS data helps the TCM determine shift points and optimize gear changes based on vehicle speed. Malfunctions or sensor errors related to vehicle speed can trigger diagnostic trouble codes (DTCs) and illuminate the "Check Engine" light. Mechanics use these codes to diagnose and repair speed sensor-related issues. Regular maintenance of wheel speed sensors, VSS, and GPS systems is essential to ensure accurate speed readings and proper operation of related vehicle systems. Cleaning connectors, inspecting sensor wiring, and replacing damaged or malfunctioning sensors are typical maintenance tasks. Vehicle speed is monitored and reported by a combination of on-board automobile sensors; including wheel speed sensors, the Vehicle Speed Sensor (VSS), and GPS systems. Accurate speed data is essential for safe and efficient vehicle operation and is used in various vehicle systems, including ABS, traction control, cruise control, and the speedometer.

Transmission gear selector position

Monitoring the transmission gear selector position is crucial for an automobile's operation and safety. It ensures that the vehicle is in the correct gear or gear mode. Various sensors and components are involved in detecting and transmitting this information to the vehicle's control systems. The Transmission Range Sensor, also known as the Neutral Safety Switch or Transmission Position Sensor, is responsible for detecting the gear selector position. It informs the vehicle's control systems about whether the transmission is in park (P), neutral (N), drive (D), reverse (R), or other gear positions. The TRS is typically mounted on or near the transmission shifter mechanism. It is directly connected to the gear selector cable or linkage. The TRS plays a critical role in vehicle safety and operation. It ensures that the engine can start in park or neutral and prevents starting in gear. It also provides information to the Transmission Control Module (TCM) and the Engine Control Unit (ECU), allowing them to adjust engine and transmission operation based on the selected gear. Accurate gear selector position detection ensures that the vehicle cannot be started in gear, reducing the risk of accidental movement when the engine is running. The information provided by the TRS allows the TCM to optimize transmission operation, ensuring smooth shifts and efficient performance. The gear selector position display on the dashboard or center console provides the driver with important information about the selected gear or gear mode. Regular maintenance of the TRS and associated wiring is essential to ensure accurate gear selector position detection and safe vehicle operation. If the TRS malfunctions, it can trigger diagnostic trouble codes (DTCs) and illuminate the "Check Engine" light, indicating the need for diagnosis and repair. Monitoring the transmission gear selector position is critical for safe and efficient vehicle operation. The Transmission Range Sensor (TRS) plays a central role in detecting the gear selector position and informing the vehicle's control systems about the selected gear or gear mode. Additionally, a shift position display provides visual feedback to the driver. Proper maintenance of the TRS and related components is essential for reliable gear selector position detection.

7.3   Home Appliance Sensors

Embedded sensors in home appliances play a pivotal role in enhancing functionality, energy efficiency, and user convenience. These sensors are integrated into various household devices to monitor and control various parameters. Here are some common types of embedded sensors in home appliances:

Temperature Sensors:
- **Thermostat Sensors**: Found in HVAC systems, these sensors monitor indoor temperature and adjust heating or cooling accordingly.

- **Refrigerator Temperature Sensors**: Maintain the desired temperature in refrigerators and freezers, ensuring food safety and energy efficiency.
- **Oven Temperature Sensors:** Help regulate oven temperature for precise cooking and baking.

Humidity Sensors:

- **Humidity Sensors in Dehumidifiers:** Detect and control indoor humidity levels for improved comfort and mold prevention.
- **Humidity Sensors in HVAC:** Optimize humidity levels in indoor air for enhanced comfort and energy efficiency.

Motion Sensors:

- **Motion Sensors in Lighting:** Automatically turn on/off lights based on motion detection, reducing energy consumption.
- **Motion Sensors in Washing Machines:** Detect load size and balance to optimize washing cycles and prevent vibrations.

Proximity Sensors:

- **Proximity Sensors in Dishwashers:** Detect the presence of dishes and adjust water usage and cycle duration accordingly.
- **Proximity Sensors in Hand Dryers:** Activate the dryer when hands are nearby to conserve energy.

Pressure Sensors:

- **Pressure Sensors in Washing Machines:** Measure water pressure to determine water levels and optimize washing cycles.
- **Pressure Sensors in Coffee Machines:** Ensure consistent brewing pressure for quality coffee.

Light Sensors:

- **Light Sensors in Automatic Blinds:** Adjust blind positions based on natural light levels to regulate indoor lighting and temperature.

- **Light Sensors in Smart Lighting:** Adjust artificial lighting based on ambient light, saving energy.

Gas Sensors:

- **Gas Sensors in Stoves and Ovens:** Detect gas leaks and shut off the gas supply for safety.
- **Carbon Monoxide (CO) Sensors:** Monitor CO levels and trigger alarms in case of dangerous levels.

Water Level Sensors:

- **Water Level Sensors in Dishwashers:** Determine water levels for efficient washing and prevent overflow.
- **Water Level Sensors in Washing Machines:** Optimize water usage based on load size.

Load Sensors:

- **Load Sensors in Dryers:** Detect the moisture level in clothes and adjust drying times to save energy and prevent over-drying.
- **Load Sensors in Dishwashers:** Monitor the dishwasher's load to optimize water and detergent usage.

Touch and Capacitive Sensors:

- **Touch Controls:** Found in many appliances, such as microwave ovens and induction cook tops, for user interaction and control.

These embedded sensors enhance the performance, safety, and energy efficiency of home appliances, contributing to a more comfortable and eco-friendly living environment. As technology continues to advance, we can expect even more sophisticated sensors and IoT connectivity in home appliances, allowing for remote monitoring and control via smart phones and smart home ecosystems.

7.4   Aerospace Sensors

Aerospace sensors play a critical role in the aviation and aerospace industry, providing crucial data for navigation, flight control, safety, and monitoring various aspects of aircraft and spacecraft performance. These sensors are often highly specialized to withstand extreme conditions and provide accurate and reliable data. Here are some common types of aerospace sensors related to embedded systems:

Inertial Measurement Units (IMUs):

- **Accelerometers**: Measure changes in velocity and acceleration, helping with flight control, navigation, and stability.

- **Gyroscopes:** Detect angular velocity and provide information about the aircraft's orientation and attitude.

Air Data Sensors:

- **Pitot-Static System:** Includes pitot tubes and static ports to measure airspeed, altitude, and vertical speed.

- **Angle of Attack (AoA) Sensors**: Measure the angle between the aircraft's wings and the oncoming air, crucial for stall warning and flight control.

Pressure Sensors:

- **Barometric Pressure Sensors:** Provide altitude information and help calculate aircraft altitude above sea level.

- **Cabin Pressure Sensors:** Monitor and control cabin pressure to ensure passenger comfort and safety.

Temperature Sensors: Thermocouples and Resistance Temperature Detectors (RTDs): Measure temperatures in various aircraft systems, including engines, avionics, and environmental control.

Position and Speed Sensors:

- **GPS Receivers:** Provide precise positioning data for navigation and flight planning.

- **Radar Altimeters:** Measure aircraft altitude above the ground for safe landing and obstacle avoidance.

- **Speed Sensors (e.g., Doppler radar):** Measure ground speed and airspeed.

Load and Strain Sensors:

- **Strain Gauges:** Measure structural load, strain, and stress in aircraft components, ensuring structural integrity.

- **Load Cells:** Measure forces acting on landing gear and other components.

Fuel and Fluid Sensors:

- **Fuel Flow Sensors:** Monitor fuel consumption and detect fuel leaks or discrepancies.

- **Fluid Level Sensors:** Measure fluid levels in hydraulic reservoirs, oil tanks, and other systems.

Environmental Sensors

- **Oxygen Sensors:** Monitor oxygen levels in cabin and cockpit to ensure crew and passenger safety at high altitudes.

- **Air Quality Sensors:** Measure air quality parameters, including CO_2 levels, to maintain a comfortable cabin environment.

Proximity Sensors:

- **Proximity Sensors in Landing Gear:** Detect the distance between landing gear components during deployment and retraction, ensuring safe landing and takeoff.

Attitude and Heading Reference Systems (AHRS): Combine data from multiple sensors (gyroscopes, accelerometers, magnetometers) to provide accurate information about the aircraft's attitude, heading, and orientation.

Environmental Sensors for Spacecraft:

- For spacecraft and satellites, sensors measure parameters such as solar radiation, radiation levels, and temperature variations in space environments.

These aerospace sensors are integrated into embedded systems and avionics equipment to provide real-time data and enhance flight safety, navigation accuracy, and performance. The aerospace industry continues to advance sensor technology to meet the rigorous demands of modern aircraft and spacecraft.

7.5   Sensors for Manufacturing

Embedded sensors play a pivotal role in modern manufacturing processes, enabling automation, quality control, data collection, and process optimization. These sensors are integrated into manufacturing equipment and machinery to monitor various parameters and provide real-time feedback. Here are some common types of embedded sensors used in manufacturing:

Proximity Sensors:

- **Inductive Proximity Sensors**: Detect the presence of metallic objects and are used for part detection and positioning.

- **Capacitive Proximity Sensors:** Detect the presence of non-metallic objects, liquids, and granular materials.

Temperature Sensors:

- **Thermocouples:** Measure temperature by the voltage difference between two different metal wires.

- **Resistance Temperature Detectors (RTDs):** Use the change in electrical resistance with temperature to measure temperature accurately.

- **Infrared (IR) Temperature Sensors:** Measure the temperature of objects remotely by detecting their emitted infrared radiation.

Pressure Sensors:

- **Piezoelectric Pressure Sensors:** Measure pressure by the change in electrical charge when pressure is applied to a piezoelectric crystal.

- **Strain Gauge Pressure Sensors**: Measure pressure by the deformation of a strain-sensitive element.

Force and Load Sensors:

- Load Cells: Measure force or weight, used in applications such as materials testing and weighing.

- Force Sensors: Detect and measure compressive or tensile forces.

Vision Sensors:

- Machine Vision Cameras: Capture images for inspection, quality control, and measurement of parts and products.

- 3D Vision Sensors: Measure the shape and dimensions of objects in three dimensions for precise inspections.

Motion Sensors:

- **Encoders:** Measure linear or rotary position and speed of moving components in machines.

- **Accelerometers:** Detect acceleration and vibration, used for condition monitoring and quality control.

Level Sensors:

Ultrasonic Level Sensors: Measure liquid or solid levels using sound waves.

Float Level Sensors: Detect liquid levels by the position of a float.

Flow Sensors:

Measure the mass flow rate of gases or liquids.

- **Magnetic Flow Sensors:** Measure the flow of conductive liquids using electromagnetic principles.

Humidity Sensors:

- **Relative Humidity Sensors:** Measure the moisture content in the air.

- **Dew Point Sensors:** Determine the temperature at which air becomes saturated with moisture.

Gas Sensors:

- **Gas Detectors:** Detect and measure the concentration of specific gases, important for safety and environmental monitoring.

RFID (Radio-Frequency Identification):

- Track and manage inventory, assets, and products using RFID tags and readers.

Sound and Vibration Sensors:

- **Microphones:** Capture sound data for quality control or acoustic analysis.

- **Vibration Sensors:** Detect and monitor vibrations in machinery to assess its condition.

Current and Voltage Sensors:

Measure electrical parameters for monitoring and control of electrical systems and devices.

Environmental Sensors:

- **Air Quality Sensors:** Monitor air quality parameters like CO2, CO, and particulate matter.

- **Environmental Sensors for Clean rooms:** Maintain controlled environments in manufacturing facilities.

Embedded sensors are essential for achieving precision, quality control, and efficiency in manufacturing processes. They enable the collection of valuable data, which can be used for process optimization, predictive maintenance, and quality assurance, ultimately contributing to improved productivity and reduced costs.

7.6   Sensors for Environmental Monitoring

Sensors for environmental monitoring play a critical role in assessing and managing various aspects of the environment, including air quality, water quality, climate conditions, and more. These sensors help monitor and collect data to assess the health of ecosystems, detect pollution, and support environmental conservation efforts. Here are some common types of sensors used for environmental monitoring:

Sensors for Air Quality:

- **Particulate Matter (PM) Sensors:** These devices monitor the concentration of airborne particulate matter, such as PM2.5 and PM10, which are crucial indicators of air pollution.

- **Sensors for Gases:** Carbon dioxide (CO_2), carbon monoxide (CO), ozone (O_3), sulphur dioxide (SO_2), and nitrogen dioxide (NO_2) concentrations must be detected and quantified.

Sensors for weather and climate:

- **Temperature Sensors:** These devices measure the ambient temperature to monitor the climate and forecast the weather.

- **Humidity Sensors:** These devices measure the amount of humidity in the air. Sensors for measuring atmospheric pressure are known as barometric pressure sensors.

- **Wind Speed and Direction Sensors:** These devices measure wind speed and direction for weather forecasting and wind energy applications.

- **Solar Radiation Sensors:** These devices measure incoming solar radiation in order to analyze solar energy and conduct climate research.

Sensors for Water Quality: pH sensors determine whether water is acidic or alkaline.

Dissolved Oxygen Sensors: Monitor oxygen levels in water, crucial for aquatic ecosystems.

- **Turbidity Sensors:** Assess water clarity by measuring the scattering of light.
- **Conductivity Sensors:** Measure the electrical conductivity of water, providing information about salinity and ion concentration.
- **Nutrient Sensors:** Detect concentrations of nutrients like nitrates and phosphates in water bodies.

Soil and Environmental Sensors:

- **Soil Moisture Sensors:** Monitor soil moisture content for agriculture, irrigation, and environmental studies.
- **Soil pH Sensors:** Measure the acidity or alkalinity of soil.
- **Soil Temperature Sensors:** Monitor soil temperature to assess its impact on plant growth and ecosystems.
- **Radiation Sensors:** Measure ionizing radiation levels in the environment, critical for nuclear safety and environmental protection.

Noise and Sound Sensors:

- **Noise Level Sensors:** Measure sound intensity and help assess noise pollution in urban and industrial areas.
- **Acoustic Sensors:** Monitor wildlife and aquatic ecosystems by detecting specific sounds or animal calls.

Remote Sensing and Imaging Sensors:

- **Satellite and Remote Sensing Sensors:** Capture data from space to monitor large-scale environmental changes, including deforestation, land use, and climate patterns.
- **Imaging Spectrometers:** Collect hyper spectral data to analyze and map land cover and

Biological and Ecological Sensors:

- **Biological Sensors:** Monitor the presence and behavior of specific organisms or species, such as fish tagging sensors.

- **Biochemical Sensors:** Detect and quantify specific biological compounds or markers in environmental samples.

Water Level and Flow Sensors:

- Water Level Sensors: Measure water levels in rivers, lakes, and reservoirs.

- Flow Sensors: Monitor water flow rates in rivers and streams to assess water resources.

References & Further Reading

1. Modern Instrumentation" By Neelapala Anil Kumar-ManTech Publications Pvt. Ltd Aug 2020.

2. Jacob Fraden, "Handbook of Modern Sensors: physics, Designs and Applications", 3rd ed., Springer, 2010.

Unit-VIII Advanced Strategies for Sensor Noise Mitigation in Software

Unit Structure

8.0 Objectives.

8.1 Introduction.

8.2 Amplifier and types

8.3 Use case

8.4 Simulation Setup

8.5 Noise reduction with aggregate and simple averages

8.6 Combining of sensor data

8.7 A running Estimate

8.8 Rate of change of predictive values

8.9 Visulisation of data

8.10 Summary

References & Further Reading

8.0 Objectives.

- Gain a deep understanding of different types of sensor noise, including random noise, systematic noise, and environmental noise, and how they affect sensor data accuracy.

- Explore and analyze the existing software-based sensor noise mitigation techniques, such as filtering, calibration, and sensor fusion, to understand their strengths and limitations.

- Investigate various sensor types) and their unique noise characteristics to tailor noise mitigation strategies for specific sensors.

- Develop or improve calibration procedures for sensors to reduce systematic errors and bias in sensor measurements.

- Optimize noise mitigation algorithms for low-power and resource-constrained sensor platforms to minimize energy consumption.

- Explore adaptive noise mitigation strategies that can automatically adjust to changing noise conditions and sensor drift.

- Define performance metrics and evaluation criteria to quantitatively measure the success of noise mitigation strategies, such as reduction in noise variance or improvement in sensor accuracy.

8.1 Introduction.

Sensor telemetry is at the heart of IoT. But while it can lead to amazing insights, it can also be noisy and inconsistent. There are two main sources of the problem. First, all sensors have hardware limitations and only measure to a certain degree of accuracy, with sequential readings having some amount of variance. (We call this variation in sensor readings, "sensor noise".) Second, even if a sensor could measure with perfect accuracy and precision, the world itself that the sensor is measuring still presents variation; for instance, an IR distance sensor is affected by sunlight. We can accept noise and inconsistency as a reality of IoT, but we can also take reasonable steps to reduce them. For instance, is there more accurate hardware available? Are there adjustable gains, sensitivity, positioning, or other calibrations to make on our sensors? Can we reduce environmental factors? Should we average out multiple readings over time? In many cases, these basic steps are enough to allow the data of interest to stand out. But when more of these basic steps have been pushed to their limits—or when they are impossible, impractical, or costly we can use software techniques to filter out the noise and variation in readings. In this 2-part series, we will look at some approaches to reducing noise and gaining insight on the underlying data. First, we will introduce a case study and attempt to solve it with the straightforward techniques of averages, running averages, and even weighted predictions using linear regression. In the second part, we will add a more robust probabilistic technique to our toolkit known as Kalman Filtering. It will allow us to factor in sensor noise, combine data from multiple sensors, and use our knowledge about what we are monitoring to develop a dynamic model of our data.

8.2 Amplifier and types

Sensor signals are in milli volts or milliamps. The analog front end for a sensor is more complex than the digital control circuitry for the sensor- actuator loop. The main issues for sensor interfaces are accuracy, noise, offset, drift and impedance.

Real op-amp varies with the ideal:

Gain is not infinite, especially to high frequency. Input impedance in not infinite. Output impedance is not zero.

Offset voltage is not zero. Output voltage takes time to change.

Basic Amplifier

V1 is the inverting input, v2 is the non-inverting input. Very high input and very low output impedance. $V_{out}=A_{ol}(v2-v1)$ where A_{ol} is the open loop gain.

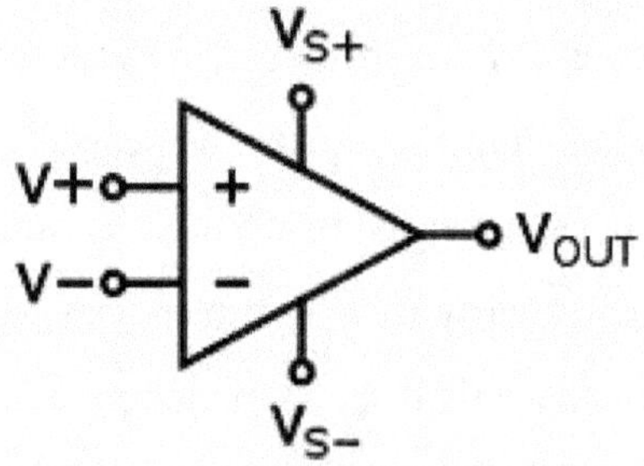

Fig 8.1 Basic Amplifier

Inverting amplifier:

Assume that input terminals have infinite impedance and draw no current. Also the summing junction has v=0. Using ohm's law, i=Vin\R1 and −i=V_{out}\R2. Solving A=gain=V_{out}/Vin=-R2/R1. Vary the resistance to set the negative gain you need.

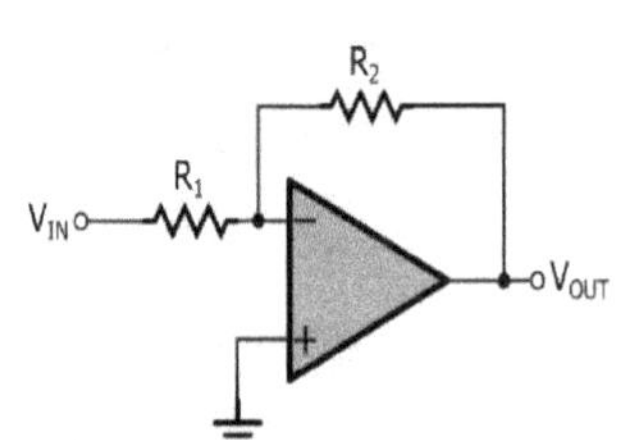

Fig 8.2 Inverting Amplifier

Non-inverting amplifier:

Assume that input terminal have infinite impedance, and draw no current. Using ohm's law $i=V_{out}(R2+R1)$ and $i=Vin/R1$. Solving, $A=gain=Vout/Vin=1+R2/R1$. Vary the resistance to set the positive gain you need.

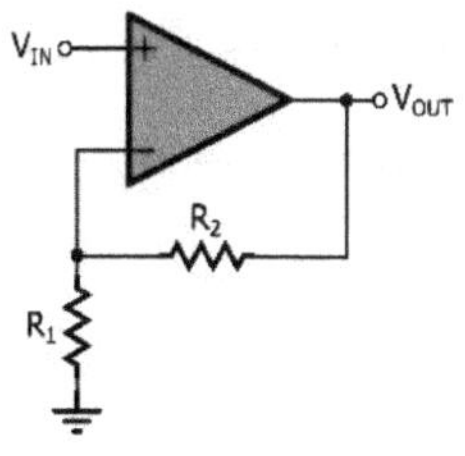

Fig 8.3 Non-Inverting Amplifier

Summing amplifier:

Input impedance has infinite impedance, draw no current. Use superposition to calculate V_{out} from V_1, V_2 nd V_N. Then sum the output voltage to find total V_{out}. $V_{out}/V_1=-R_f/R_1=gain$ for loop1, repeat for other loops. $V_{out}=-(Rf/R1 \times V1 + Rf/R2 \times V2 + \ldots + Rf/Rn \times Vn)$

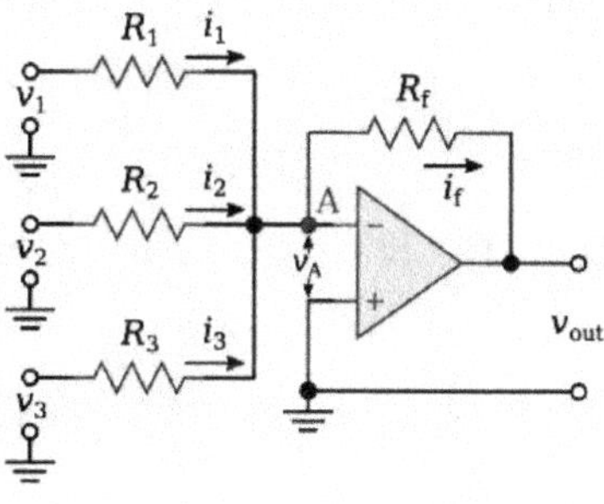

Fig 8.4 Summing Amplifier

Instrumentational amplifier:

Special type of variable gain, differential amplifier with high input impedance and single output. Commonly used to amplify small differential signals for thermocouples, strain gauges and current sensors.

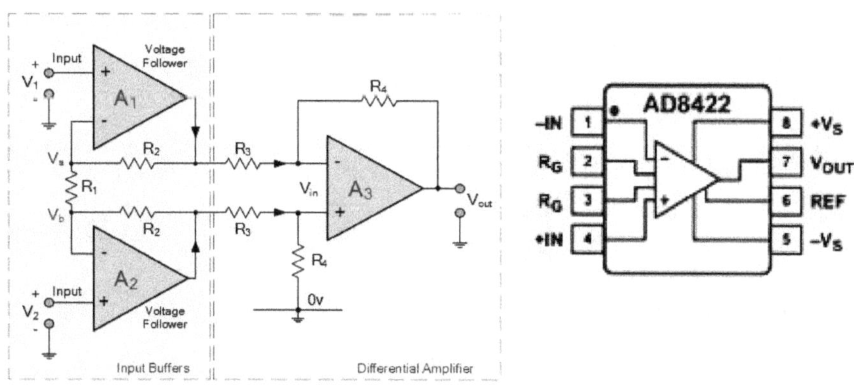

Fig 8.5 Instrumentational Amplifier (b) AD8422

Deriving the gain equation:

R1 is a variable gain resistor.

Step 1: Set V2=0, calculate component of Vout from V1.

Step 1(a): Use differential gain equation using V3 and V4

- Vout= (R4/R3) x (V4-V3)

Step 1(b): Solve for V3

- Vb is a virtual earth, A1 acts as a non-inverting amplifier
- V3= V1(1+R2/R1)

Step 1(c): Solve for V4 in terms of V3

- I= V3/(R1+R2) = -V4/R2
- V4= -V3(R2/(R2+R1))

Step 1(d): Solve for Vout1 in terms of V1

- Vout1 = (R4/R3) x (V4-V3)
- Vout1 = (R4/R3) x (V1(1+R2/R1)) – (V1(1+R2/R1)) x (R2/(R2+R1))
- Vout1 = (R4/R3) x (V1) x ((R1+R2)/R1 + (R2/R1))
- Vout1 = -V1 x (R4/R3) x (R1+2R2)/R1)

Step 2: Set V1=0, calculate component of Vout from V2

Step 2(a): Use differential gain equation using V5 and V6

- Vout2 = (R4/R3) x (V5-V6)

Step 2(b): Solve for V5

Va is a virtual ground, A2 acts as a non-inverting amplifier

- V5 = V2(1+R2/R1)

Step 2(c): Solve for V6 in terms of V5

- I = V5/(R1+R2) = -V6/R2
- V6 = -V5(R2/(R2+R1))

Completing the gain equation:

Step 2(d): Solve for Vout2 in terms of V2

- Vout2 = (R4/R3) x (V5-V6)

- Vout2 = (R4/R3) x (V2(1+R2/R1)/R1+(R2/R1)) x (R2/(R2+R1))

- Vout2 = (R4/R3) x (V1) x ((R1+R2)/R1 + (R2/R1))

- Vout2 = V2 x (R4/R3) x (R1+2R2)/R1)

- Vout = (V2-V1) x (R4/R3) x((R1+2R2)/R1)

AD 8422 Instrumentational Amplifier

- R1 is an external resistor, user settable, to allow amplifier gain between 1 and 100

- High Common Mode Rejection Ratio(CMRR)

- Very low input offset voltage.

- Low noise distortion is important for low voltage sensor signals.

Instrumentational amplifier pinout:

Vout(V2-V1) = Gain = (R4/R3) x (1+(2R2)/R1)

Amplifier imperfection:

Imperfection #1: input offset voltage

- The ideal op amp output is zero when both inputs are at equal voltage.

- A real op amp will saturate in one direction .

Input offset voltage model:

Input offset voltage can be modeled as a voltage source in series with the non-inverting input

Input offset voltage implications:

- Vos gets multiplied by the gain to produce an error in the amplified signal, can be significant

- Critical spec when you have small differential input and you need a high gain for the output.

- Vos has a base component and a value that depends on temperature, see examples below.

- PSOC kit: 0.5mV with 30µV/°C thermal drift

- LM358 Op Amp: 7.0 mV with 25µV/°C thermal drift

- AD8422: Inst. Amp: 0.06mV with 0.3µV/°C thermal drift

Input offset voltage amplified error:

- Offset voltage(Vos) error at 100x gain for these amplified shown here

- PSOC kit: 50mV at 25°C

- LM358 Op amp: 700mV AT 25°C, 812mV at 70°C

- AD8422: Inst. Amp: 6mV at 25°C. 7.4mV at 70°C

- Reason #1 to use an instrumentational amplifier for low voltage sensors!

Imperfection #2: Input Bias Current

The inputs of all op amps will draw a small amount of current unlike an ideal op amp. This current draw cannot be accurately modeled as simple resistive impedance. It happens because the inputs to an op amp have finite impedance. Input bias current caused a voltage drop across your input resistors. The bigger the resistor, the more the voltage drop

Input bias current compensation:

Otherwise, meaningless resistor added to equalize the voltage drop, usually seen only in high bias current op amp designs

How large is the input bias current?

- PSoC: not specified!

- LM741: 1.5µA

- LM358: 0.5µA

- AD8422: 0.0005µA

Imperfection #3: Common Mode Rejection

There should be no change in output signal if identical; in phase input signals are applied. In real op amp the change in output consists of the sum of a large differential gain and a very small common mode gain. The common-mode rejection ratio (CMRR) of a differential amplifier measures its ability to reject common-mode signals. CMRR gets worse at high frequencies.

Common mode rejection formula:

- Vout = Aol(V2-V1) is the differential gain

- Vcm = 1/2Acm(V2+V1) is the common mode gain

- CMRR = Aol/Acl

$$= 20 \log10(Aol/Acm)dB$$

Common mode rejection implications:

When measuring sensor voltages, RF noise appears as an offset on both wire leads, making it a common mode signal. The CMRR of the amplifier determines the attenuation applied to the noise. High CMRR's reduce the impact of noise on the sensor accuracy. LM358 Op Amp: 80dB at 25°C

8.3 Use Case

Monitoring the Water Level of a Storm Drain

Let's imagine we are monitoring a municipality's storm drain system, and we want to know the current level of water at a certain point.

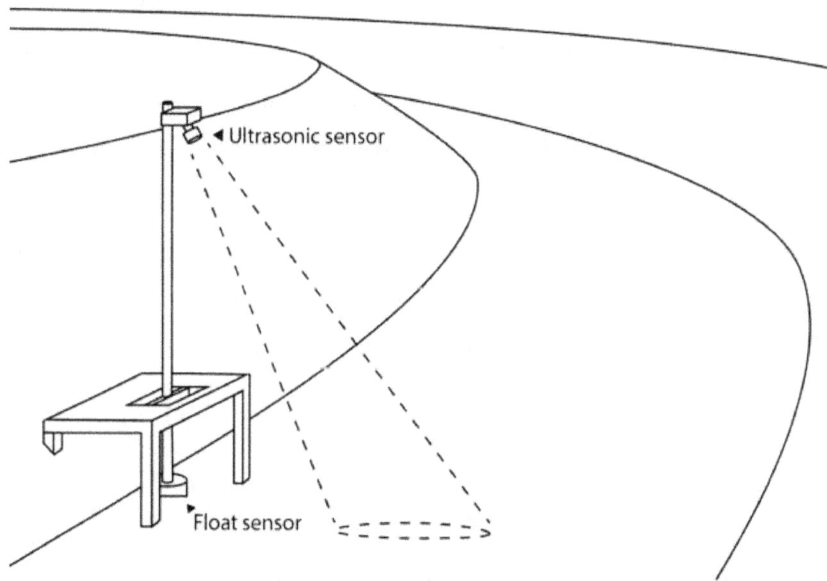

Fig 8.6 Use case model with Ultrasonic and Float sensor

We also know that the water level tends to move in one direction or the other based on recent weather. Aside from small variations from surface turbulence, the water level will either be stable, rising, or falling, and won't switch rapidly from one to another. So, in addition to filtering out some of the sensor noise to get a more accurate reading, we'd also like to get a sense of the water level's current rate of change something our sensors can't directly measure without getting misled by small variations in sensor readings. This could help us plan preemptive actions as the water approaches a critical depth.

8.4   Simulation Setup

Let's talk about setting this up in Losant. In our water level example, we have two sensors measuring the same thing. This could be set up as either two separate devices in Losant (one for each sensor) or as a single device reporting two depths attributes. We'll choose the latter, as this would likely be data from out in the field, and there's a good chance both sensors would report through a single gateway. So we add float Depth and ultrasonic Depth as device attributes to a single device. Finally, because this is a simulation, we will track the actual simulated depth of the water level and the actual rate of change. A production implementation would not have these values, and they are only ever shown in light gray on the dashboard charts. If our imaginary remote gateway supports MQTT, we can have it report device state directly to Losant. Then, without even having to set up a workflow, we can view the reported data using a Losant Dashboard with a Time Series Graph Block

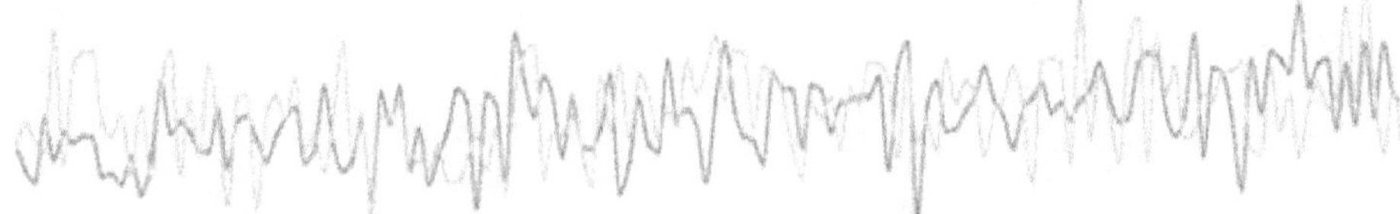

Fig 8.7 Losant Dashboard with a Time Series Graph Block

Here we see both sensors' readings in green, with the natural variation and inaccuracy showing up early in the reported values. The light green line, representing the ultrasonic sensor, has more variance because the lower level of the water is not in its favor. More to the point, the water level is slowly rising here! It's a gradual rate of only 2cm / minute, but because of all the sensory noise, that's very hard to tell visually. Our hope is to draw this feature out more clearly with the techniques below.

8.5   Noise Reduction with Aggregations and Simple Averages

Losant already provides us with some powerful aggregation features. The above chart was a 5-minute time series with a 1 second resolution and no aggregation. If we lower the resolution, we can choose to visualize the data using the mean, median, min, max, or several other aggregation methods.

Fig 8.8   Noise reduction Aggregations and Simple Averages of sensor data

Using a 10 second resolution with the 'mean' aggregation method, we've already reduced a fair amount of the noise. However, this is a visual representation only and does not allow us to do much with the data. These are also both measuring the same depth, so a combined value would be even better. To accomplish this, we'll set up a third device attribute called combined Depth.

8.6   Combining Sensor Readings

The gateway is not reporting a combined Depth for us, so we'll need to listen to the reported state and calculate it ourselves. We can easily do this in a workflow with the Device State Trigger. When float Depth or ultrasonic Depth are reported, the workflow will trigger with that data. We are only interested if both sensors report, as we are calculating their average. Then we simply average them together and report the average to the new attribute. We are careful to select "Use the time of the current payload," which will match the reporting time of the original state. Adding this third, computed attribute to our chart shows us that we have indeed combined our values together into a nice average:

Fig 8.9 Combined sensor data

The individual sensor noise is balanced out by the other sensor. Still, when both sensors happen to report low or high together, we get artificial bumps in our average.

8.7   A Running Estimate

Since we are now tracking a computed value, we can go ahead and add a little more logic to it. One approach is to make this value more than an instantaneous average. It can instead look back at the previous values and combine them with the new readings for a running average. This should allow us to filter out some of the sensor noise by downplaying the variation in new values. We add time series blocks to our workflow to query the past data for each of our sensor readings. One parameter here is how far back we want to look. For instance, we might choose to have a 30 second running average. We can let the Time Series Node provide us with the sum and count if we use one of the predefined resolutions and set the aggregation method to "mean". We won't use the mean value it gives us, because we want to first add in the new sensor readings. But the node helpfully provides both the "sum" and the "count" for us to add the new sensor readings to.

Since the Time Series returns an array of points, we pull out the most recent one since that's the one with values we are interested in.

Then we divide the result to get a running average:

{{Working. last Float Time Series Point.sum}} +

{{working. last Ultrasonic Time Series Point.sum}} +

{{data. float Depth}} + {{data. ultrasonic Depth}}

{{working. Last Float Time Series Point. count}} +

{{working. Last Ultrasonic Time Series Point. count}} + 2

Adding this new value to our chart, we see a slightly less variable line. Here it is pictured in purple:

Fig 8.10 Running estimate.

If we return our sensor readings (green) to their actual values we can see just how well the running average is performing. Overall, this is giving us the best visual estimate so far.

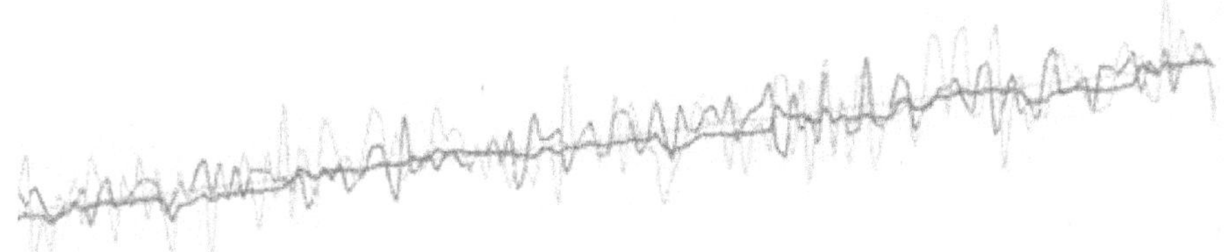

Fig 8.11 Over all best visual estimate.

We may notice, however, that it tends to be slightly low. That's because our water level is rising, and incorporating past data will always drag a running average a bit into the past. We can address this with a different technique that involves estimating the rate of change in something we wanted to track anyways and using it to make predictions.

8.8   Rate of Change to Predict Values

The rate that the water depth is changing is essentially a velocity, the formula for which is the change in value divided by the change in time:

$$V = \Delta x / \Delta t$$

In our existing workflow, we can add a calculation of this by comparing past data across time. If we just use the last two data points to do this, though, the velocity will rapidly fluctuate due to the sensor noise. Instead, we'd like to get an average recent velocity. There's more than one way to do this, but a sensible method is using simple linear regression. With the slope and intercept of the best-fitting line, we can now extend the line of best fit to the current time, and we'll be looking at a loose but reasonable prediction of the value. Then we can average this prediction with sensor readings to create an estimate. This approach should allow good estimates even when the depth is rising or falling:

Fig 8.12 rate of change of predictive values.

The prediction depth initially performs worse than the running average. Because the running average gives equal weight to each of the past data points and the new sensor readings, while the prediction depth combines all the past data into a single point. Instead of new sensor readings making up of the new value with a running average, the new value with the prediction. However, we can easily adjust the weight of our prediction. In fact, giving it the same ratio as the running average results in a similar value, but one that is aware of rate of change.

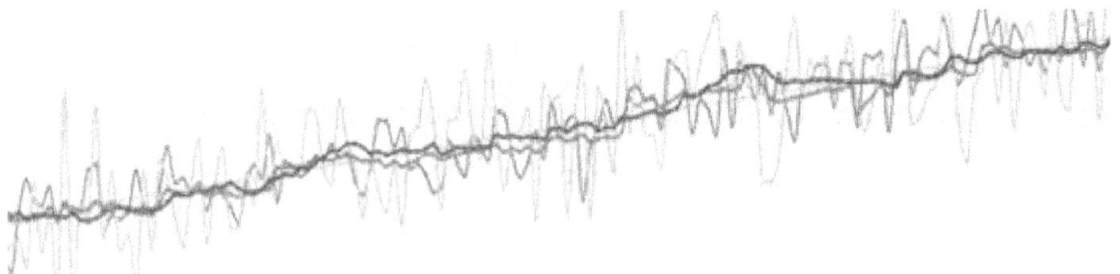

Fig 8.13 Responsive of new data

That's not bad, and we could play around with this weight more to find a value that is smooth but still responsive to new data.

8.9   Visualisation of data

Since we are already calculating the line that best fits the recent data, we can use its slope as an estimate of the water level's rate of change, or velocity. We add another attribute to our device, velocity Estimate, and save the value as state at the same time as our prediction.

We'll show this estimate in a few different ways on our final dashboard: as a simple value using a Gauge, as a value over time with a Time Series Graph, and as a human friendly summary using an Indicator:

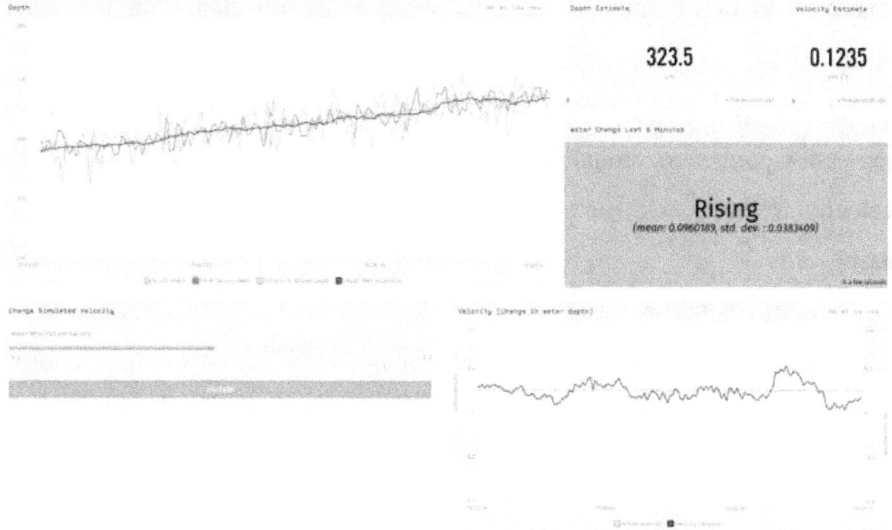

Fig 8.14 Value over time with a Time Series Graph

However, that specific value is a little too variable, because it's constantly adjusting our estimated depth up and down to track the water level. We need to average this out a little over time and consider how much it's deviating. We consider both the mean of the estimated velocity as well as its standard deviation over a period. If the standard deviation is larger than the velocity's distance from 0 (say, a mean of 0.1 with a standard deviation of 1) we can't be very confident about whether the level is rising or falling. So, if we have a high standard deviation, we choose to report this as "Fluctuating" rather than give a bad estimate.

8.10 Summary

We've taken 2 sensors giving quite noisy data and used various techniques to filter it out and derive actionable insights. First, we used the dashboard blocks' built-in aggregation to get a smoother visualization of the data. Next, we created a combined depth reading that factored in both sensors. Then we brought in past data to smooth out the combined value as a running average. Finally, we used linear regression to estimate the depth's rate of change and create a predicted value, which we were able to weigh with the actual observations.

All of these techniques allowed us to view our data with less noise. The linear regression prediction, though, also gave us a deduced value of the water depth's velocity. With this we were able to add a simple, actionable indicator to our dashboard.

References & Further Reading

1. https://www.sciencedirect.com/topics/computer-science/noise-cancellation

Unit-IX Sensor Development Process

9.0 Objectives.

9.1 Introduction.

9.2 Concept Generation and Feasibility Study

9.3 Design and Prototyping

9.4 Testing and Calibration

9.5 Manufacturing and Production

9.6. Packaging and Distribution

9.7 Ongoing Improvement and Support

9.0 Objectives.

- Outline the key stages involved in sensor development.

- Explain the importance of identifying the need for a new sensor.

- Discuss the process of researching existing technologies and conducting feasibility studies.

- Describe the design and prototyping phase, including the selection of sensing elements, transducer design, and signal conditioning.

- Highlight the significance of testing and calibration in ensuring sensor accuracy and precision.

9.1 Introduction.

The development of a sensor involves a systematic process that encompasses various stages, from concept generation to ongoing support. This process begins with identifying the need for a new sensor to measure a specific physical quantity and researching existing technologies to assess their limitations. Feasibility studies are conducted to evaluate the technical and economic viability of developing a new sensor.

Once feasibility is established, the design and prototyping phase commences. This involves selecting a suitable sensing element, designing the transducer to convert the physical signal into an electrical signal, and considering signal conditioning techniques to improve the signal quality. A prototype is then created to test the sensor's functionality and performance. Rigorous testing and calibration are carried out in controlled laboratory environments to ensure accuracy and precision. The sensor is then evaluated in real-world conditions to assess its performance under varying operating parameters. The development of a sensor involves several key stages, the detailing is given under subsequent sections shown in fig 9.1

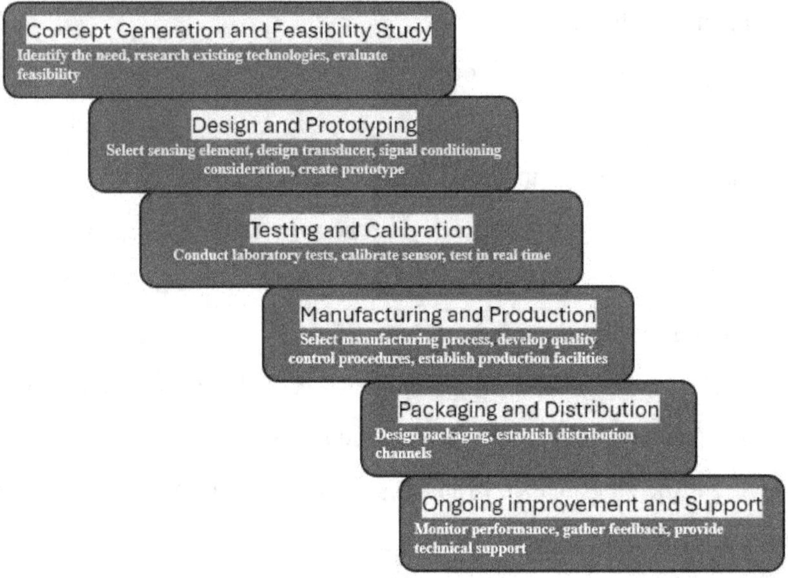

Fig 9.1 Key Stages for Sensor Development Process.

9.2 Concept Generation and Feasibility Study

Identifying the Need

The first step in the development of any new sensor is to clearly define the need it will fulfil. This involves:

- Understanding the application: Identifying the specific use case or industry where the sensor will be deployed.
- Defining the target market: Determining the potential customers or industries that could benefit from the sensor.

- Analyzing existing solutions: Examining the current state of the art and identifying the limitations or gaps in existing sensors.
- Identifying the key performance indicators (KPIs): Defining the critical metrics that the sensor must measure or monitor to be valuable.

Researching Existing Technologies

Once the need has been identified, it is essential to research existing technologies to understand the current state of the art and potential alternatives. This involves:

- Literature review: Examining published research papers, patents, and industry reports related to sensor technology.
- Market analysis: Studying the competitive landscape to identify existing sensors and their strengths and weaknesses.
- Technology assessment: Evaluating the feasibility and limitations of different sensing principles and materials.
- Identifying potential suppliers: Exploring the availability of components and materials required for the sensor.

Evaluating Feasibility

Based on the identified need and the research conducted, it is necessary to evaluate the feasibility of developing a new sensor. This involves:

- Technical feasibility: Assessing the availability of suitable materials, components, and manufacturing processes.
- Economic feasibility: Estimating the potential costs associated with research, development, manufacturing, and marketing.
- Market feasibility: Analyzing the potential market size, competition, and pricing strategies.
- Regulatory compliance: Considering any relevant regulations or standards that the sensor must meet.

- Risk assessment: Identifying potential risks and challenges that may arise during the development and commercialization process.

By carefully considering these factors, it is possible to determine whether a new sensor concept is viable and worth pursuing. If the feasibility study is positive, the next step is to proceed with the design and prototyping phase.

9.3 Design and Prototyping

The transducer converts the physical signal from the sensing element into an electrical signal that can be processed by electronic circuitry. The choice of transducer depends on the type of sensing element and the desired output signal. Common transducer types include:

- Resistive transducers: These transducers change their resistance in response to the physical quantity being measured. Examples include strain gauges, thermistors, and photo resistors.

- Capacitive transducers: These transducers change their capacitance in response to the physical quantity being measured. Examples include accelerometers and humidity sensors.

- Inductive transducers: These transducers change their inductance in response to the physical quantity being measured. Examples include magnetic field sensors and proximity sensors.

- Piezoelectric transducers: These transducers generate an electrical voltage in response to mechanical stress or deformation. Examples include microphones and force sensors.

Considering Signal Conditioning

Signal conditioning is the process of modifying the electrical signal from the transducer to make it suitable for further processing or display. This may involve amplification, filtering, or other signal processing techniques. Factors to consider when designing signal conditioning circuitry include:

- Noise reduction: The circuitry should be designed to minimize noise and interference that can degrade the signal quality.

- Linearity: The signal conditioning circuitry should maintain a linear relationship between the input and output signals.

- Accuracy: The circuitry should ensure that the processed signal accurately represents the physical quantity being measured.

- Stability: The circuitry should be stable over time and resistant to environmental factors.

Creating a Prototype

Once the sensing element, transducer, and signal conditioning circuitry have been designed, it is time to create a prototype of the sensor. The prototype is a physical model that can be tested and evaluated to assess its performance and identify any design flaws. Factors to consider when creating a prototype include:

- Materials: The prototype should be constructed using materials that are compatible with the sensing element and transducer.

- Manufacturing methods: The prototype should be manufactured using techniques that can be scaled up for mass production.

- Testing procedures: A plan should be developed for testing the prototype under various conditions to evaluate its performance.

- Feedback: The prototype should be evaluated by experts and potential users to gather feedback and identify areas for improvement.

The design and prototyping phase are a critical step in the development of a sensor. By carefully selecting the sensing element, designing the transducer, considering signal conditioning, and creating a functional prototype, it is possible to develop sensors that are accurate, reliable, and meet the needs of specific applications.

9.4 Testing and Calibration

Testing and calibration are crucial stages in the development of sensors. These processes ensure that the sensor functions accurately and reliably in real-world applications.

Conduct Laboratory Tests

Laboratory tests are conducted under controlled conditions to evaluate the sensor's performance. These tests typically involve measuring the sensor's output over a range of input values. The following parameters are commonly evaluated:

- Accuracy: The ability of the sensor to measure the correct value of the physical quantity.
- Precision: The consistency of the sensor's measurements.
- Sensitivity: The ability of the sensor to detect small changes in the physical quantity.
- Response time: The speed at which the sensor responds to changes in the physical quantity.
- Linearity: The relationship between the input and output of the sensor should be linear.
- Hysteresis: The difference between the sensor's output when the input is increasing and decreasing.
- Repeatability: The ability of the sensor to produce consistent results under identical conditions.
- Stability: The ability of the sensor to maintain its calibration over time.

In addition to these basic parameters, other tests may be required depending on the specific application of the sensor. For example, temperature sensors may be tested over a wide range of temperatures, while pressure sensors may be tested at different pressures and frequencies.

Calibrate the Sensor

Calibration involves determining the relationship between the input and output of the sensor. This is typically done by comparing the sensor's output to a known standard. The calibration process may involve adjusting the sensor's settings or using mathematical models to compensate for non-linearity or other deviations.

There are several methods for calibrating sensors, including:

- Point calibration: The sensor is calibrated at a few specific points within its operating range.
- Curve fitting: A mathematical function is fitted to the sensor's calibration data to interpolate values between the calibration points.
- Least squares fitting: A statistical method is used to find the best-fit curve to the calibration data.

Calibration is essential for ensuring that the sensor produces accurate and reliable measurements. It is typically performed at regular intervals to account for changes in the sensor's characteristics over time.

Test in Real-World Conditions

Once the sensor has been calibrated, it should be tested in real-world conditions to evaluate its performance in actual operating environments. This involves exposing the sensor to various environmental factors, such as temperature, humidity, vibration, and electromagnetic interference.

Real-world testing can help to identify potential issues that may not be apparent in laboratory tests. For example, a sensor may be sensitive to vibrations that are present in a particular application, but not in a laboratory setting.

Real-world testing is also important for ensuring that the sensor is compatible with the rest of the system in which it will be used. For example, a sensor may need to be interfaced with a microcontroller or other electronic components.

In conclusion, testing and calibration are critical steps in the development of sensors. These processes ensure that the sensor functions accurately and reliably in real-world applications. By conducting laboratory tests, calibrating the sensor, and testing in real-world conditions, developers can ensure that the sensor meets the requirements of its intended application

9.5 Manufacturing and Production

The manufacturing and production phase of sensor development involves the transformation of sensor prototypes into large-scale, commercially viable products. This stage requires careful consideration of several factors, including the selection of appropriate manufacturing processes, the development of robust quality control procedures, and the establishment of efficient production facilities.

Select Manufacturing Process

The choice of manufacturing process depends on various factors, such as the sensor's complexity, required accuracy, production volume, and cost constraints. Some common manufacturing methods for sensors include:

- Micro fabrication: This technique is widely used for producing miniature sensors, such as those found in micro electro mechanical systems (MEMS). It involves etching and patterning materials on a silicon wafer.

- Thick-film technology: This method involves printing layers of conductive and resistive materials onto a ceramic substrate. It is often used for producing pressure sensors and temperature sensors.

- Thin-film technology: Like thick-film technology, this method involves depositing thin layers of materials onto a substrate. However, the layers are typically thinner and more precise.

- Bulk manufacturing: This method is suitable for high-volume production of simple sensors. It involves machining and assembly of components from bulk materials.
- Hybrid manufacturing: This approach combines multiple manufacturing techniques to produce complex sensors.

Develop Quality Control Procedures

Ensuring consistent product quality is crucial in sensor manufacturing. Quality control procedures should be implemented throughout the production process to identify and address defects early on. Some key quality control measures include:

- Incoming inspection: Inspect raw materials and components to verify their quality and conformance to specifications.
- In-process inspection: Monitor the manufacturing process at various stages to identify and correct defects.
- Final inspection: Conduct a thorough inspection of the finished sensors to ensure they meet all quality requirements.
- Statistical process control (SPC): Use statistical methods to monitor and control the manufacturing process, identifying trends and variations.
- Calibration: Regularly calibrate sensors to ensure their accuracy and precision.

Establish Production Facilities

The establishment of production facilities is essential for large-scale sensor manufacturing. The facilities should be designed and equipped to accommodate the chosen manufacturing processes and meet quality control standards. Key considerations include:

- Facility layout: Design the layout of the production facility to optimize workflow and minimize waste.

- Equipment selection: Select appropriate equipment and machinery for the manufacturing processes.

- Clean room environment: For sensitive sensors, a clean room environment may be necessary to minimize contamination.

- Inventory management: Implement effective inventory management systems to ensure a steady supply of raw materials and components.

- Training and development: Provide training to production staff to ensure they have the necessary skills and knowledge.

By carefully selecting manufacturing processes, developing robust quality control procedures, and establishing efficient production facilities, sensor manufacturers can ensure the consistent production of high-quality sensors that meet market demands.

9.6. Packaging and Distribution

Designing packaging for sensors is a crucial step in ensuring their protection, functionality, and marketability. Effective packaging should not only safeguard the sensor from damage during transportation and storage but also provide essential information to users and enhance the product's overall appeal.

Key considerations for sensor packaging design include:

- Protection: The packaging should be robust enough to withstand potential shocks, vibrations, and environmental factors such as temperature extremes, humidity, and contaminants. Materials like cardboard, plastic, or metal can be used, depending on the sensor's fragility and the shipping conditions.

- Functionality: The packaging should facilitate easy handling, opening, and closing. It may also need to include features like tamper-evident seals or specific compartments for accessories.

- Information: The packaging should clearly label the sensor's type, model number, specifications, and any relevant warnings or instructions. This information can be printed directly on the packaging or included in a separate insert.

- Branding: The packaging should align with the overall branding and marketing strategy of the sensor manufacturer. Consistent design elements, colors, and logos can help create a strong brand identity.

- Sustainability: Consider using environmentally friendly materials and packaging practices to reduce the product's ecological footprint. This can include minimizing packaging waste, using recyclable materials, and opting for sustainable sourcing.

Examples of packaging features for sensors:

- Blister packs: These are commonly used for small, delicate sensors and provide good protection against damage.

- Cardboard boxes: These are suitable for larger sensors or multiple units and can be customized with various printing options.

- Protective cases: For sensors that require extra protection, cases made of materials like plastic, metal, or neoprene can be used.

- Bubble wrap or foam inserts: These provide cushioning and shock absorption for the sensor inside the packaging.

- Labels and barcodes: These helps identify the sensor and facilitate inventory management and tracking.

Establish Distribution Channels

Once the sensors have been packaged, the next step is to establish effective distribution channels to reach the target market. The choice of distribution channels depends on various factors, including the nature of the sensor, the target market, and the geographic reach desired.

Common distribution channels for sensors include:

- Direct sales: The manufacturer can sell sensors directly to end-users or customers through its own website, sales representatives, or physical stores. This channel provides the highest level of control over the sales process but may require significant marketing and sales efforts.

- Distributors: Distributors are intermediaries who purchase sensors from manufacturers and resell them to retailers or end-users. Distributors can help expand the market reach and provide logistical support.

- Retailers: Retailers, such as electronics stores, hardware stores, or specialty shops, can sell sensors to end-users. This channel provides convenient access for customers but may involve lower profit margins.

- Online marketplaces: Platforms like Amazon, eBay, or Alibaba can be used to reach a wider audience and facilitate online sales. However, competition can be fierce, and there may be additional fees associated with selling on these platforms.

- Original equipment manufacturers (OEMs): Sensors can be sold to OEMs who incorporate them into their products or systems. This can provide a steady stream of revenue but may require customization or certification.

Factors to consider when establishing distribution channels:

- Target market: Identify the specific industries or customer segments that the sensor is intended for.

- Geographic reach: Determine the regions or countries where the sensor will be sold.

- Sales channels: Evaluate the suitability of different distribution channels based on the target market and geographic reach.

- Partnerships: Consider partnering with distributors or retailers who have established relationships with the target market.

- Logistics and fulfilment: Ensure that there is a reliable system in place for shipping, handling, and fulfilling orders.

By carefully designing packaging and establishing effective distribution channels, sensor manufacturers can optimize the sales and marketing of their products, reaching a wider audience and maximizing revenue.

9.7 Ongoing Improvement and Support

Monitoring Sensor Performance

The ongoing performance of a sensor is crucial for ensuring its reliability and accuracy. This involves a continuous tracking process that involves:

- Data collection: Gathering sensor data at regular intervals or in response to specific events.

- Data analysis: Evaluating the collected data for trends, anomalies, or deviations from expected performance.

- Comparison with benchmarks: Comparing the sensor's performance against established standards or reference values.

- Identifying performance degradation: Detecting signs of sensor drift, noise, or other issues that may affect its accuracy.

- Implementing corrective actions: Taking steps to address any identified performance problems, such as recalibration, maintenance, or replacement.

Gathering Feedback

User feedback is invaluable for improving sensor design, functionality, and usability. It provides insights into real-world applications and helps identify areas for enhancement. Effective feedback gathering strategies include:

- Surveys and questionnaires: Collecting quantitative and qualitative data through surveys or questionnaires sent to users.

- Customer interviews: Conducting one-on-one interviews to gain in-depth feedback and understanding of user experiences.

- Online forums and communities: Monitoring online discussions and forums where users discuss sensors and their applications.

- Technical support interactions: Analyzing customer support inquiries and complaints to identify common issues and areas of concern.

- Field trials and demonstrations: Conducting field trials or demonstrations to observe sensor performance in real-world settings and gather feedback from participants.

Providing Technical Support

Offering comprehensive technical support is essential for ensuring customer satisfaction and maximizing sensor utilization. Effective technical support services include:

- Installation assistance: Providing guidance and support for proper sensor installation, including hardware and software setup.

- Operational training: Offering training programs or tutorials on sensor operation, data interpretation, and troubleshooting.

- Maintenance guidance: Providing recommendations for routine maintenance tasks, such as cleaning, calibration, and component replacement.

- Troubleshooting assistance: Helping customers diagnose and resolve sensor-related problems, including hardware failures, software errors, or environmental factors.

- Remote support: Offering remote access or assistance to troubleshoot issues and provide timely solutions.

- Knowledge base and documentation: Creating a comprehensive knowledge base or documentation to provide users with information and resources.

By effectively monitoring sensor performance, gathering user feedback, and providing technical support, organizations can ensure the long-term reliability, accuracy, and value of their sensor products. This fosters customer satisfaction, strengthens brand reputation, and drives continuous improvement in sensor technology.

SELF TEST
Multiple choice questions

TEST-1

1. Which of the following is not a type of sensor in your smart phone?
    a) Gyroscope
    b) Pressure
    c) Temperature
    d) Capacitive Touch Screen
    e) GPS

2. What advantage does a thermocouple have over the NTC thermistor?
    a) It is more accurate than the NTC thermistors.
    b) It can measure lower temperature than the NTC thermistors.
    c) It curves of temperature vs. voltage is more linear, and can be used without complex calibration.
    d) It can measure higher temperature than the NTC thermistor.

3. Which of the following is true about an NTC thermistor?
    a) It has an excellent accuracy of 0.1%-0.2%.
    b) The range: -100 degree C to 300 degree C.
    c) None of the above
    d) Common base resistance is 20,000 Ohms and 100,000 Ohms.
    e) It is made out of transistors and memory circuits.

4. What is the Steinhart Hart Equation?
    a) None of the above
    b) An equation that compares the thermistor voltage to the thermocouple voltage
    c) A highly nonlinear equation that models the behavior of thermistor
    d) A cubic polynomial equation that models the highly nonlinear behavior of thermistor
    e) An equation that compares the thermistor voltage to the RTD voltage

5. Which fact is not true about RTD's?
    a) DIN/IEC 60751 is the global standard for RTD's
    b) The Class A resistance tolerance is smaller than the Class B tolerance
    c) They have a temperature coefficient of resistance(TCR) of 3.85 ohms/ohms/degree C
    d) They have a range of -200 degree to 800 degree C
    e) They have a nearly linear temperature vs. resistance curve

6. Suppose we include the lead resistance in the calculation of temperature for an RTD. If R3=5000 ohms, RA=50 Ohms, V0=3 ohms and V=6.5Volts. What is R?

   Given:

   R3= 5000 ohms

   RA= 50 ohms (lead resistance)

   V0 = 3 volts

   V = 6.5 volts

   In an unbalanced bridge:

   V = V0 xR/(R + 2RA) -R3/(R + 2RA)

   We need to solve for R.

   Rearranging the equation to group the terms with R on one side:

   V = V0x(R)/(R + 100)-(R3)/(R + 100)

   Substituting the given values:

   6.5 = 3x(R)/(R + 100)-(5000)/(R + 100)

   To find the value of R, let's rearrange and solve the equation:

   6.5 = 3 x (R)/(R + 100)-(5000)/(R + 100)

   Multiplying everything by \((R + 100) \):

   6.5(R + 100) = 3R - 5000

   Expanding:

   6.5R + 650 = 3R - 5000

   Combining like terms:

   3.5R = -5650

   Now, divide both sides by 3.5:

   R = -1614.29

The result is a negative resistance, which doesn't make physical sense in this context. It's possible that there was an error in the given data or in the way the bridge was described. Please review the data or the context in which this formula is being used.

7. What happens if you don't perform cold junction compensation in a thermocouple circuit?

a) Noting. The reading will be accurate anyway

b) The temperature reading will be inaccurate because the ice bath reference temperature will not be maintained

c) The accuracy will be improved because you are doing away with an unnecessary process measurement step

d) The temperature reading will be inaccurate because you have no way to compensate the circuit for thermoelectric voltages created at the junction of dissimilar metals

e) The temperature reading will be inaccurate because the table lookup curve for thermoelectric voltage vs. temperature will be thrown off

8. Which is the most common thermocouple in use?
   - a) Type T
   - b) Type K
   - c) Type E
   - d) Type J
   - e) Type N

9. In what temperature measurement application are thermocouples used?

a) When accuracy of worse than 1% is acceptable

b) When it is acceptable to do periodic calibration checks

c) Measuring temperatures above 1400 degree C

d) Where a large number of measurement points are needed to keep the total cost of the sensors down

10. You are using a 2252 ohms thermistor, Beta=3940 and you measure a resistance of 672.5 ohms. What is the temperature in degree C that you are measuring?

ANSWER: GIVEN:

$1/T = T0\ 1 + \beta 1\ \ln(R0\ R\ )$

$1/T = 298.151\ + 39401\ \ln(2252672.5\ )$

$\ln(0.2984) = -1.2103$

$1/T = 0.003354016 + (-0.000307204)$

$1/T = 0.003046812$

$T = 1/0.003046812$

$T = 328.23K$

Now, converting from Kelvin to Celsius:

$°C = T - 273.15$

$°C = 328.23 - 273.15$

$°C = 55$

ANSWER KEY TEST-1

1	2	3	4	5	7	8	9
b	b	a	c	c	d	b	a,b,c,d

TEST-2

1. Which of the following files are stored in the Workplace Explorer Module of the Cypress PSOC Creator 4 workplace?
   a) All of the files for the hardware schematic and source code solely related to the components you placed in the schematics
   b) All of the source code that relates to pins, ADC's and DAC's
   c) All of the source code that relates to pins
   d) All of the files for the hardware schematics
   e) All of the files relates to your project

2. Under which circumstances will you need to use an oscillator with your PSOC system? There are multiple correct answers?
   a) To study the sensor noise in a system after a SAR ADC
   b) To study the sensor noise in a system as manifested by the digital signal of the sensor
   c) To study the sensor noise in a system before and after any type of purely hardware filter
   d) To study the low frequency sensor noise in a system before and after an RC filter

3. What code is stored in the PSOC file main.c when you first start your project?
   a) A series of very useful and generic function for your project. You enable them by deleting the /* and */ character which comment them out at the beginning.
   b) All of the possible API's that Cypress creates for a project
   c) No executable code because you haven't created the project yet
   d) The executable for a few simple digital components like clocks, pins and counters
   e) None of the above

4. Which of the following is not an on-board component, available for selection from Cypress Component Catalog?
   a) DAC
   b) Amplifier
   c) 16 gigabyte memory
   d) Digital pin
   e) Comparator

5. Which of the following is not an off-chip component, available for selection from the cypress component catalog?
    a) Battery
    b) Thermocouple
    c) None of the above
    d) Motor controller
    e) Fuse

6. Which items are configurable for a digital pin in the PSOC system? There are multiple correct answers.
    a) Interrupt
    b) Sync mode
    c) Threshold

7. You are using a 2252 ohms thermistor, Beta=3940 and you measure a resistance of 672.5 ohms. What is the temperature in degree C that you are measuring?
    a) The SAR ADC resolution be configured between 8 and 20 bits in intervals of 1, while that of the Delta Sigma ADC can be configured to 8, 10, or 12 bits.
    b) The SAR ADC resolution be configured between 8 and 20 bits in intervals of 1, while that of the Delta Sigma ADC can be configured between 8 and 16 bits in intervals of 2.
    c) The SAR ADC resolution can be configured between 8 and 24 bits in intervals of 2, while that of the Delta Sigma ADC can be configured between 8 and 16 bits in intervals of 1.
    d) The Delta Sigma ADC resolution can be configured between 8 and 20 bits in intervals of 1, while that of the SAR ADC can be configured to 8, 10, or 12 bits.
    e) The resolution of both the SAR and Delta Sigma ADC's can be configured between 8 and 20 bits in intervals of 1.

8. The resolution of both the SAR and Delta Sigma ADC's can be configured between 8 and 20 bits in intervals of 1.
    a) Use the pull down menu to assign a schematic number on the chip
    b) Use the Generated Source tab in Workspace Explorer, double-click on the appropriate pin
    c) Pin mapping is done in the pins tab (selected from workspace explorer). You click on the "Port" and "Pin" drop down, and

select the appropriate port and pin number. Then the physical pins are connected to the pins in the schematic.

   d) None of the above

9. Pn mapping is done in the pins tab (selected from workspace explorer). You click on the "Port" and "Pin" drop down, and select the appropriate port and pin number. Then the physical pins are connected to the pins in the schematic.

   a) Use Cydelay () or other methods to make sure you don't write to the LCD too fast for it to respond

   b) Set where the cursor is on the LCD using the function LCD_Position (0,0)

   c) All of the above

   d) Insert the function LCD_Start () into main.c

   e) Write a string of characters (contained in double quotes) to the LCD using LCD_PrintString ()

10. What type of software protocol is implemented in a UART?

   a) RS-232

   b) RS-485

   c) 4-20mA

   d) Ethernet

   e) SPI

ANSWER KEY TEST-2

1	2	3	4	5	6	7	8	9	10
e	c,d	c	c	d	a,b,c	d	c	c	a

TEST-3

1. A two-channel encoder counts the leading and trailing edges of the pulse trains of its two channels. Suppose the resolution of a single encoder is 300PPR. If you add a second channel to the encoder, and change no other specs, how much can you improve the resolution of the encoder?
   a) Increase it from 300 PPR to 450 PPR
   b) Increase it from 300 PPR to 2400 PPR
   c) None of the above
   d) Increase it from 300 PPR to 600 PPR
   e) Increase it from 300 PPR to 1200 PPR

2. An absolute encoder is mounted to the motor driving the x-axis lead screw of a CNC machine. If the encoder has a spec of 1250PPR, a lead of 1.5mm and the lead screw moves a distance of 250mm, how many revolutions of the lead screw will the encoder count and what is the resolution of the Y-axis?
   a) 166.7 revolution of the lead screw and the resolution is 0.0012mm
   b) 250.0 revolution of the lead screw and the resolution is 0.0012mm
   c) 166.7 revolution of the lead screw and the resolution is 0.0018mm
   d) 166.7 revolution of the lead screw and the resolution is 0.0024mm
   e) 250.0 revolution of the lead screw and the resolution is 0.0024mm

3. A multiple speed resolver has 64 sets of secondary windings. Relative to a single speed resolver of the same basic design, how much more accurate will it be?
   a) The same accuracy as the single speed resolver
   b) 64 times as accurate
   c) 16 times as accurate
   d) 32 times as accurate
   e) 8 times as accurate

4. Your resolver has a maximum tracking rate of 27 revolutions per second and gives rotational accuracy of 15.3 arc minutes. If you need a rotational accuracy of 0.2 degrees and your motor shaft rotates at 1140 rpm, can you use your resolver? Why or why not?
   a) No. The resolver accuracy of 15.3 arc minutes is worse than the required accuracy of 0.2 degrees, and the tracking rate of 27 rps is slower than the motor speed of 1140 rpm.

    b) No. The resolver accuracy of 15.3 arc minutes is better than the required accuracy of 0.2 degrees, and the tracking rate of 27 rps is slower than the motor speed of 1140 rpm.

    c) Yes. The resolver accuracy of 15.3 arc minutes is better than the required accuracy of 20 arc minutes, and the tracking rate of 27 rps is faster than the motor speed of 1140 rpm.

    d) Yes. The resolver accuracy of 15.3 arc minutes is better than the required accuracy of 0.2 degrees, and the tracking rate of 27 rps is faster than the motor speed of 1140 rpm.

    e) No. The resolver accuracy of 15.3 arc minutes is worse than the required accuracy of 0.2 degrees, and the tracking rate of 27 rps is faster than the motor speed of 1140 rpm.

5. You want to measure the flow rate of air of density 1.225kg/m3 in a differential pressure meter. The upstream pressure is 30 N/m2 and the downstream pressure is 27 N/m2. The meter has an area of 0.2m2 . What is the flow rate?

    a) 0.443 m^3 / sec m3/sec

    b) 0.990 m^3 / secm3/sec

    c) 0.286 m^3 / secm3/sec

    d) *0.221* m^3 / secm3/sec

    e) It cannot be calculated with the information provided

6. A vortex meter used to measure the flow rate of steam has an accuracy of +/- 1.5% of rate. If the true mass flow rate of the stream is 20kg/sec, what is the maximum error in the reading?

    a) 0.13 Kg / sec

    b) 0.1 Kg / sec

    c) 20.3 Kg / sec

    d) 0.3 Kg /sec

    e) 0.2 Kg / sec

7. An ultrasonic flow meter has more than enough flow capacity to measure the flow rate of any flow in a process area. However, the maintenance department notes a leaky pipe, and replaces it with a much larger than the previous one. The pipe material is extremely expensive because it must not rust when in contact with corrosive fluid inside. Now the flow meter does not fit on the outside of the pipe. You can no longer measure the flow rate. How do you solve this problem?

    a) You buy a larger clamp for the flow meter than can fit on the larger pipe.

    b) You have the maintenance department cut out the large diameter Module of pipe where the flow meter clamps on, and replace it with a smaller diameter Module. This will also involve adding adapter fittings and pipes to neck down the diameter of the pipe smoothly.

    c) None of the above

    d) You tell the maintenance department to do their job a second time, and replace the brand new larger pipe with a brand new smaller pipe of the same dimension as originally.

    e) You buy a new ultrasonic flow meter which fits on the larger pipe.

8. The k-factor for a turbine meter for flow in a 3/4" (19.1 mm) diameter pipe is 689 pulses per litre. Your magnetic pickup assembly recorded 1000 pulses in a period of 1 second. What is the flow rate in the pipe?

    a) 87 liters per minute

    b) None of the above

    c) 70 gallons per minute

    d) 1.45 liters per minute

    e) 0.087 liters per minute

9. Suppose the temperature differential between downstream and upstream flow meters at constant flow is represented by ΔT. If the flow in the pipe decreases, what happens to ΔT?

    a) ΔT stays the same

    b) ΔT decreases

    c) None of the above.

    d) ΔT increases exactly by the ratio of the new flow rate to the steady state flow rate.

    e) ΔT increases

10. What does zero-point stability mean in a coriolis meter?

    a) Very little. It takes your attention away from the main sources of error

    b) Zero-point stability measures the oscillation of the flow meter electronics around a zero reading. You add it to the accuracy spec to get the true accuracy of a Coriolis meter.

    c) Zero-point stability is another way of stating repeatability.

d) Zero-point stability is another way of stating accuracy.

e) Zero-point stability measures the oscillation of the flow meter electronics around a zero reading. You subtract it from the accuracy spec to get the true accuracy of a Coriolis meter.

ANSWER KEY TEST-3

1	2	3	4	5	6	7	8	9	10
e	a	d	e	a	d	a	a	b	b

TEST-4

1. How does a real op amp differ from the ideal op amp?
   a) Input impedance is not infinite in a real op amp
   b) The output of a real op amp ramps up at the slew rate
   c) A real op amp does not have infinite band width.
   d) All of the above
   e) Open loop gains are not infinite in a real op amp

2. An inverting op amp has Vin = .236 volts, R2 = 1000 ohms and R1 = 100 ohms. What is Vout in volts? (Type in a two-decimal number)

   ANSWER: Given:

   Vin=0.236 v

   R1=100 ohms

   R2=1000 ohms

   Vout= -(R2/R1)Vin

   Substitute the values in equation-

   Vout= -(1000/100)x0.236

   Vout= -2.36 v

3. A summing amplifier with N=3 has RF = 1000 ohms, V1 = 0.285 volts, R1 = 500 ohms and V2 = .516 volts, R2 = 100 ohms, and V3 = .651 volts and R3 = 200 ohms. What is Vout in volts?

   ANSWER: Given:

   RF= 1000 ohms

   V1   = 0.285 volts

   R1= 500 ohms

   V2= 0.516 volts

   R2= 100 ohms

   V3= 0.651 volts

   R3= 200 ohms

   Vout=−R F(R1/V1+R2/V2+R3/V3+...)

   Vout   =−1000(0.285/500   + 0.516/100   + 0.651/200)

   Vout=-8.9 v

4. A differential amplifier has R4 = 1000 ohms, V1 = 0.583 volts, R3 = 200 ohms and V2 = .312 volts. What is Vout in volts? (Type in a two-decimal number.)

   ANSWER: Given:

   RF=1000 ohms

   V1=0.285 volts

R1=500 ohms
V2=0.516 volts
R2=100 ohms
V3=0.651 volts
R3=200 ohms
Vout= R3/R4(V2−V1)
Vout=1000/200(0.312-0.583)
Vout=4.47v

5. You are using an instrumentation amplifier with V1 = 21.23 mV, V2 = 43.54 mV, R4 = 3000 ohms, R3 = 500 ohms, R2 = 2000 ohms and R1 = 200 ohms. What is Vout1 in millivolts? (Type in an integer.)

ANSWER: Given:
V   0=(1+2R2/R1   )×(R4/R3   )×(V2−V1)
V1=21.23mV
V2=43.54mV
R4=3000ohms
R3=500ohms
R2=2000ohms
R1=200ohms
V0=(1+2x2000/200)x(3000/500)x(43.54-21.23)
V0=(1+20)x6x22.31
V0=21x6x22.31
V0=2805.84mV
When we invert V1 and V2-
V0=(1+2x2000/200)x(3000/500)x(21.23-43.54)
V0=21x6x(-22.31)
V0=-2674.98mV

6. You are using an instrumentation amplifier with V1 = 21.23 mV, V2 = 43.54 mV, R4 = 3000 ohms, R3 = 500 ohms, R2 = 2000 ohms and R1 = 200 ohms. What is Vout in millivolts?

ANSWER: GIVEN:
V   0=(1+2R2/R1   )×(R4/R3   )×(V2−V1)
V1=21.23mV
V2=43.54mV
R4=3000ohms
R3=500ohms

    R2=2000ohms

    R1=200ohms

    Using the provided formula:

    V0=(1+2x2000/200)x(3000/500)x(43.54-21.23)

    V0=(1+20)x6x22.31

    V0=21x6x22.31

    V0=2805.84mV

7. Your raw sensor signal is 6.5 mV, and you are using an instrumentation amplifier to process it. The amplifier has a CMRR of 80 dB and a differential mode gain of 40 dB. If the RF noise on the leads from the thermocouple sensor to the data logger is 79 mV, what will the noise level be on the amplified signal in mV? (Type in a two-decimal number.)

    ANSWER: Given:

    CMRR (dB) = 80 dB

    Gain (dB) = 40 dB

    RF noise = 79 mV

    CMRR (linear)=10(CMRR (dB)/20)

    Gain (linear)= 10(Gain (dB)/20)

    CMRR(linear)=10(80/20) =10^4=10,000

    Gain(linear)=10(40/20) =10^2=100

    Common-Mode Noise after CMRR=RF/CMRR(linear)

    Common-Mode Noise after CMRR=79/10,000=0.0079mV

    Noise level on amplified signal =Common-Mode Noise after CMRR x Gain(linear)

    =0.0079 mV x 100=0.79 mV

8. An op amp with a slew rate of 0.2 V/μs is amplifying the signal 5 sin (2,000,000t) mV. What is the ratio of the slew rate spec to $2\pi fV0$?

    ANSWER: GIVEN:

    Slew rate SR = 0.2 V/μs = 2x10^5 V/s.

    vi(t) = 5sin(2,000,000t) = 5x10^-3sin(2,000,000t)V.

    f= 2,000,000 Hz.

    The output voltage V0(t)=AVi(t)

    The peak of the output voltage is V0 is:

    V0=A(5x10^-3)

    V0=5Ax10^-3V.

    The condition that determines the maximum frequency for the op-amp given a specific amplitude is:

SR>2πfV0

2×105≥2π(2×106)(5A×10−3)

2×105≥20πA×103

Now, to find the ratio of the slew rate spec to 2πfV0   :

Ratio=SR/2πfV0   SR

Ratio= 2 x10^5/20πAx10^3

Ratio = 10/πA

We have,

10≥πA

10   /π≥A

A≤ 10   /π

Since A (the gain) is maximum when it's 10/π   , plugging this back into the ratio formula gives:

Ratio=10/πx10/   π

   Ratio=20

9. The Johnson-Nyquist noise in a resistor in a circuit of 1Mhz bandwidth is 70 nV / √hz. What is the magnitude of the noise in the resistor in μV? (Type in a one-decimal number)

ANSWER: Given:

Noise bandwidth $\Delta f = 1\ Mhz$

Noise voltage = 70n V/√hz

$$\frac{V_{rms}}{\sqrt{\Delta f}} = 70n \frac{V}{\sqrt{hz}}$$

$$V_{rms} = 70n \times \frac{V}{\sqrt{hz}} \times \Delta f$$

Where, Δf = noise bandwidth

Put the value into the formula

$$V_{rms} = 70 \times 10^{-9} \times \sqrt{10^6}$$

$$V_{rms} = 70\ \mu V$$

Hence, The magnitude of the noise in the resistor is 70 μV.

ANSWER KEY TEST-4

1	2	3	4	5	6	7	8	9	10
d	Refer Q for Ans								

TEST-5

1. You determine the resistance in a thermistor in two ways. First, you use a voltmeter to measure the voltages across the precision resistor and calculate the measured current with your calculator. Then, using the same voltmeter, you measure the voltage across the thermistor and calculate its resistance using the current found previously. Then you use the thermistor component in PSoC Creator to calculate the same resistance. Unfortunately, the two values of thermistor resistance are not the same. What are likely reasons for the discrepancy?

   a) The precision resistor is well out of specification.

   b) Poor contact between components added some unexpected resistance.

   c) You mixed up the voltages you manually measured when you calculated the resistance.

   d) The value of the precision resistor drifted significantly in the 1 hour it took for you to perform the experiment.

2. Why is using an analog multiplexer in our thermistor circuit to feed in both voltages to the Delta Sigma ADC as accurate a way to perform the measurement as using two independent ADC's?

   a)   None of these choices are correct.

   b)   The resistance of the thermistor does not change so any need for two ADC's.

   c)   The resistance of the precision resistor does not change.

   d)   The multiplexer constantly maintains the connection of both voltages measured by the ADC.

   e)   The multiplexer switches so fast that the resistance of the thermistor will not change appreciably while the multiplexer connects the ADC to the voltage across the precision resistor.

3. Why is self-heating of a thermistor a problem in obtaining a precise measure of environmental temperature? Select all that apply.

   a) Being a non-linear device, the thermistor is incapable of calculating any temperature if it is not maintained at ambient temperature

   b) Thermistor linearity is lost as it heats up.

   c) If the thermistor heats up above the environmental temperature, it will give you a reading that is higher than what it is supposed to measure

4. How does the PSoC thermistor API calculate thermistor resistance?

a) The API divides a measured current through the 10K precision resistor by its resistance to get the current in both the resistor and the thermistor. Then it takes the current measured through the thermistor to get the resistance in the thermistor.

b) The API uses as its input the voltages across both the precision resister and the thermistor.

c) The API uses the ratio of the current through the thermistor to the current through the thermistor, and multiplies by the resistance of the fixed resistor

d) None of the above

e) The API divides a measured voltage across the fixed resistor by its resistance to get the current in both the resistor and the thermistor. Then it takes the voltage measured across the thermistor divided by that current to get the resistance in the thermistor.

5. How do you add a thermistor to the PSoC schematic?

a) None of the above

b) Go to the Component Catalog on the right side of the screen and click on the tab for Thermal Management. Click on the + sign in front of Sensors, click on Thermistor and drag it to the schematic.

c) Go to the Component Catalog on the right side of the screen and click on the tab for Thermal Management. Click on the + sign in front of Thermistor Calculator and drag it to the schematic.

d) Go to the Component Catalog on the right side of the screen and click on the tab for Off-chip. Click on the + sign in front of Sensors, click on Thermistor and drag it to the schematic.

e) Go to the Component Catalog on the right side of the screen and click on the tab for Off-Chip. Click on the + sign in front of Thermistor Calculator and drag it to the schematic.

6. Which of the following are process steps when directly measuring the resistance in the thermistor in your thermistor lab? Select all that apply.

a) Take the voltage measured across the thermistor divided by the thermistor current to get the resistance in the thermistor

b) Multiply the thermistor current by 10K ohms to get the thermistor voltage, then divide by the resistor current to get the resistance in the thermistor.

    c) Divide the measured voltage across the 10K precision resistor by its resistance to get the current in both the resistor and the thermistor

7. Why did you put the loop counter in your code for the thermistor lab? Select all that apply.
    a) You could stop the code at any time and see how many times you had gone through the loop
    b) You could stop the code at any time and see how many times the thermistor had measured temperature
    c) For debugging purposes, you could compare the loop counter with how long it should have taken to execute the code
    d) For debugging purposes, you could compare the loop counter with the number of counts in the thermistor calculator

8. Why did we use an analog multiplexer in the thermistor circuit? Select all that apply.
    a) Only the Delta Sigma ADC has enough precision for this measurement, and the PSoC only has one of these so it must be shared.
    b) The PSoC system does not have a SAR ADC, which would have been more useful to measure the voltage across the 10K resistor
    c) The temperature changes slow enough, so that the multiplexer has enough time to switch the voltage signal across the 10K resistor and the thermistor before a change occurred

9. Why did we add two analog test points to the thermistor circuit schematic? Select all that apply.
    a) None of these choices are correct
    b) It allowed us to use an oscilloscope (or your nScope) to verify the voltages that the ADC reads
    c) Once you know the voltages that the ADC reads, you can determine if there is a problem with the ADC configuration, or if your voltage input is at fault
    d) It allowed us to use an oscilloscope (or your nScope) to verify the voltages that analog multiplexer outputted

10. What is the value of the thermistor calculator in PSoC?
    a) It saves you from having to write your own software to solve the Steinhart Hart equation
    b) It prevents the thermistor from overheating.

c)   It's faster than a table lookup

d)   It reduces the power draw when doing this measurement

e)   It is no more useful than measuring the voltages with a voltmeter

ANSWER KEY TEST-5

1	2	3	4	5	6	7	8	9	10
b,c	e	c	b	d	a,c	a,c	a,c	b,c,d	a